PERFORMANCE, POPULAR CULTURE, AND PIETY IN MUSLIM SOUTHEAST ASIA

Performance, Popular Culture, and Piety in Muslim Southeast Asia

Edited by

Timothy P. Daniels

First published in 2013 by
PALGRAVE MACMILLAN®
in the United States—a division of St. Martin's Press LLC,
175 Fifth Avenue, New York, NY 10010.

Where this book is distributed in the UK, Europe and the rest of the world,
this is by Palgrave Macmillan, a division of Macmillan Publishers Limited,
registered in England, company number 785998, of Houndmills,
Basingstoke, Hampshire RG21 6XS.

Palgrave Macmillan is the global academic imprint of the above companies
and has companies and representatives throughout the world.

Palgrave® and Macmillan® are registered trademarks in the United States,
the United Kingdom, Europe and other countries.

ISBN: 978–1–137–32002–5

Library of Congress Cataloging-in-Publication Data

Performance, popular culture, and piety in Muslim Southeast Asia /
edited by Timothy P. Daniels.
    p. cm.
    Includes bibliographical references and index.
    ISBN 978–1–137–32002–5 (alk. paper)
    1. Islam and the performing arts—Malaysia. 2. Islam and the
performing arts—Indonesia. 3. Islam and culture—Malaysia. 4. Islam
and culture—Indonesia. 5. Popular culture—Malaysia. 6. Popular
culture—Indonesia. I. Daniels, Timothy P., 1960–

BP190.5.P4P47 2013
297.2'670959—dc23   2012038717

A catalogue record of the book is available from the British Library.

Design by Newgen Imaging Systems (P) Ltd., Chennai, India.

First edition: March 2013

10 9 8 7 6 5 4 3 2 1

Contents

Figures and Table

Figures

Table

Acknowledgments

I would like to thank all the people—performers, directors, producers, audience members, friends, and family—in Malaysia and Indonesia who have helped me and the authors of this volume to experience, appreciate, and understand various forms and aspects of performance. Without their assistance this volume would not have been imaginable.

I would like to take this opportunity to express my deep gratitude to all the contributors to this volume. An edited volume such as this requires a good deal of coordination and teamwork. I have been so fortunate to have assembled a highly talented and responsive group of scholars. This volume has grown out of our collaboration over the past two years, including discussions before and after our panel, "Performance, Popular Culture, and Piety in Southeast Asia," convened during the annual meetings of the Association for Asian Studies in Toronto, Canada, in 2012. In fact, when I was in Malaysia over the summer conducting research in 2011, Laurie Margot Ross uploaded the panel proposal for me because I was experiencing difficulties with uploading it in Kuala Lumpur, Malaysia. Special thanks go out to Laurie for her kind support throughout the process of organizing the panel and producing this volume. Following the conference, we constructed an informal electronic forum in which we generously shared ideas on each other's papers as we worked toward revisions. I am so grateful that we were able to benefit from each other's commentaries, and I think this volume is much better because of it.

James L. Peacock, the panel discussant at the conference and author of the Afterword commentary in this book, was a steady and consistent motivator throughout this process. Having discussions with Jim over breakfast and lunch were a delight for several of us. His perspective spanning several periods and momentous events in Southeast Asian history has been a benefit to all of us. Moreover, when Jim shared his photograph taken in front of a stadium on the occasion of the 2010 Muhammadiyah Congress in Yogyakarta, Indonesia, with me and other contributors we all felt that it would be perfect as a cover photo for our volume. I would like to thank Jim for granting us permission to use it and for all of his kind support and motivation.

Back at my university home, Hofstra University, I would like to thank the Executive Committee for partially funding my research projects over the past two summers. My colleagues in the Department of Anthropology are a friendly and flexible group. I am thankful that they covered some of my university service duties while I was abroad trying to maximize my time in the field. I also want to thank Alexander Smiros for his technical support.

I greatly appreciate recognition from the Malaysia, Singapore, and Brunei Studies Group and the Indonesian and East Timor Studies Group of the Association for Asian Studies. Special thanks to the latter for sponsoring and endorsing our panel at the annual meetings in 2012. I also appreciate the questions and feedback from several colleagues at the meetings, and from an anonymous reviewer of earlier drafts of several chapters of this volume.

Introduction: Performance, Popular Culture, and Piety in Malaysia and Indonesia

Timothy P. Daniels

This book explores the complex intersections of public cultural forms—performing arts and popular culture genres—and Muslim piety in Indonesia and Malaysia, the two largest Muslim-majority nations of Southeast Asia. There is also significant minority populations of Muslims scattered across the region living in Burma, Cambodia, Thailand, Vietnam, Singapore, and the Philippines, as well as the small Muslim-majority state of Brunei (see figure I.1). Although Malaysia and Indonesia do not constitute all of Muslim Southeast Asia, they are a highly important segment in terms of political influence and sheer numbers. Indonesia is the fourth largest population in the world and the single most populous Muslim country, with over 200 million Muslims; while Malaysia, with its greater economic development and influence, has often lauded itself, and is often viewed, as a model Muslim nation. There is a growing awareness early in the twenty-first century that these two nations, in particular, and Muslim Southeast Asia, in general, must no longer be sidelined in studies of Islam.

Indonesia and Malaysia, currently led by Muslim nationalist elites, have experienced more than three decades of Islamic revival and pious social and political movements (Nagata 1980; Banks 1990; Hefner and Horvatich 1997; Chinyong Liow 2009). In Indonesia, secular nationalists succeeded, during the struggle for political independence from 1945 to 1949, to eliminate any formal ideological relationship between Islam and the state. Muslim activists, who argued for including the clause "with the obligation for the adherents of Islam to practice Islamic law" in the Jakarta Charter of the new republic's constitution, were defeated (see Yudi Latif 2008:222–225). *Pancasila*, a secular nationalist ideology that officially recognized five large "religions" in the country, was

Figure I.1   Map of Southeast Asia.

institutionalized and widely promulgated. Belief in *Tuhan*—the Lord of the civic religion that became shared by many Muslims, Buddhists, Taoists, Christians, and Hindus—and a commitment to continuing the Dutch civil court system, held precedence over Muslim activists' calls for the nation-state to stress belief in *Allah* and implement *shari'a* (Islamic laws and norms). Indonesia's Muslim majority, marginalized in power struggles and modern education, developed "the majority with minority mentality" syndrome (W. F. Wertheim 1980; cited in Latif 2008:228). Moreover, the Muslim majority was fragmented not only as secularists and advocates of political Islam, but also into countless *pribumi* (indigenous) ethnicities and traditionalist, modernist, Sufi, and syncretistic religious orientations (Geertz 1960; Woodward 1989; Bowen 1993; Daniels 2009). Whereas Sukarno, Indonesia's first president, attempted to include Islamic organizations in an alliance with nationalists and communists, Suharto, his successor and architect of the New Order regime, adopted an approach of eliminating communists and repressing Muslim activists.

Nahdlatul Ulama and Muhammadiyah—the two largest Muslim mass organizations—and several smaller ones restricted from politics concentrated on cultural, educational, and social welfare projects. These older organizations were joined by several new Islamic organizations in the 1980s and 1990s, many active in piety movements and political activism on university campuses. Before the fall of Suharto's autocratic rule in 1998, he moved to facilitate more of a public presence and institutionalization of Islam with legal initiatives, financial institutions, the Council of Indonesian Islamic Scholars (MUI, *Majelis Ulama Indonesia*), and the Association of Indonesian Muslim Intelligentsia (ICMI, *Ikatan Cendekiawan Muslim Se-Indonesia*). During the post-Suharto *Reformasi* (Reformation) era, there has been an intensification of the influence of Islam in the public sphere, a multiplication of Islamic political parties and piety movements, and the emergence of several radical Islamic "splinter groups" (Azra 2005; Daniels 2007). Yet there is an apparent paradox presented by the results of recent surveys that indicate widespread support for the implementation of *shari'a* when considered alongside consistently weak electoral results for Islamic parties. If support for implementation of Islamic laws is so strong, then why don't people vote in higher numbers for Islamic political parties with this goal as a key part of their ideological platforms? Hefner (2009:95) suggests that the "public's commitment to shari'a is real but also, so to speak, procedurally vague." This procedural vagueness, or lack of clarity about exactly how to go about implementing *shari'a*, may very well be a telling effect of the diverse and highly fragmented character of the Indonesian Muslim majority.

In Malaysia, the Muslim majority obtained official recognition of Islam as the religion of the federation and special rights for *Bumiputera* (indigenous peoples), especially Malays, written into the Federal Constitution. Malay sultans, though much less powerful than prime ministers, remained influential symbolic figures viewed as protectors and leaders of Islam in each state. Malaysian secular nationalists maintained the dual judicial system constructed under British colonialism with federal civil courts presiding over all manner of cases and state-level *shari'a* courts only adjudicating Muslim family and personal morality cases.[1] PAS, the Islamic Party of Malaysia, separated from the secular nationalist UMNO (United Malays National Organization) during the 1950s transition to political independence, and campaigned for greater adherence to and implementation of *shari'a*. Malaysian Muslim and non-Muslim conflicts over special rights and symbolic advantages bestowed on *Bumiputera* persisted and exploded in the racial riots of 1969. In the aftermath of the riots, new economic policies were formulated and institutionalized aimed at securing a larger share of material resources and benefits for the Malay Muslim majority. During the turbulent 1970s, PAS joined the UMNO-led National Front but in the 1980s returned to being an opposition party with a newly formulated leadership of Islamic scholars (*ulama*).

Unlike the Muslim majority in Indonesia, which is fragmented into numerous ethnicities and a spectrum of religious orientations, Malaysian Muslims are more unified in ethnicity and religious orientation. Muslims who would be divided into traditionalist and modernist camps in Indonesia are united within the Islamic Party of Malaysia. Moreover, PAS and UMNO, although fiercely divided politically over secularism and the extent of Islamic laws, remain very much alike theologically and in terms of adherence to traditional jurisprudential opinions.[2] The UMNO-led federal government, PAS, and several Islamic nongovernmental organizations have led piety campaigns for several decades. Although the Malaysian government has championed the certification of *halal* products and outlets, established "Islamic" banks and financial regulations, and raised the jurisdiction of *shari'a* courts, PAS and many Islamic NGOs still campaign for greater Islamization and fuller implementation of *shari'a*. PAS, through electoral politics, regained control of the state of Kelantan in 1990 and won Terengganu in 1999 and Kedah in 2008. Meanwhile, Pakatan Rakyat—the opposition coalition of PAS, DAP (Democratic Action Party), a socialist-leaning majority Chinese party, and PKR (People's Justice Party), a multiethnic nationalist party, led by the former deputy prime minister Anwar Ibrahim— threatens to electorally defeat and topple the UMNO-led National Front that has controlled the federal government of Malaysia since political independence in 1957.

MULTIPLE LIVES OF AESTHETIC PRACTICES

These are some aspects of the broader social and political contexts relevant to understanding the aesthetic texts—dance, music, song, ritual theater, television series, and films—examined in this volume. Contributors move back and forth between aesthetic practices and sociocultural contexts in the process of identifying and explicating a range of issues in Malaysian and Indonesian societies. Victor Turner, an early proponent of "performance studies," helped move the study of aesthetic practices away from static structuralism and toward more dynamic fluid approaches. Discussing the relationship between aesthetic practices and sociocultural contexts, he wrote:

> My thesis is that this relationship is not unidirectional and "positive"—in the sense that the performative genre merely "reflects" or "expresses" the social system or the cultural configuration, or at any rate their key relationships—but that it is reciprocal and reflexive—in the sense that the performance is often a critique, direct or veiled, of the social life it grows out of, an evaluation (with lively possibilities of rejection) of the way society handles history. (1987:21–22)

Turner strikes a delicate balance shifting from a focus on structural constraints performances "grow out of" to the agency of artists who critique, evaluate, and reflect upon society and culture. Many contemporary practice theorists attempt to build upon this insight. Moreover, Turner modeled his thesis quoted above on linguistic anthropologists' attempts to bridge their dual focus on the formal qualities of language and the *use* of language in sociocultural contexts. Indeed, taking this cue from Turner, performance studies can gain further theoretical insights from linguistic anthropological studies of speech performances. Everyday human conversations have several layers of meanings and embedded knowledge, including those at the level of sound, basic units of meaning, syntactic ordering of sentences, semantic meanings of words and sentences, strategies of language use in social contexts, and metalinguistic or ideological views of language itself. Although it is not essential for any single study of a human speech event to examine every level of knowledge, it is important not to make the error of reducing one layer of knowledge to another. For instance, one might be prone to reduce basic units of sound or meaning to social actions in particular contexts or the literal meaning of a statement to its intended social meaning (F. K. Lehman 1997). In this volume, we attempt to move across various dimensions of meanings of aesthetic practices without committing the semiotic fallacy of reducing one dimension to another.[3]

Those engaged in aesthetic practices, including performers, directors, writers, and audiences, work across several layers of ideas and meanings. On one layer there are techniques, masks, costumes, and repertoires, and on another layer interpretations of self, body, and ways of healing, and still others reflect and respond to wider societal norms and values, including those of religious piety. Thus, this volume delves into the multiple lives of aesthetic forms of practice, the ways they represent, express, and embody cultural knowledge and articulate with negotiations of social relationships. It builds upon the work of contemporary scholars of anthropology, sociology, ethnomusicology, cultural studies, and other disciplines, who have noted that performing arts and popular culture genres are active events that entail these multiple layers of meaning.

Moreover, this multidisciplinary volume examines constructions and connections of other strands of ideas and meanings with those of religious piety. The chapters in this proposed volume will address the critical role the performing arts and popular culture play in responding to and creating changes in the broader context. Keeping in mind the diversity of social actors and the spectrum of notions of religious piety, one aim of this volume is to highlight this multiplicity and its relationship to forces in society. For instance, Patricia A. Hardwick and Laurie M. Ross, in their respective chapters, examine the notions of piety of government officials as well as of the performers. Similarly, Christina Sundari describes the senses of religious piety of cross-gender performers and some people in their social networks. These aesthetic practices are never divorced from their contexts. Building upon the insight that such enactments are valuable sites of inquiry, these case studies will underscore how various social actors experience and understand these performances in particular contexts.

PERFORMANCE AND RELIGION

There are several fine studies about religion and popular culture such as those by Forbes and Mahan (2000), Stout and Buddenhagen (2001), Weintraub (2011), and Lynch, Mitchell, with Strhan (2012). These collections make important contributions to the study of religion and media, in general, as well as in its particular forms. This volume builds upon such collections that help us to understand how media forms influence and embody everyday religious life. However, these tend to focus on text and context without extensive concern for local perspectives. *Performance, Popular Culture, and Piety in Muslim Southeast Asia* attempts to rectify these shortcomings by explicating text, context, and local cultural understandings through its deployment of *ethnographic* methods. Although contributors to this volume bring varied disciplinary perspectives and methods of analysis, we share awareness of the significance of local interpretations of performances and their various levels of meanings, concepts, and discourses.

This literature on religion and popular culture also tends to consider religion more broadly rather than concentrating on religious piety. For instance, Weintraub's edited volume *Islam and Popular Culture in Indonesia and Malaysia*, one of the most relevant to the topic at hand, focuses upon Muslim heterogeneity on a range of topics such as modernity, media interests, religious identity, sex, gender, and sexuality. His collection makes an important contribution to the literature through addressing popular culture and Islam in Southeast Asia, and as such, provides a resource for our studies. However, our concentration on religious piety facilitates important insights into a region that has experienced several decades of Islamic revival and the current proliferation of Islamic movements and political contests (see Hefner and Horvatich 1997; Daniels 2009). Karin van Nieuwkerk's volume (2011) demonstrates how significant a greater concentration on Islamic piety and popular culture can be for insights into sociopolitical dynamics. Nieuwkerk's works connect aesthetic practices to various social quandaries Muslims are confronted with in North America, Europe, and several Middle Eastern countries. Similarly, contributors to this volume show how pious Islamic discourses are encoded and embodied in public cultural forms, delving into the meanings of signs and symbols of piety, and how these forms, in turn, influence and mediate everyday lives and social processes. *Performance, Popular Culture, and Piety in Muslim Southeast Asia* fills a crucial gap in the literature by highlighting these topics in the Malayo-Indonesian region that has its own particular history of Islamization, local culture and Islam syntheses, piety movements, and emergence of a Muslim public sphere.

This volume also builds upon several ethnographic studies of performing art and ritual forms such as those by Peacock [1968] (1987), Geertz (1973), Bowen (1993), Hellman (2006), Frisk (2009), Rasmussen (2010), and Harnish and Rasmussen (2011). These and several other ethnographic works are valuable resources for the study of religious piety in relation to performance, context, and local culture. This volume contributes to this trajectory of work in Muslim Southeast Asia. Moreover, we extend upon the insights proffered by these works through our consideration of performing arts *and* popular culture forms, and live and electronic performances. Although performing arts and popular culture are often mediated by the market and mediate religion in different ways, our readings and contextualizing of both will enhance our understanding of contemporary Muslim Southeast Asia. This volume demonstrates that through studying performing arts *and* popular culture we can discern how performance mediates religious piety in a variety of ways in different sites.

PERFORMANCE, PIETY, AND SOCIAL
CULTURAL PROCESSES

In addition, this edited volume sheds light on the complex roles performing arts and popular culture genres play in a variety of religious and sociopolitical contexts in the contemporary world. Although the contributors to the volume focus on the Muslim-majority societies of Malaysia and Indonesia, many of the findings of this volume are of comparative value for those studying Islam and other religions in other regions of the world. This volume not only contributes ethnographically with detailed case studies, but also theoretically propels the emerging literature on religions in practice through delineating the diverse ways Muslims draw upon and interpret textual sources in their lives and societies, and the ways in which religion in everyday life is *performance-mediated*.

Rasmussen (2010) and Harnish and Rasmussen (2011) resonate at times with the studies in this volume. Despite a broader focus on Indonesian Islamic culture and the ways Islam intersects with gender or nationalist discourses, these works offer some insights into how particular performance genres articulate with pious religious projects and sociopolitical dynamics. In her detailed ethnographic study of Indonesian female Qur'an reciters and Islamic music, Rasmussen makes some important observations of connections between aesthetic practices, piety, and sociopolitical projects. For instance, she notes how some Indonesian Arabic-language song and music genres are used to articulate "authentic" senses of religious piety and *dakwah* (Islamic proselytizing) to national identity (2010:171, 194–198). She also notes that the pious gamelan *dakwah* of Emha Ainun Nadjib and Kiai Kanjeng express intense religiosity as well as sharp critiques of state politics and corruption, while the *nasyid* boy bands embody neomodernist reformism and express an agenda of clean and virtuous development and progress (198–210). Similarly, Harnish and Rasmussen's edited volume *Divine Inspirations: Music and Islam in Indonesia*, a fine and thoughtful collection that adds to the study of performance and Islam in a broad range of settings in contemporary Indonesia, touches upon the crucial topic of art forms and piety. In this volume, Sumarsam (2011) examines the historical contrast between the two largest Islamic mass organizations' approaches to traditional cultural arts, while Cohen (2011) and Pätzold (2011) explore aesthetic practices, *brai* mystical music and *pencak silat* self-defense arts respectively, that embody Sufi senses of piety.

The contributors in *Performance, Popular Culture, and Piety in Muslim Southeast Asia* attempt to explicate the multifaceted influence of forms of Islamic piety upon aesthetic practices, and more deeply penetrate the connections between aesthetic practices, piety, and sociopolitical projects. Laurie Margot Ross' chapter, "Performing Piety from the Inside Out: Fashioning Gender and Public Space in a Mask 'Tradition' from Java's Northwest Coast," examines *topeng cirebon*, a masked dance genre, underscoring the matrix of gender, dancer costume, and performance arena from 1850 to 2012. *Topeng* performances over time have blended several senses and methods of Sufi piety expressed in the elevated role of female performers and embodied in the dance costumes and performers' bodily comportment. Ross makes important insights pertaining to the analysis of the complex and often intertwining influence of forms of Hindu and Muslim mysticism on cultural arts, masks, and costumes. Normative piety-oriented criticism, which first impinged on this aesthetic form during the late Sukarno era, returned as part of an internal debate within *topeng* circles in the 1990s. As *topeng* performances were shifted from village squares to spaces under the authoritarian control of the Suharto regime, discourses of normative piety influenced the genre with performers even being required to adhere to the schedule of five daily prayers. During the late Suharto era, *topeng cirebon* was launched at the Al-Zaytun University led by an Islamic scholar linked to the radical Islamic movement, *Darul Islam*, which several decades earlier sought to establish an Islamic state. *Topeng* performances at this Islamic university staged in a massive outdoor arena exhibit changes in costume and clothing and indicate a shift from mystical practices to normative piety.

In his chapter, "Islamic Revivalism and Religious Piety in Indonesian Cinema," Eric Sasono describes several films from the late 1950s to 2012 relating forms of religious piety represented in the films to aspects of the sociopolitical contexts at the times of their production. Asrul Sani and Chaerul Umam's three films, the 1983 remake of the 1959 film *Titian Serambut Dibelah Tudjuh*, *Al Kautsar* (1977), and *Nada and Dakwah* (1991), attempt to refute the New Order regime's negative stereotype of Islam as unsuitable for modern development through depicting "modernized/substantialist" Muslims as protagonists correcting the social ills "traditionalist/scripturalist" Muslims help to perpetuate. Forms of "modernized/substantialist" piety, which emphasize the rational application of Islamic teachings to a range of social problems, hold sway in these film narratives over traditionalist/scripturalist forms that stress memorization of Arabic religious texts and formal symbolism. However, several post–New Order films with Islamic themes, such as *Ayat-ayat Cinta* (2008) and *Ketika Cinta*

Bertasbih (2009), shifted to concentrate on embodying piety in personal relationships. Some audiences of these films were critical of the gaps in piety between that expressed in the film and that embodied in the real lives of performers and filmmakers. There was also controversy over Hanung Bramantyo's two recent films, *Perempuan Berkalung Sorban* (2009) and *Sang Pencerah* (2010), that criticized traditionalist Islamic scholars for treating women unfairly and the Muslim majority for intolerance toward minority religious groups.

Patricia A. Hardwick's chapter, "Embodying the Divine and the Body Politic: *Mak Yong* Performance in Rural Kelantan, Malaysia," is an outgrowth of her earlier research on *mak yong* and *main puteri* in which she participated as a dancer in rural dance troupes in Kelantan. The Islamic Party of Malaysia (PAS) banned these traditional art forms in 1991 following their state-level electoral victory. They interpreted *mak yong* as being of pre-Islamic origins, encouraging polytheism, and objectifying women. On the other hand, the United Malays National Organization (UMNO) attempted to appropriate *mak yong* as a symbol of Malay identity in their nationalist projects. However, Hardwick describes complex forms of heterodox piety in which performers conceptualize the human body as a divine kingdom ruled by Dewa Muda, embody Islamic monotheism and other pillars with hand positions, and enter into healing trances through repeating the name of God. Placing her in-depth research in dialogue with previous research in the region, Hardwick points out some important aspects of current socioreligious dynamics. Performers negotiate their sense of personal piety with the heterodox piety embodied in these aesthetic forms and the normative piety widespread in Kelantan society.

In chapter 4, "Islamic TV Dramas, Malay Youth, and Pious Visions for Malaysia," Timothy P. Daniels explores the encoding of forms of liberal and normative Islamic piety in several recent television dramas and a film based on one of them, along with several films directed by the late Malaysian filmmaker, Yasmin Ahmad. Whereas Malay youth tended to view Yasmin Ahmad's films as being about "controversial" racial issues, they considered *Nur Kasih*, and other such TV dramas, to be "Islamic." Yasmin Ahmad films, depicting intimate relations between Muslim Malays and Malaysians from other ethnic and religious backgrounds, encode notions of ethnic and religious pluralism, bottom-up multiculturalism, and liberal Islamic piety. On the other hand, "Islamic" TV dramas and *Nur Kasih the Film*, portraying Muslim Malay relations in all-Malay rural and urban settings with diffuse Islamic symbolism, encode Malay and Islamic primacy and normative Islamic piety. These films and TV dramas not only reflect and continue long-term social struggles over race, religion, and nation, but also express hopes, dreams, and fears of what Malaysia can be.

Christina Sunardi's chapter, "Complicating Senses of Masculinity, Femininity, and Islam through the Performing Arts in Malang, East Java," examines cross-gender dance genres, such as *Ngremo, Beskalan,* and *Tayub,* and the complex senses of gender and piety expressed and embodied onstage and offstage in the everyday lives of performers. Building upon the theoretical concept of "contingent" gender, Sunardi describes particular forms of female masculinity and male femininity produced in various contexts, which subvert the dominant gender ideology in Indonesian society that weds gender to sex in an uncomplicated fashion. Orthodox Islamic piety has influenced these aesthetic forms but not as destructively as many have suggested; in fact, cross-gender performers note receiving emotional and financial support from *fanatik* Muslims who strictly adhere to Islam. Moreover, cross-gender performers actively negotiate varied approaches and orientations to Islam in their performances and offstage social relations. Those males who live as women in their everyday lives experience the greatest difficulty with being accepted in the broader society; nevertheless, they, like other cross-gender performers, create ways of understanding their gender in relation to religiosities.

In chapter 6, "Social Drama, *Dangdut,* and Popular Culture," Daniels explores the social drama surrounding the emergence of Inul Daratista as a national pop star and *dangdut* as the most popular and highly televised cultural art form. The social drama involves a broad array of normative Islamic forces that aligned themselves against Inul arguing that her style of performance, which flouted norms of public modesty, called for a religious struggle or *jihad* of the pious to protect society from its harmful effects. On the other hand, many of her fans and a prominent leader of the largest traditional Muslim organization in the world, NU (*Nahdlatul Ulama*), supported Inul arguing for her freedom of expression, even declaring it a human rights issue. Building upon Victor Turner's notion of "social drama," this chapter examines the dramatic episode of contention over Inul Daratista's provocative *dangdut* performance style as part of ongoing conflict and contradictions over visions for Indonesia's future. It also addresses the cultural politics of using *dangdut* in the national election and its relevance to contests between secular and Islamic parties and processes of equalization.

Finally, James L. Peacock writes the afterword. Peacock is one of the pioneering scholars of performance and Islam in Southeast Asia. His works on *ludruk* ritual theater in East Java and on the modernist piety movement, Muhammadiyah, have influenced several generations of researchers in the region and beyond. In his afterword, he provides a commentary on all the chapters in the volume drawing upon his extensive research and experiences in the region, and ruminates on the complexities of Islamic piety, performance, and cultural diversity in the contemporary age of globalization.

NOTES

1. State-level *shari'a* courts have jurisdiction over Muslim family matters, such as marriage, divorce, custody, support, and personal morality matters that include penalties for drinking alcoholic beverages, gambling, ingesting substances during the fasting month, and engaging in sexual relations outside of marriage.
2. Scholars affiliated with Sisters in Islam, a Muslim feminist nongovernmental organization in Malaysia, have noted that UMNO and PAS consistently embrace the same "fundamentalist" or "neotraditionalist" perspectives in regard to the rights and obligations of Muslim men and women in matters connected to marriage and divorce (see Norani Othman 2005:5–6).
3. Many social scientists, including structuralists and post-structuralists, have modeled their approaches on studies of human language. Many contemporary linguistic anthropologists, arguing that their predecessors paid too much attention to the ways language is organized, emphasize how language is used to do things in social contexts (see Duranti 1997; Ahearn 2012). F. K. Lehman, a formal linguist and cultural anthropologist, cautions against analyzing linguistic performances without some knowledge of linguistic structures. In order to better understand language as a social *tool*, we must understand how this particular tool is organized.

Performing Piety from the Inside Out: Fashioning Gender and Public Space in a Mask "Tradition" from Java's Northwest Coast

Laurie Margot Ross

Introduction

Cirebon, on Java's northern littoral or *pasisir*, was an important port of transnational exchange in the Indian Ocean region, where Sufi artist guilds devoted to carving and textile industries flourished in the seventeenth century.[1] The historic trade routes that we today call the "silk road" carried not only silk and other goods, but also cultural and religious ideas, of which many were linked to Sufism. In western Java, the two most important nodes of transnational exchange were Cirebon, on the cusp of Central Java, and Banten,[2] just southeast of Sumatra and the Sunda Strait. Both Cirebon and Banten had mask theater traditions and were home to Java's two oldest Muslim courts, of which only Cirebon's remains now. Through these two portals Chinese, Arabs, Persians, Indians, Siamese, Central Asians, and Europeans gained access to the interior. In the early seventeenth century, Batavia (Jakarta) was built between them by the Dutch.[3]

Sufism appears to be immoderately male—both in terms of its practitioners and its lexicon[4]—yet, as Annemarie Schimmel elegantly argues in *My Soul Is a Woman*, women enjoy full equal rights in the mystical branch of Islam.[5] Virtually all of the classical works on early Sufism position one woman as its early central figure: Rabi'a al-'Adawiyya. For Rabi'a, who introduced the absolute love of God[6] into Sufism in the eighth century, beauty was not of the lateral world; rather, it existed in the interior life of the heart. As Schimmel also notes, women are seldom referred to in the *Quran*, yet the important term *nafs* ("soul") is a feminine noun used numerous times in the *Quran*. Although its meaning is often pejorative, it also refers to the mother of mankind.[7]

The gender equity that Sufism provides has afforded both female and male pedigreed mask dancers from Java's rural northwest coast equally vibrant spiritual and artistic roles spanning multiple generations. These artists, called *dalang topeng (dalang)*, trace their lineage to Sunan Kalijaga, one of the nine legendary Sufi saints (*walisongo*), who wandered the countryside performing with masks and puppets as instruments of *dakwah* (proselytization).

Topeng cirebon is different from the *topeng malang* described by Onghokham[8] and Sunardi (chapter 5). While both are inherited forms that enjoyed great popularity before 1965, qualitative differences exist that are constellated around class, gender, and age: most *dalang topeng* are day laborers and predominantly female, while *Malang* troupes are comprised of men and children from well-heeled families. Furthermore, whereas the *Cirebon* practitioners trace their genealogy (*keturunan*) to a Sufi apostle, *Malang* artists view their art as a family business.[9] Thus, the debate about displays of piety in *topeng cirebon* pertains chiefly to women, including the importance of concealing those parts of the body considered private, *aurat*.

Even with the thoughtful engagement about piety, the debate about doctrinal injunctions on figurative art hotly contested throughout much of the Islamicate remains off of most Cirebon citizens' radar. This is likely due to the region's idiosyncratic blend of Sunni and Shia mysticism.[10] Shia Muslims have a long tradition of figurative art, including copious depictions of Prophet Muhammad. Moreover, one of Java's most prominent and controversial Muslim figures, Shaykh Siti Jenar,[11] is often compared to Junayd al-Baghdadi, both in terms of ideology and fate—both men were accused of extremist Shiism and executed for heresy. Siti Jenar, whose burial site resides on the outskirts of Cirebon, is considered the "eighth *wali*" by some adherents.[12] While most *dalang* are Sunni and trace their lineage to Sunan Kalijaga, some recognize Siti Jenar's disciple, Pangeran Panggung (Prince of the Stage), who met the same fate as his teacher, to be the founder of *topeng*. That those claiming this genealogy are often women signals a sharp contrast with other Islamic masking traditions, notably those of Sumatra and sub-Saharan Africa, where it is chiefly the domain of males.[13]

HISTORICAL CONTOURS

Masking was well established in the pre-Islamic Java,[14] and at least as far back as the sixteenth century women are known to have performed with masks in popular entertainments.[15] There is a lacuna in our knowledge of gendered mask dance in western Java until the mid-nineteenth century, when E. Hardouin's 1855 illustration of a female *dalang topeng/ronggeng*[16] and two clowns appeared in a chapter on itinerant mask performance, *topeng babakan* (mask acts) in *Java Tooneelen uit het Leven Karakterschetsen en Kleederdragten van Java's Bewoners in afbeeldingen naar de natuur geteekend.*[17]

Three centuries of Dutch control came to a close when Japanese troops entered Java near Indramayu in 1942 and quickly gained control of the region. Following Japan's defeat at the end of World War II, Dutch attempts to reclaim their hold of the Archipelago led to the Indonesian revolution and its eventual Independence in 1950.

It appears that the debate about visual representation in Islam first entered the *topeng* discourse during the last decade of Sukarno's presidency, when three organizations were vying to succeed him in the late 1950s and early 1960s: Indonesia's communist party, Partai Kommunis Indonesia (PKI); Indonesia's nationalist party, Partai Nasional Indonesia, and; the separatist Darul Islam and Islamic Army of Indonesia (Darul Islam/Tentara Islam Indonesia, or DI/TII) movement, which aimed to establish an Islamic state governed by *shari'a*. Although the peasant-based art form appealed to the PKI and its aligned socialist art organization, Lekra (Lembaga Kebudayaan Rakyat, or People's Cultural League), suspicions ran high between the organization and artists. PKI was reportedly concerned about the artists' potential link with members of DI/TII, who, likewise, were suspicious of the frequency of *topeng* performances at PKI events. According to the late *dalang topeng*, Sujana Arja (d. 2006), who frequently performed for both groups, DI/TII took issue with the mask itself, which they viewed as heresy.[18] Yet, in DI/TII's bid to dominate the region, *topeng* continued to be an important part of members' *hajatan* (life cycle events). The critique of masks lay dormant with the execution of its leaders in west Java by the Sukarno administration in 1962.

Soon after the Suharto's 1965 coup, referred to here as *Gestok*,[19] when he had wrested control of the government from Sukarno and the furore over the massacres quieted, martial law silenced the itinerant dancers. This might have been a permanent state of affairs for *topeng* practitioners were it not for Suharto's wife, Ibu Tien, who took up the mission of promoting Indonesia's cultural diversity by creating the neocolonial theme park, Taman Mini Indonesia Indah (TMII, Beautiful Indonesia Miniature Garden), on the outskirts of east Jakarta in the mid-1970s. Her conception of TMII was based on both the colonial fairs and, more to the point, her personal observations at the New York World's Fair in 1964.[20] TMII showcased Indonesia's rich visual and performing arts, including *topeng cirebon*. However, its once overt *tasawwuf* (Sufi) nuances were now muted with heavy restrictions placed on the use of public and private space. By removing *topeng* from its natural milieu, a secularized, stripped-down version was created. However, with the first overseas *topeng* tour that soon followed in 1977, *topeng* was back in circulation, albeit now under the watchful eye of the authoritarian Suharto regime.

By the late 1990s, nearly forty years after the Darul Islam movement was suppressed in west Java and with Suharto's days numbered, piety in the public sphere was again ripe for debate and *topeng* involved in the conversation. This time, however, the debate was not merely externally driven, but was organically taking place within *topeng* circles. Perhaps not surprisingly, it is not female *dalang* with pedigree, but young mask dancers without it, who are the most conflicted and rigorous debaters. That the polemic reached rural artists before social media was entrenched at the village level was no doubt influenced by Suharto's tacit (and not so tacit) support of DI/TII's heirs. Its ripples are most clearly felt at the massive, reformist *Pesantren Al-Zaytun* in the village of Mekerjaya in Gantar, Indramayu, which will be examined shortly.[21]

PERFORMING *TASAWWUF* FROM THE INSIDE OUT

With the destruction of traditional networks of Sufi transmission in Mecca and Medina as a result of the Wahhabi movement in the early nineteenth century, Sufi orders throughout the Islamicate became indigenized; yet Wahhabism became a serious topic of debate in Indonesia only with their second conquest in Mecca in 1924, when Javanese Muslims' beliefs were attacked. Its most significant inroads into Javanese religio-political thought began in the 1970s and are increasingly felt in Cirebon today.[22] Increased pressure from the Salafi community over the past few years has prevented performances in the village of Ciliwung, home to the Palimanan style of the late Wentar, Dasih, and Sudji, who were among the most important *dalang topeng* of the twentieth century.

One consequence of the breakdown in transmission of the Sufi orders (*tarekat*)[23] was that the *silsilah*—the spiritual chain of initiation—became blurred, most notably in Southeast Asia and the Balkans.[24] Malays began borrowing from and influencing one another and, in so doing, created indigenous practices in which the principles of different *tarekat* were combined. As might be expected, the guiding principles of a given order's eponym were not always in sync,[25] particularly pertaining to the devotional act of *dzikir* (Arabic: *dhikr*) for inducing remembrance of God.[26] This is no small matter, for the kind of *dzikir* employed is the primary way the orders are differentiated. There are two basic forms: silent (Cirebon Javanese: *sirri*; Arabic: *khafī*)[27] and vocal (Cirebon Javanese: *dhohir*; Arabic: *jahrī*). The starting point of the silent *dzikir* is the heart (*kalbu*)—the center of one's being. It is performed in solitude, shuns use of the voice, and involves all but minimal motion. Vocal *dzikir*, alternately, starts with the tongue. It frequently leads to body motion and is communal. Proponents of silent *dzikir* argue that theirs requires greater focus and is fully embodied, and that vocal remembrance is too easy to achieve. Hamid Algar contends that the general preference for vocal *dzikir* corresponds to the needs of the masses,

> who can emerge from their submersion in the bodily state only by the use of bodily means. A certain transmutation of bodily powers takes place that is frequently described by traditional writers in the language of alchemy, and the *dhikr* comes to serve as a transition or bridge (*bar-zakh*) between the corporeal state and those higher states that lie behind it.[28]

Tensions between proponents of the vocal and silent *dzikir* are poignantly illustrated in the early nineteenth-century Surakarta mystical court poem attributed to Sultan Pakubuwana V, *Serat Centhini*,[29] which describes the fate of the progeny of one of the *walisongo*, Sunan Giri of Giri/Gresik. *Dzikir* is mentioned in the context of a celebration prior to a wedding, in conjunction with Islamic texts, accompanied by tambourines (*terbang*) and Arabic songs. The decisive encounter between masking and mystical Islam is realized when two *dalang* perform the character, Klana, which inspires an ecstatic response in the *santri* (normatively pious Muslims), who begin singing. At one point, the bride's younger brother feels compelled to put down his tambourine and dance Klana, but upon seeing his elder brother he is frightened to do so and resigns himself to playing the tambourine.[30] The character, Klana—a madman (see figure 1.1)—has a clear *tasawwuf* context. The individual who descends into madness (*majnun*) is the equivalent of someone who embarks on the *tarekat* without the benefit of a guide.[31] Such individuals are perceived as reckless and inviting madness (*gila isim*).

Correspondences between madness and sound and between ecstasy and control so beautifully described in the *Serat Centhini* are echoed in the relationship between the *dalang topeng* and musicians who accompany her. The Sufi order, *Naqshbandiyya*, is the chief proponent of the silent *dzikir*, and while few traces of this *tarekat* are visible in Cirebon today, it can't be denied that their guiding principles exerted a deep, intractable influence in *topeng* culture, as did the *Shattariyya*, a still-prominent *tarekat* in Cirebon *kraton* circles and one of the most indigenized of the orders in the Archipelago. Throughout Java, the two *tarekat* were often combined. The relationship to *dzikir sirri* is clearly articulated in the *dalang*'s silence, her voice muted by biting into a piece of leather to secure the mask in place. One might deduce that the *dalang*, whose relationship to God is alternately achieved through rigorous asceticism *and* bodily motion, would be at odds with the ascetic *Naqshbandiyya*; yet this is not the case. Ecstatic movement (trance) is shunned by the *dalang*, whose rigorous focus on controlled breathing necessary to hold the mask in place is how remembrance is induced while dancing.

The *dalang*'s silence is countered by the musicians' distinctive whoops and hollers that distinguish the Cirebon gamelan's soundscape. Their vocal pyrotechnics, not found in any other gamelan culture in Java today, suggest a link to the *Rifaʿiyya tarekat* that spread to Cirebon and Banten. These musicians are sometimes referred to as "howling dervishes" in response to their ecstatic utterances during *dzikir* meetings.[32] Their howls stand in sharp relief to the *dalang*'s utter silence invoked by the beating of her heart. Endo Suanda shares a wonderful anecdote, wherein the late *dalang topeng*, Dasih binti Wentar (d. 1985), described the role of the heart in transmitting emotions between the *dalang* and the spectator: "When you dance, you should feel like *geregeteun*; *geregeteun* here...while she circled her fingers around her heart...so the audience will also be *geregeteun*."[33] Not only is the heart the center of her relationship to the Divine and, in this world, humanity, it also conveys the madness and intense longing that frequently accompanies *tarekat*. The tensions between proponents of the vocal and silent *dzikir* laid out in the *Serat Centhini* and realized in *topeng* suggest that in the case of the latter—keeping in mind that most members of *topeng* troupes were kin—the musicians' hollers and *dalang*'s silence were a compromise.

SPATIAL CONSTRUCTS AND THE
POLITICIZATION OF ISLAM

Before itinerancy was banned in Indonesia in 1965, *topeng* was a "happening" that played out in the *alun-alun* (village square)—a bubbling geyser of gossip, plotting, political unrest, and rebellion. While this bustle made for exciting social experiences, the performance space is not neutral. Kenyan playwright, Ngũgĩ wa Thiong'o, stresses that it memorializes time in terms of "what has gone before—history—and what could follow—the future."[34] It is thus a contested space—a magnet for tensions and conflicts—not only in Java, but also in colonial territories throughout the developing world. Wherever it took place, it expressed tangible and metaphoric contingencies of power and nationhood.[35] For performers from the Cirebon region, that space (then and now) oscillates between expansion and contraction: between government promotion and control and between the village square and global spectacles. It is thus as much about the geography traversed as the physical space where neighbors gather to participate in a shared experience. This held true whether they were day laborers traveling to Europe and America to participate in the colonial expositions; curious, privileged travelers from Europe and the United States who came to watch the Natives perform in the "Java Village";[36] or members of small itinerant *topeng* ensembles who walked for miles in their heavy costumes, stopping in each *alun-alun*, their instruments and cooking utensils in tow.

If you were a male *dalang*, the performance space is where you changed into your *topeng* attire in full view of the audience, removing your "veil" in the presence of God. Piety, however, dictates that women change in private, entering the public space only in full costume. It is also where the musicians set up their instruments while the *dalang* chewed *sirih*,[37] recited mantras, and created a universe of interactions that bridged the performers, spectators (ancestral and living), and God.

The realities of the space and the artists' preparations dictated that live *topeng* performances were both shared and intimate. As open spaces go, this one is unforgiving. The *dalang* must navigate through narrow eye slits carved in the mask in order to avoid obstacles in her path: children clamoring, giggling, and impinging closer and closer upon the *dalang*'s finite physical sphere; babies crying; and the musicians who are at times only inches from the dancer. They are almost always outside her visual field, yet her focus remains fixed on her breath and her eyes are fervently on the ground. This interiority, acutely unique to *topeng*, illustrates another core principle of the *Naqshbandiyya*: maintaining solitude in the public sphere.[38] For female practitioners it signals modesty as well, even as all eyes gaze upon her.

When *topeng* was reintroduced to Indonesians and to the world as part of Indonesia's national heritage in accordance with Suharto's fledgling nationalist narrative, the contours of the performance space shifted with it. Military-sponsored identification cards to track artists followed (*tanda kenyataan* or "certificate of proof"), which gradually gave way to artist identification cards (*kartu seniman*), both of which were designed to control the physical space and who utilized it.[39] Moreover, in acknowledging the critical role Muslims played in the eradication of the communist party, PKI,[40] Suharto required performers to rigorously adhere to *shalat* (daily prayers) during scheduled performances. Performances in the evening could begin no earlier than 8 p.m., approximately one hour after evening prayer, *Isa*, and conclude no later than 3:30 a.m., approximately one hour prior to morning prayers, *Subuh*. Breaks from 12:30 to 1 p.m. for noon prayers, *Duhur*, and at 3:30 p.m. for afternoon prayers, *Asar*, had to be observed.[41]

The important role anticommunist Muslim organizations played in securing Suharto's place in Indonesian history sheds light on the timing of *topeng*'s inauguration at Al-Zaytun. *Topeng* was introduced into their art curriculum in conjunction with the opening of Al-Zaytun's university, *Universitas Al-Zaytun*, on the fortieth anniversary of Gestok. The event unfolded with great fanfare, including a brief appearance by the then-ailing ex-president Suharto, who arrived in time to witness the unveiling of the university's new building that bears his name.[42]

Al-Zaytun is under the leadership of the Islamist Shaykh Panji Gumilang (alias Abu Toto), whose ties to the violent, underground wing of *Darul Islam, Negara Islam Indonesia KW9 Darul Islam*, reach back to 1978.[43] A deeper secularization of the mask "tradition" followed, both at the school and in the village from which it came. One is hard-pressed to imagine two more disparate entities coming together than when Panji Gumilang hired a *topeng* troupe from rural Slangit, Cirebon, to teach mask dance to their students and faculty. It was not a static experience. The two young, male village *dalang* were teaching pious female students; hence, their teaching technique and behavior was modified. Discernable shifts in how the form was taught upon their return home followed, including less corrective touching and costume alterations.

Today, *topeng* performances at Al-Zaytun are held in their massive outdoor arena every Friday night following soccer games, which in itself is a contested space. Once a rich source of teak wood, the sprawling 1,200-hectare campus (approximately 3,000 acres), which was home to an agrarian community that was forcibly displaced in the late 1990s so that the campus could be built, comprises one of the most deforested regions in the district today. The performance space takes on a very different meaning within this Golkar-funded,[44] religion-based context.

FASHIONING THE *TOPENG* PANTHEON

The *topeng* characters often strike outsiders as "Hinduized," both in name and personality. Yet the primary stories they vibrate to—the *Ramayana* and *Mahabharata*—have over the centuries not only been Javanized, but also Islamicized. In no place is this more evident than in the characters' dress and temperament. The first character is Panji, whose eggshell-white color is associated with semen, indicating a fertile, potent male. He is also associated with *mutmainah* (calmness, refinement). His movements are concealed behind a rectangular batik *sarung* (*kaen lancar*) that is draped like a long skirt. In the legendary Panji tales known throughout the Malay world and which rival the Indic epics' popularity in Cirebon,[45] the refined Panji is a Javanese Hindu prince in search of his lost love, Candra Kirana.

Within the frame of *topeng*, Panji is a transitional character that bridges Hindu and Muslim Java. Although his sarong is unquestionably pre-Islamic, he is not stuck there. He has converted to Islam, signaled by Panji's movement that corresponds to *adzan* (the call to prayer). Panji is the only character whose *batik* is draped long like a skirt. With the second character, Samba, who is painted white or pink and represents adolescence, the *batik* is folded between the legs and tucked in the waist so that the knickers and legs are visible. The costume remains this way for the remaining three characters. Samba is alternately joyous, light, and coquettish, though narcissistic. Once the mask is donned, the adolescent giggles, gazes at his reflection in his hand as if it were a mirror, prepares betel nut paste (*sirih*), and applies it as makeup. Samba unequivocally represents a seeker, whose movements alternate between confusion and giddiness.

The flirtatious Rumyang is usually painted rose and follows Samba chronologically, although some *dalang* perform it last if time allows. This sequential deviation suggests Rumyang may be a late addition to the *topeng* canon and is used to sanctify the space, suggesting a pre-Islamic Javanese connection to number "five."[46]

The next character, Tumenggung, signifies a warrior—a positive force, though not in possession of Panji's profundity. In the context of life cycle, Tumenggung represents adulthood, with bold, but con-trolled movements connoting his stamina and determination. His energy is external and directed toward the audience.[47] Tumenggung's costume exudes colonial influence: the sacred headdress, called the *sobrah*, is replaced by a visor (*peci*), collar (*kelambi kerah*), and nar-row tie (*dasi*). By the 1970s, some *dalang* wore sunglasses during the unmasked part of the dance, a cosmopolitan flourish that also implies deception.[48] Yet, in previous generations, clear glasses were the norm. Their appearance at a time when prescription eyeglasses were rare in Indonesia suggests the focus was on the Divine and external forces, for example, colonial hegemony. His strong (*gagah*) and precise movements demonstrate the importance of unwavering clarity on the Sufi path.[49] The final character, the beet-red, lusty, greedy king, Klana (figure 1.1), lacks full control of his faculties. Like those who precede him, Klana is more nuanced than meets the eye. Dwelling beneath his anger is an impulse toward deeper consciousness. And so the cycle begins anew.

The five main characters are male; yet the importance of women is encoded in the second character, the androgynous Samba, whose rela-tionship to the clown-servant Tembem is least understood. Tembem, who is the only clown (*bodor*) character still performed in *topeng cire-bon*, has the additional distinction of being the only female character (although her role must be performed by a man). Her swollen third eye and exaggerated mole define her as homely, yet her "clown" des-ignation confirms she is a friend of God (*wali*). In some versions of the dance, Samba—who is associated with death[50]—nods off, awak-ens, and nods off again while dancing. His awakened, trance-like state confers the diffused focus of an individual embarking on *tarekat* and, in particular, the Sufi notion that one must "die before dying." When finally revived by Tembem, Samba's movements suggest a bird grooming its feathers.

The tropes of the bird and its disguise are consistent with Sufi alle-gories: notably, Farid ud-Din Attar's (Persian poet) twelfth-century allegory, *The Conference of the Birds*,[51] wherein a group of birds hold a conference to seek their leader and designate a colorful bird (hoopoe) to lead the way. The birds have as many questions of the hoopoe as excuses for why they should not participate before starting on the pilgrimage. They pass through seven valleys, which represent the dif-ferent stages of *tarekat*. The story is constellated around the dilemma of those birds that still have not yet fully committed themselves to the journey. It is through the birds' self-doubt, a litany of questions about the journey, the hoopoe's responses, and, ultimately, the "death" of many of the birds along the way, that lead them to realize that the *shaykh* they sought existed already within them. The story is rooted in two connected ideas: the necessity to destroy the Self and the importance of passionate love. The love Attar celebrates flies in the face of social, sexual, and religious convention, for example, love between a superior and an inferior. This point is clearly portrayed in the clown's loquacious banter and the chief characters' silence, the silence that is grounded both in *topeng*'s gestural lexicon and, as will be discussed in the next section of this chapter, in the *lokcan* cape worn by the *dalang*. The relationship further suggests the character reversals of the Javanese *wayang punakawan* clown characters, who also represent the *wali*.[52]

THE FACE AND BODY AS A MEDIUM

Anthony Reid's description of the human body as the most important medium of art that particularly transitions into adulthood that incorporates "decoration and artifice, often of a painful kind"[53] is central to the *topeng* mask. The aesthetics of illusion is the stuff of intense relational encounters between artist and disciple, performer and audience, and the living and the dead. It is incumbent upon the *dalang* to know her way around her mind and heart and to allow others access to both.

As the first part of most *topeng* characters is performed sans mask, audiences expect the artist's face to be pleasing to watch, regardless of either party's gender. To this end, a yellow facial powder, *bedak kuning*, was often applied to give the face a special glow.[54] The feminized, often eroticized, human face was thus as studied and critiqued as the characters being portrayed. During the first part of the dance, the spectator had ample time to fantasize about the *dalang*, both as an object of beauty and a potential mate. The most successful performers combined charisma with exceptional talent. Not surprisingly, spectators frequently fell in love with the *dalang* while watching them dance, prompting many a marriage and nearly as many divorces.[55] When unions between female *dalang* and their nonartist husbands dissolved, the division of property was based on local imams' interpretation of shari'a. Since female *dalang* often married wealthy patrons and entered marital unions with few worldly goods, their soon-to-be ex-husbands reaped the greatest financial benefit. Lacking the financial resources to face the situation, *dalang* typically returned to the home of a family member until they either resurrected their careers or remarried. Usually, the career came first. The reason is twofold. First, performing is the *dalang*'s raison d'étre and, second, it was the best opportunity where they were most likely to attract a new mate. In this way, the circulation of performance opportunities and potential partners energized *topeng*, with practitioners cycling between working and nesting.[56]

The other face under discussion is, of course, the mask itself, whose outer dimensions have complex interior counterparts. Just as *sirih* has mystical, aesthetic, and relational values, strategically placing precious stones on the outer face of some masks has its internalized counterpart, with *dalang* inserting precious metals (*susuk*) subcutaneously in the identical location. Whereas the external appearance of stones is overt beautification, placing it beneath the flesh is believed to enhance the *dalang*'s stamina and skill (inner) while attracting someone or something to her, most commonly, an audience or a mate. The increasingly rare appearance of amulets on the inner face of older masks impregnate the mask and its wearer with power, bringing the external world of form (*zahir*) into constant conversation with the internal world of meaning (*batin*). Its external elements are intended for the spectator, while internalized manifestations are for the *dalang* alone.

Figure 1.1   Klana mask made by the maskmaker, Waryo. This mask incorporates three green stones in the crown, black molars, and golden teeth. *Photo*: Laurie Margot Ross.

Another human aesthetic captured in the outer face of the mask—teeth filing—is one of the most widespread Southeast Asian devices of human body beautification. Although less common today, it is still performed on young girls in parts of Indramayu. Historically, the rationale was to differentiate human beings from feral animals and demons of the spirit world, who also have white teeth, so as not to be mistaken for an evil spirit upon death.[57] Likewise, leveled teeth convey human beings in *topeng* as opposed to the fanged animal and demonic types portrayed in the dance drama, *wayang wong*.

In addition to the filing of teeth, *sirih* use is also depicted in the mask's iconography in the form of blackened dental molars and lower teeth. When combined with golden upper teeth, the character's charisma and power are accentuated (figure 1.1). *Sirih* was the most common way to transfer dye to the lips before cosmetics became widely available. The ingredients *gambir/apu* in *sirih*, when combined with saliva, reddens the lips, which symbolizes idealized beauty.[58] While in its earlier context it is believed to have bridged local agricultural and spiritual beliefs, *sirih* enjoyed tremendous staying power long after Islam became the dominant discourse and is still integrated into the ritual preparations of elder *dalang*, who chew it while reciting silent *dzikir* next to the *kotak topeng* (the plain wood chest where the masks are stored). They do so in plain view of the audience. *Sirih*, then, not only had cosmetic properties; it also heightened the *dalang*'s focus. To the attentive observer, it also signaled that the *kotak topeng* served as far more than the home of the masks. It was a portable altar.

Jean Gelman Taylor stresses that modification in costume "is the outward sign of change in religion, government, and availability of trade goods."[59] There is no doubt that *topeng* attire has proved highly adaptive to the zeitgeist. During Japan's occupation of Java, Claire Holt noted the substitution of inexpensive Japanese ready-made scarves used by itinerant *wayang wong* troupes in West Java, which she chalked up to the wartime scarcity of hand-drawn batik.[60] More recently, *dalang* from Losari, Cirebon, on the cusp of Central Java, crossed the border to buy their *sarung*—not because Central Javanese designs were favored over those from Cirebon, but because they were less expensive. While in past generations when full-day performances were the norm in conjunction with ritual events, a single top and a pair of pants were used for all characters. Today, the color of the costume is different for each character; yet, due to Klana being the most oft-requested dance today, most *dalang* wear red costumes, the color associated with him. Furthermore, the old Chinese *mega mendung* (cloud) motif *kaen lancer* that, today, is considered an important aspect of the *topeng* costume is, in fact, a relatively new addition. Its emergence over the past generation reinforces, somewhat anachronistically, Peranakan Chinese patronage of *topeng* prior to the 1965 massacres, at which time itinerancy and Chinese New Year celebrations were banned. The reasoning behind the recent addition of the *mega mendung* motif, though unclear, suggests the *reformasi*-generation's interest in revisiting the close bond these two communities once enjoyed. Thus, while more recent costume alterations seem out of sync with the past, they are, instead, consistent with it.

EXPRESSED PIETY, CLOTH, AND THE BODY

By all accounts, the tradition of professional improvisational dancers (*ronggeng*) in Java is very old and shares symmetry with India's *devadasi* court dancers (including the shared connotation of court prostitution, often noted by outsiders).[61] While seemingly an odd fit with *topeng*'s masculine energy, the launch of official *ronggeng* schools at Cirebon's royal court (and taxed by Dutch administrators) bridged the two forms.[62] A warm drink composed of ginger, *air serbat*, was an integral part of the *ronggeng* experience. According to the late prominent Cirebon *kraton* scholar, T. D. Sudjana (died c. 2010), the drink was consumed to heat up the body and ignite passion in the performer and spectator-participant, which included members of the royal court.[63] The drink was eventually replaced with alcohol under Dutch hegemony. Since alcohol consumption is prohibited in Islam, female *dalang* who doubled as *ronggeng* were increasingly linked to prostitution by the early twentieth century.

Contemporary definitions notwithstanding, both the *ronggeng* and *dalang*'s alliance is mystical. According to the *Babad Cerbon* (the Chronicles of Cirebon), written by Abdul Kahar, the seventeenth-century *pengulu* (chief mosque official) at the Agung Mosque, *ronggeng* is the performed translation of *marifat* (knowledge). It is the zenith of the *tarekat*, the culmination of the previous three levels: *shari'a, tarekat* (the way), and *hakekat* (truth). Each level has its counterpart in the Cirebon performing arts beginning with *wayang* (puppetry) and then progressing to *berokan* (full body mask), and *topeng*, respectively. *Ronggeng* is exalted because it combines the first three stages finally in unveiled form,[64] replicated in the male *dalang* who undresses in view of his audience.

E. Hardouin's 1851 *topeng babakan* illustration (published posthumously in 1855) shows a *dalang topeng* performing *ronggeng*, so noted by the fan in her right hand as well as her gesture. The *sarung* hugs her body from the chest to the ankle, anchored by a silver belt and obscured by a variety of patterned handkerchiefs that, tucked into the belt, create a skirt effect (figure 1.2). This early presentation suggests that the uncut cloth, so long touted as sacred to the people of Java, was either not as meaningful as the visible parts of the costume, or, in fact, more sacred in its concealment.

The *ronggeng/topeng* combination highlights the important role attractiveness plays in the careers of these dancers. During Japan's occupation of Java (1942–1945), female *dalang*, some of whom were forced to serve as "comfort women," had more opportunities to be hired by Japanese troops than their male counterparts.[65] Whenever the sound system failed (which was often), the *dalang* slipped back into her *kebaya* (blouse) and *sarung* and entertained the troops with her *ronggeng* moves.[66]

Figure 1.2 *Topeng babakan* performance. Female *dalang* and male *bodor* (clown). From Hardouin et al. *Java Tooneelen uit het Leven Karakterschetsen en Kleederdragten van Java's Bewoners in afbeeldingen naar de natuur geteekend.* 1855.

We cannot point with certainty to a date when pants became a de rigueur part of *topeng* attire, although they were likely standardized following the opening of the Suez Canal in 1869, when more Muslim Malays performed the haj than ever before.[67] Pilgrims' contact with the larger Muslim community in Mecca and Medina expanded their worldview, including diverse expressions of Muslim attire, particularly the preference for stitched cloth, in contrast with Java's traditional garments, which were made up of rectangular cloth, notably the *sarung* and *selendang* (shawl).

The material transition from Panji to the second character in the pantheon, Samba, makes this point quite clearly. Panji's sensuously enveloping cloth is cleverly reconfigured to mimic pants, which are draped over knickers for Samba.[68] This has historical precedent in the traditional dress of Saudi Arabia, wherein both men and women wear loose-fitting pantaloons with a drawstring waist, called *sirwaal*, beneath the *thawb*, an ankle-length shirt.[69]

A matching short-sleeved top that is partially obscured by the silk cape, *lokcan*, has replaced the breast wrap and exposed arms that were hidden in the past. *Lokcan* is a Chinese term for "blue silk," so-named because the silk derived from the province of Shantung, had a bluish hue.[70] Due to the rarity of this particular silk, the term now refers to its Chinese-inspired iconography, notably the phoenix, sea creatures, and other oceanic motifs. Today's *lokcan*, which is often made of silk crepe or imported fine cotton, remains one of the most important possessions of the *dalang*. Those considered most spiritually imbued have been handed down intergenerationally. Those *dalang* who are not on the receiving end of an heirloom *lokcan* seek one of comparable age and condition—the more weathered, the better. Although its meaning is lost today, the *lokcan* likely represents the initiatic cloak (*khirqa*) that symbolizes the transmission of knowledge and nonmaterial power from the *shaykh* to disciple—a practice known to both Sunni and Shia mystics.[71] Among the Naqshbaniyya, it symbolizes the garment of poverty Gabriel gave to Muhammad during the *Miraj*.[72] Annemarie Schimmel describes its significance thus:

> In investing the *murīd* with the patched frock, Sufism has preserved the old symbolism of garments: by donning a garment that has been worn, or even touched, by the blessed hands of a master, the disciple acquires some of the *baraka*, the mystic-magical power of the sheikh.[73]

The late Cirebon religious scholar and artist, Kandeg, shared a story with Endo Suanda about the character Aki-Aki, who represents an old priest of Chinese ancestry and embodies the sacred teacher-student relationship and the secret system of knowledge, which sheds considerable light on the important role of the *lokcan* in *topeng* culture. In Kandeg's version, Aki-Aki is unsteady on his feet and leans on the *kotak*. He complains to the musicians that his back aches and requests them to massage him. A musician comes forward and kneads the sore area. The *bodor* subsequently places Aki-Aki's costume over his own (mimicking Aki-Aki's action). Here, as in the Samba/Tembem dyad described earlier, there is a clear role reversal in place wherein the clown serves as the guru/*shaykh*.

Aki-Aki is clearly a transformative figure as indeed are all of the characters in the pantheon to one degree or another. What distinguishes him from the others is his dual role as healer and the healed. For example, he asks a musician to massage his ailing body, just as the *murid* asks a *shaykh* for psychic healing. Moreover, Aki-Aki wins the battle against the protagonist through his now able body (*pencak*). That the *murid* portrays the old (experienced) teacher is consistent with the Samba/Tembem inversion. It is also revelatory for it indicates the implicit interdependence of all mentoring relationships, which are based on reciprocity, mutuality, and emotional sustenance.

The *lokcan* cape's former blue hue further defines it as a *tasawwuf* object of exchange. Similar to it, the Sufi *khirqa* that is passed from the *shaykh* to *murid* is usually dark blue, which, it has been suggested, is the color of mourning, demonstrating that "the Sufi had separated himself from the world and what is in it."[74] This makes it not only a physical, but also a spiritually imbued garment. By the late eighteenth century, transferring the cloak indicated the student was both worthy of succession and had, in fact, been formally initiated. That the *lokcan* is stitched at the center and proudly worn—holes and all—further supports a *tasawwuf* interpretation that positions the *dalang*'s lineage and her repudiation of the material world, front and center.

Dasih, with whom I trained with in the late 1970s, gave me her *lokcan* when I completed my studies. She did not explain, nor did I understand, the significance of her gesture at the time, since I not only lacked pedigree, I was an American. Even so, I treasured the tattered cloth that she, her father, and grandfather had worn before her. The reality was that I was her only student who had learned all five *topeng* characters in her family's style (*gaya Palimanan*). It was also unusual for a guru and non-*keturunan* student to share a bedroom: we shared hers for nearly one year. In that tiny space, we faced each other every evening on our respective beds, where I asked her about her life and about the form I was studying. She withheld nothing.

In our bedroom, my ailing guru recited the Divine Names in her heart, while her still nimble fingers counted each bead on her *tasbih* (rosary). Perhaps I became the custodian of Dasih's sacred heirloom (*pusaka*) cloth because she was unable to bear children and was, thus, chosen to perform the rigorous, ascetic practices expected of one's progeny.[75] What was once opaque is now transparent: I was initiated, *khirqa* and all.

SOBRAH POWER

Some *dalang* refer to the *sobrah* (headdress) as the "center" or "home." In past generations there were five styles, one for each of the characters in the *topeng* pantheon. Most important to this discussion is the *sobrah* reserved for Panji, the first and most spiritual character. The name of the *sobrah* designated for him is *tekes Panji*. The etymology of *tekes* is understood to be Javanese, in reference to both the headdress and Panji in Old Javanese literature, with examples in the fourteenth-century Hindu-Buddhist text, *Nāgarakrtāgama*,[76] and the fifteenth-century chronicle of the Javanese Majapahit kingdom, *Pararaton*. While both texts are considered to be of pre-Islamic origin, the purpose of the *tekes Panji* (keeping in mind that Muslim traders and merchants were present on the island during this period) suggests it might correspond to the Turkish word *tekke*,[77] which designates an intimate place of respite and learning for Sufi *shaykhs* and their disciples, a concept related to the Javanese *rumah suluk*.[78]

The *sobrah*'s significance to the *dalang* parallels that of the Muslim turban's significance in designating different *tarekat* in Ottoman lands, which is clearly translated in their tombs of *shaykhs*, mullahs, and other prominent Sufis. There, the three-dimensional carved turban of the deceased's *tarekat* affiliation is signaled by its placement atop a male's tombstone.[79] While *tarekat* in the Cirebon region do not have specific turbans, I located two twentieth-century headstones at *Astana Gunung Jati* in Cirebon (figure 1.3), whose designs are executed in relief near the head of the stone and synthesize the motif of the turban with the tree of life (*pohon hayat*) iconography common to Cirebon graves. While the Cirebon stones are not three-dimensional turban renderings, they do correspond to Ottoman tombstones that designate important female dervishes, whose designs are also incised near the top of the stone.

Just as turban designs may indicate a particular Sufi order in some regions, the design of the *sobrah* is equally iconic and critical for the smooth performance. Yet, because it is prepared from human hair, it

Figure 1.3   Double-headed tombstone at *Astana Gunung Jati* in Cirebon. *Photo:* Laurie Margot Ross.

sparks strong reactions in some Muslims, even though animal skin has long been featured in the head coverings worn by Muslims in Turkey and Iran.[80] There is a gendered component to using hair in the making of the *sobrah*. Because it must be long enough to weave into the frame and cannot be dyed, the pool of candidates from whom it can be taken is limited to young women. In a culture where long hair is prized, persuading women to part with theirs is costly, making the headdress one of the most important financial investments in a *dalang*'s career.

Over the past decade, *dalang* are increasingly commissioning *sobrah* made from black wool yarn. Although the use of wool in this context may be little more than a coincidence since the terms Sufi and Sufism are not part of most *dalang*'s vocabulary, it is important to note that the word *tasawwuf* translates as "Sufism," which is derived from *suf,* or "wool." Other possible translations of *suf* are certainly plausible; however, in its Sufi context, it is widely believed to refer to the coarse

woolen robes worn by early Muslim ascetics representing their disregard for worldly goods.[81] Substituting wool for those practitioners
may thus be more aligned with economics than mystical attunement:
it costs a fraction of the price and is indistinguishable from hair when
looked from a distance.

The late *sobrah* maker, Nawi, argued against using wool, stating that human hair was specified by the *wali*. He stressed it "lacks
charisma,"[82] an idea in agreement with Anderson's claim that charisma
assumes political force within mystical and magical cosmologies.[83] It is
also an exemplar of the Javanist-*tasawwuf* conceptualization of power,
with charisma residing fervently at the center and a synthetic expression of the horizontal axis of Islam,[84] demonstrating that even in her
role as conduit, the *dalang* is of this world.

The double-icon third eye, *picisan*, which rests on the *dalang*'s
forehead, is referred to by performers as simply *topeng*[85] (figure 1.4).
The two "eyes" are sewn together at the innermost connection point
of the *sobrah*: the center. The antiquity of this feature is unknown;
however, the Sufi fascination with binaries suggests it is a highly adaptive icon.[86] Ricklefs describes how binaries are fused in pre-Islamic
Java, in his discussion of Pakubuwana II's *Serat Wulang*:

> The left eye is synonymous with Javanese literature and the right eye
> with Arabic literature. The left eye thus provides an interior perspective
> on the self, and the right eye an external view of the self. "Both were
> needed for a complete view of reality, just as one must be both Javanese
> and Muslim to achieve a full identity."[87]

Elder *dalang* and musicians understand the *picisan* in similar binaries
based on the Javanese word for "eye," *mripat*, which is believed to be
derived from *marifat* that, as previously noted, constitutes the highest
level of the Sufi path. "The left eye (*narakah*) symbolizes impoverish-
ment of the soul, while the right eye (*sorgah*) connotes the positive
path...We must always remember the good path. There is only one
God. *Topeng* [*picisan*] is the state of constant remembrance."[88] The
late puppeteer Kalim (d. 2009) stressed that the *dalang topeng* is one
form of God because of the *picis* and that it is named *topeng* because
it has already entered the heart. The genealogy of how one acquires
knowledge trumps any other lineage.[89] Musician Miska Lukmanul
Hakim echoes this, stating that it is the equivalent of the mask before
it is worn. During the unmasked part of the dance, it provides the
context for *ilmu* (spiritual knowledge) and automatically migrates to
the heart once the mask is worn.[90]

Figure 1.4   Drawing of Tekes Panji by Kandeg Patmadjawinata. Courtesy of Irawati Durban Ardjo, Bandung, West Java, Indonesia.

Dasih offered a different explanation: "One eye gazes upon Allah, while the other eye is fixed on the earth,"[91] a fine-tuned blending of Islam's vertical and horizontal axes in the performer/spectator/Divine matrix. She described the *picisan* as *khafi*, a mystical reference to perception and intuition associated with the color of the *sobrah* (black) and the vehicle for understanding the heart (*kalbu*)—the organ of perception.

In addition to the significance of human hair and the *picisan*, several strands dangle from each side of the *sobrah* composed of beads and cotton balls, called *rawis* (figure 1.2). Its symmetry replicates the same dichotomy integral to the Javanese *Weltanschauung* of balance and harmony.[92] In past generations the beads totaled ninety-nine, one for each of the Divine Names—a *tasbih* in motion. Though it is

beyond the scope of this chapter, it is nonetheless tantalizing to consider that the *rawis* may have a linguistic correlation with the Arabic
word for a reciter or storyteller (the preserver of lost knowledge),
rāwī. Certainly, its function is similar to the rawis-as-rosary.

Not only has the shape of the *sobrah* changed over generations,
so, too, have other parts of the costume. Female mask dancers began
modifying their costumes as a response to growing concerns about
covering *aurat* by the early 2000s. The *jilbab* (head covering) was
embraced and along with it, the short-sleeve top (*klambi*) was extended
below the wrists, or at least modified by wearing a long-sleeve shirt
beneath it; the knickers that fall just below the kneecap were being
extended to the ankle; and the feet increasingly covered with socks.[93]

The City of Cirebon's Department of Culture and Tourism's
increased sponsorship of cultural affairs ushered in a contemporary version of *topeng*, called *rampak topeng* (group *topeng*) that features one
character from the pantheon (usually Klana) in synchronized form. In
order to give it the look of gender symmetry, *dalang* and nonlineage
mask dancers[94] perform side by side. The latter, thus, became de facto
dalang topeng in a culture that has long distinguished the two.

The *topeng* style put on the national and global map by the late
Sujana bin Arja since the first *topeng* tour in 1977 is the dominant style
today, asserting the form's masculinity in a culture disproportionately
composed of women, who, like their male counterparts, trace their
lineage to the *wali* patriarchy. This duality confirms a powerful correlation between female agency and Islam along Java's northwest coast,
one that is swiftly distancing itself from mystical praxis and toward
normative Islam.

NOTES

1. H. J. de Graaf, *Chinese Muslims in Java in the 15th and 16th Centuries:
The Malay Annals of Semarang and Cerbon.* Trans. and comments,
G. Pigeaud. Ed. M. C. Ricklefs, *Deśawarnana (Nāgarakrtāgama)*
(Melbourne, Australia: Monash Papers of Southeast Asia, No. 12, 1984),
181. Graaf and Pigeaud speculate that the stone reliefs on some Islamic
tombstones along the *pasisir* were carved by Chinese Muslim crafts-
men. Chinese and Arab traders who supplied cotton and other goods
pertaining to textile production also had contact with the coastal Sufi
guilds, with many Peranakan Chinese carvers said to be guild members.
Harmen C. Veldhuisen, *Batik Belanda, 1840–1940. Dutch Influence in
Batik from Java: History and Stories* (Jakarta: Gaya Favorit, 1993), 28;
Alit Veldhuisen-Djajasoebrata, *Weavings of Power and Might: The Glory of
Java* (Rotterdam: Museum voor Volkenkunde, 1988), 27.

2. Banten was formerly part of the province of West Java. It was established as a separate province in 2000.

3. Bruce W. Carpenter, *Javanese Antique Furniture and Folk Art* (Singapore: Editions Didier Millet, 2009), 22; Engseng Ho, *The Graves of Tarim: Genealogy and Mobility Across the Indian Ocean* (Berkeley: University of California Press, 2006): 183–187; M. C. Ricklefs, *Mystic Synthesis in Java: A History of Islamization from the Fourteenth to the Early Nineteenth Centuries* (Norwalk: East Bridge, 2006), 3.

4. For example, the noun "man" designates any person who strives toward God, without reference to the gender of the individual.

5. Annemarie Schimmel, *My Soul Is a Woman: The Feminine in Islam* (New York: Continuum, 1997), 15.

6. Absolute love is grounded in the *Quran*. See *Surah* 5, Verse 54: "Bring forth those whom He loves and who love Him."

7. Schimmel, *My Soul Is a Woman*, 19–21; 69–70.

8. Onghokham, "The Wayang Topèng World of Malang." *Indonesia* 14 (1972).

9. Ibid., 117–120.

10. *Babad Djalasutra: Njarijosaken Lampahanipun Pangeran Panggung Ladjeng Karan Kijai Djalasutra* (Yogyakarta: Sumodidjojo, Mahadewa, 1956); D. A. Rinkes, *Nine Saints of Java* (Kuala Lumpur: MSRI, 1996), 21–22, 42–48. Java is predominantly Sunni; however, there is a marked Shia presence.

11. See, for example, Eric Sasono's description of the film, *Sang Pencerah* in this volume, in which Siti Jenar (Djenar) is blamed for Islam's failings.

12. Rinkes, *Nine Saints of Java*, 29–38.

13. Simon Ottenberg and David A. Binkley, eds. *Playful Performers: African Children's Masquerades* (Edison, NJ: Transaction, 2006); René A. Bravmann, "*Gyinna-Gyinna*: Making the *Djinn* Manifest." *African Arts* 10, 3 (1977): 46; Paul Mason, "The End of Fasting: Evolving Performances at *Hari Raya* Celebrations Are a Window into Deeper Cultural Change." *Inside Indonesia* 93 (July–September 2008). http://insideindonesia.org /content/view/1126/47/

14. Clara Brakel, "Masked Dances, Spirit Worship and the Introduction of Islam in Java." *Assaph: Studies in the Theatre* 9 (1993): 20; Claire Holt, *Art in Indonesia. Continuities and Change* (Ithaca: Cornell University Press, 1967), 281; Soedarsono, *Wayang Wong: The State Ritual Dance Drama in the Court of Yogyakarta* (Yogyakarta: Gadja University Press, 1984).

15. Holt, *Art in Indonesia*, 281; Tomé Pires, *The Suma Oriental of Tomé Pires*, 2 vols. (London: Hakluyt Society, [1515], 1944), 177; Stuart Robson, trans. *Deśawarnana (Nāgarakrtāgama)* by Mpu Prapañca (Leiden: KITLV Press, 1995). The first concrete mention of masked dance in Java is in the fourteenth-century (1365) Hindu-Javanese pan-egyric about King Hayam Wuruk of Majapahit, *The Nāgarakrtāgama of Rakawi Prapañca*.

16. A female *dalang topeng* who also performs sans mask as an improvisational dancer.

17. The French set designer, Ernest Alfred Hardouin (1820–1854), came to Java with a theater troupe in 1842 and traveled throughout West Java after the troupe dissolved. Although the book was first published in 1855, the drawings were executed c. 1851. Y. M. de Jager, *Excerpta Indonesia* 44 (1991): 42; Ensiklopedi Jakarta, "Ernest Alfred Hardouin." Dinas Komunikasi, Informatika dan Kehumasan Pemprov DKI Jakarta: http://www.jakarta.go.id/jakv1/encyclopedia/detail/538

18. Much has been written about this debate in Islamic art, although no Quranic *surah* support such injunctions. Thoughtful treatment of the subject is presented in Sir Thomas Arnold, *Painting in Islam* (New York: Dover, [1928], 1965), 1–40. See, too, K. A. C. Creswell's extensive bibliography on this topic in "The Lawfulness of Painting in Early Islam." *Ars Islamica* 11, 12 (1946): 159. Also, Eva Baer, *The Human Figure in Islamic Art: Inheritances and Islamic Transformations* (Costa Mesa, CA: Mazda, 2004); Oleg Grabar, *The Formation of Islamic Art* (New Haven: Yale University Press, 1973).

19. *Gestok*, the acronym for *Gerakan Sabtu Oktober* (October 1 Movement), reflects the actual date of the coup attempt in which six generals and one army officer were killed in an effort to overthrow President Sukarno. The term was introduced by Sukarno in his (unsuccessful) bid to stop use of the pejorative acronym initiated by the Suharto regime, *Gestapu* (September 30 Movement), which places the date of the event as one day earlier, September 30. Hersi Setiawan, *Kamus Gestok* (Yogyakarta: Galang Press, 2003), 99–100.

   Two theories persist about who initiated the *putsch* that swiftly led to Suharto's coup and ultimate control. Anderson and McVey's early report points to dissatisfied junior officers as likely behind it. The second theory—and the official version promoted by the Suharto regime—places disgruntled PKI members as its driving force. The second theory has gained currency in recent years with compelling new evidence by Boden and Roosa. Benedict R. O'G. Anderson and Ruth McVey, *A Preliminary Analysis of the October 1, 1965 Coup in Indonesia* (Ithaca, NY: Cornell University Press, 1971); Ragna Boden, "The 'Gestapu' Events of 1965 in Indonesia: New Evidence from Russian and German Archives." *Bijdragen tot de Taal-, Land- en Volkenkunde* 163 (2007): 507–528; John Roosa, *Pretext for Mass Murder. The September 30th Movement & Suharto's Coup d'État in Indonesia* (Madison: University of Wisconsin Press, 2006).

20. According to Bandung dancer, Irawati Durban Ardjo, who performed at the New York World's Fair in 1964, Ibu Tien was part of the Indonesian Pavilion there, where she sold textiles. Personal Communication, August 27, 2012. For more on the Indonesian pavilion in 1964, see Ardjo (2008).

21. Administratively, Indramayu is part of the Cirebon region. When I first visited Al-Zaytun in 2005, it was the largest *pesantren* in Indonesia. Its

enrollment has steadily declined since then, although the current numbers are impossible to verify.

22. Martin van Bruinessen, "Wahhabi Influences in Indonesia, Real and Imagined" (summary of paper presented at the *Journée d'Etudes du CEIFR (EHESS-CNRS) et MSH sur le Wahhabisme*. Ecole des Hautes Etudes en Sciences Sociales / Maison des Sciences de l'Homme. Paris, June 10, 2002). http://www.archivesaudiovisuelles.fr/11/163/martin _van_bruinessen-7.pdf

23. *Tarekat* has two meanings. In this context it refers to the Sufi orders or fraternities. It also means the Sufi path.

24. Hamid Algar, "Some Notes on the Naqshbandī Tarīqat in Bosnia." *Die Welt des Islams.* New Series 13, 3–4 (1971): 168–203. Martin van Bruinessen, "Origins and Development of the Sufi Orders (Tarekat) in Southeast Asia." *Studia Islamika* 1, 1 (1994): 1–23.

25. Hamid Algar, *Wahhabism: A Critical Essay* (Oneonta, NY: Islamic Publications International, 2002); Azyumardi Azra, *The Origins of Islamic Reformism in Southeast Asia. Networks of Malay-Indonesian and Middle-Eastern "Ulamā" in the Seventeenth and Eighteenth Centuries* (Honolulu: University of Hawaii Press, 2004), 148–153.

26. I am indebted to Hamid Algar for his insights on the nuances of dzikir.

27. The earliest important figure in the Naqshbandi lineage, 'Abd al-Khāliq Ghidjuvānī, introduced the eight principles of the Naqshbandiyya and a silent form of *dzikir* at the turn of the thirteenth century. However, the practice became normative only with the crystallization of the order and those practices endorsed by its spiritual master and eponym, Bahā' ad-Dīn Naqshband. See Hamid Algar, "Silent and Vocal Dhikr in the Naqshbandī Order." *Akten des VII. Kongresses für Arabistik und Islamwissenschaft. Göttengen 15. Bis 22.* (1974) (Göttingen: Vandenhoeck & Ruprecht, 1976), 42–43.

28. Algar, "Silent and Vocal Dhikr in the Naqshbandī Order," 40–41.

29. R. Ng Soeradipoera et al. eds., *Serat Tjentini* (Batavia: Ruygrok, 1912–1915).

30. Poerbatjaraka, "De Geheime leer van Sunan Bonang (soeloek Woedjil)." *Djawa* 18 (1938). Trans. and cited in Brakel, "Masked Dances, Spirit Worship and the Introduction of Islam in Java," 24–25.

31. Michael W. Dols, *Majnūn: The Madman in Medieval Islamic Society.* Ed. Diana E. Immisch (Oxford: Clarendon Press, 1992).

32. Annemarie Schimmel, *Mystical Dimensions of Islam* (Chapel Hill: University of North Carolina, 1975), 176; Martin van Bruinessen, "Shaykh 'Abd al-Qadir al-Jilani and the Qadiriyya in Indonesia." *Journal of the History of Sufism* 1–2 (2000): 361–395; Bruinessen, "Origins and Development of the Sufi Orders (Tarekat) in Southeast Asia."

33. Sundanese: *Ari ngibing teh kudu siga anu geregeteun; geregeteun di dieu yeuh...ngarah anu lalajo oge milu geregeteun.* Suanda translates the Sundanese word *geregeteun* as being emotional and full of intensity in

both madness and love. Endo Suanda, "Dancing in Cirebonese Topeng." *Balungan* 3, 3 (1988): 7–15.

34. Ngũgĩ wa Thiong'o defines three schemas for understanding performance space: as "a self-contained field of internal relations" or "the totality of its external relations to these other centres and fields," or "in its entirety of internal and external factors...in its relationship to time." Ngũgĩ wa Thiong'o, *Penpoints, Gunpoints, and Dreams. Towards a Critical Theory of the Arts and the State in Africa* (Oxford: Clarendon Press, 1998), 39–41.

35. Penny Edwards, "Half-Cast: Staging Race in British Burma." *Postcolonial Studies* 5, 3 (2002): 281–282; James D. Scott, *Domination and the Arts of Resistance: Hidden Transcripts* (New Haven: Yale University Press, 1990); Laurie J. Sears, *Shadows of Empire: Colonial Discourse and Javanese Tales* (Durham: Duke University Press, 1996); Thiong'o, *Penpoints, Gunpoints, and Dreams*, 69.

36. Marieke Bloembergen, *Colonial Spectacles: The Netherlands and the Dutch East Indies at the World Exhibitions, 1880–1931* (Singapore: Singapore University Press, 2006); Carolyn Schiller Johnson, "Performing Ethnicity: Performance Events in Chicago 1893–1996" (PhD Dissertation, University of Chicago, 1998).

37. *Sirih* circulated throughout the Muslim world. It was exported from India to the Middle East at least as far back as the thirteenth century where it enjoyed some notoriety in Mecca and Yemen, but proved too fragile for the long, arduous journey. Some conservative Muslims contend that sirih, in its comparisons to alcohol and stimulants, violates Islamic doctrine, which resulted in its being banned in much of the Arabian Peninsula and among many Indian and Pakistani Muslims. In Java, *sirih* has a long history as an aphrodisiac. This reputation, which has contributed to betel nut's prominent role in courtship and marriage throughout the Malay world, is found in the lingua franca, Malay. The Malay word for areca, *pinang* (Cirebon Javanese: *nginang*), is the root of *pinangan* and *memingan*, the words for engagement and to propose marriage, respectively. Furthermore, *pinang muda* is the young nut, whose two halves, when combined, represent a perfect match. Brownrigg, *Betel Cutters from the Samuel Eilenberg Collection*, 30; Laurie Margot Ross, "Journeying, Adaptation, and Translation: *Topeng Cirebon* at the Margins" (PhD Dissertation, University of California, Berkeley, 2009), 236, 250–255; Huan Ma, *Ying-yai Sheng-Lan: The Overall Survey of the Ocean's Shores* (Cambridge: Cambridge University Press, 1970), 92–93.

38. The *Naqshbandiyya* refer to this as *khalvat dar anjuman* (isolation in gathering).

39. Laurie Margot Ross, "The Artist Registry. Tracking Itinerant Artists Before and After Suharto's 1965 Coup d'état in the Cirebon Region, West Java." *Indonesia and the Malay World* 39, 114 (2011): 163–166.

40. For the role of Nahdlatul Ulama (NU) and other groups, including Muhammadiyah in the 1965–1966 massacres, see Greg Fealy and

Katharine McGregor, "Nahdlatul Ulama and the Killings of 1965–66: Religion, Politics and Remembrance." *Indonesia* 89 (2010).

41. Endo Suanda, "The Social Context of the Cirebonese Performing Artist." *Asian Music* 13, 1 (1981): 38–39.

42. Ross, "Journeying, Adaptation, and Translation," 408–437.

43. Abu Toto eventually rose to become its Ninth Regional Commander in 1993. Following an organizational split in 1996, he launched his own faction, *KW9 al-Zaytun*. Martin van Bruinessen, "'Traditionalist' and 'Islamist' Pesantren in Contemporary Indonesia" (paper presented at ISIM workshop, Leiden, "The Madrasa in Asia," May 2004); Al Chaidar, *Sepak terjang KW. IX Abu Toto Syech A.S. Panji Gumilang menyelewengkan NKA-NII pasca S.M. Kartosoewirjo* (Jakarta: Madani Press, 2000); International Crisis Group, "Recycling Militants in Indonesia: Darul Islam and the Australian Embassy Bombing." *Asia Report* 92 (February 22, 2005): 15, 26–27. http://www.crisisgroup.org/~/media/Files/asia/south -east-asia/indonesia/092%20Recycling%20Militants%20in%20Indonesia %20Darul%20Islam%20and%20the%20Australian%20Embassy%20 Bombing.pdf

44. Founded in 1964, the organization claimed to be apolitical, yet was supported by senior army officials in response to the PKI's growing influence. When Suharto made his first "official" presidential run in 1968, he joined Golkar. From that point forward, Suharto and Golkar have been virtually synonymous. The organization took swift control of artist activities in the immediate decade.

45. Panji is also widely known as Damar Wulan. The tales are described in Poerbatjaraka, *Tjerita Pandji dalam perbandingan* (Jakarta: Gunung Agung, 1968).

46. Examples being the four cardinal points and the center; the five days of the Javanese calendar (*Pon, Wage, Kliwon, Legi,* and *Pahing*); the victorious five Pandava brothers of the *Mahabharata*; and associations to Bhima's magic *Pancanaka* nails.

47. Kathy Foley, "My Bodies: The Performer in West Java." *TDR: The Drama Review* T126 (1990): 69.

48. Sunglasses are also worn in a variety of female and male trance dances in Cirebon, notably *sintren, warilais,* and the old seafaring dance form, *angklung bungko*. In the context of trance, sunglasses are employed to enhance concentration and conceal the rolled-back eyes of the performer.

49. Sukarta Chandra, personal communication, August 31, 2012.

50. Foley, "My Bodies: The Performer in West Java," 68.

51. Farid ud-Din Attar, *The Conference of the Birds* (London: Penguin, 1984).

52. James Peacock, "Symbolic Reversal and Social History: Transvestites and Clowns of Java." In *The Reversible World: Symbolic Inversion in Art and Society*. Ed. Barbara A. Babcock (Ithaca, NY: Cornell University Press, 1978).

53. Anthony Reid, *Southeast Asia in the Age of Commerce*, vol. 1: *The Land Below the Winds* (New Haven: Yale University Press, 1988), 75.

54. Yellow is associated with *supiyah* (possessiveness, but also fertility, e.g., water), and the androgynous Samba.

55. Serial marriages are ubiquitous in rural Cirebon. First unions are often prearranged between families or as a "practice" marriage prior to the onset of menses.

56. Today, divorces are more difficult to attain in rural Cirebon, where conservative Islam is firmly entrenched. According to several *dalang topeng* that I interviewed in 2012, *ulama* are increasingly reticent to grant them. Combined with increased monetary costs, it is nearly impossible for rural dancers to attain a divorce without a wealthy benefactor.

57. Reid, *Southeast Asia in the Age of Commerce 1450–1680*, 1:75.

58. Brownrigg, *Betel Cutters from the Samuel Eilenberg Collection*, 21.

59. Jean Gelman Taylor, "Costume and Gender in Colonial Java, 1800–1940." In *Outward Appearances: Dressing State and Society in Indonesia*. Ed. Henk Schulte Nordholt (Leiden: KITLV Press, 1997), 85.

60. *Wayang wong* and *topeng* troupes were often composed of the same artists. The Claire Holt Collection of Indonesian Dance. New York Public Library for the Performing Arts. "Photographs of Indonesia: Java, East and West: Dances (Miscellaneous)": Image 1122589.

61. Liesbeth Hesselink, "Prostitution: A Necessary Evil, Particularly in the Colonies: Views on Prostitution in the Netherlands East Indies." In *Indonesian Women in Focus: Past and Present Notions*. Ed. E. Locher-Scholten and A. Niehof (Leiden: KITLV Press, 1992); A. de Braconier, "Het Prostitutie-vraagstuk in Nederlandsch-Indië." *Indische Gids* 55 (1933): 916; Thomas Stamford Raffles, *The History of Java* (Kuala Lumpur: Oxford University Press, [1817], 1965), 1:342; Henry J. Spiller, *Erotic Triangles: Sundanese Dance and Masculinity in West Java* (Chicago: University of Chicago Press, 2010), 76–103; W. F. Stutterheim, "A Thousand Years Old Profession in the Princely Courts on Java." In *Studies in Indonesian Archeology*. Ed. W. F. Stutterheim (The Hague: Martinus Nijhoff, 1956); R. Anderson Sutton, "Who Is the *Pesindhen*?: Notes on the Female Singing Tradition in Java." *Indonesia* 37 (1984): 119–133.

62. F. De Haan, *Priangan: De Preanger-Regentschappen onder het Nederlandsch Bestuur tot 1811* (1910–1912). In 2009 Governor-General Daendels restored *ronggeng* schools at Cirebon's royal courts. An extensive overview of the *ronggeng* in Java is found in Spiller, *Erotic Triangles*, 76–103.

63. Heating up the body is often related to dzikir practices. Persian Sufi poets often describe drunkenness metaphorically in the *shaykk/murid* dyad, since alcohol consumption is prohibited in Islam.

64. Hadisutjipto, trans. *Babad Cerbon* (Jakarta: Department of Education and Culture, 1979); Sharon Siddique, "Relics of the Past? A Sociological Study of the Sultanates of Cirebon, West Java" (PhD Dissertation,

Universität Bielefeld, Germany, 1977), 79–80; P. J. Zoetmulder, *Pantheism and Monism in Javanese Suluk Literature: Islamic and Indian Mysticism in an Indonesian Setting.* Trans. M. C. Ricklefs (Leiden: KITLV Press, 1995), 248–249.

65. Rasinah, pers. comm., May 26, 2005.
66. Wita, personal communication, June 20, 2005.
67. During the 1850s roughly 2,000 pilgrims were said to have left the Dutch territories for Mecca. The numbers grew steadily after the Suez Canal opened.
68. Robyn J. Maxwell, *Textiles of Southeast Asia: Tradition, Trade, and Transformation* (Melbourne and New York: Australian National University and Oxford University Press, 1990), 306, 334; Taylor, "Costume and Gender in Colonial Java, 1800–1940," 92; Stephen Vernoit, *Occidentalism: Islamic Art in the 19th Century* (London and New York: Nour Foundation and Oxford University Press, 1997), 62.
69. U.S. Committee for Saudi Arabian Cultural Heritage, *Palms and Pomegranates: Traditional Dress of Saudi Arabia* (Washington, DC, 1989), 9–10.
70. Judi Knight-Achjadi and Asmoro Damais, *Butterflies & Phoenixes: Chinese Inspirations in Indonesian Textile Arts* (Jakarta: Mitra Museum Indonesia, 2005), 10.
71. *Kisa* is the term employed by Shia Muslims.
72. Patricia Baker, *Islam and the Religious Arts* (London and New York: Continuum, 2004), 184.
73. Schimmel, *Mystical Dimensions of Islam*, 102.
74. Ibid., 102. The color blue has far-reaching significance. According to Jasleen Dhamija, the "use of checkered cloth in the slave trade for buying and selling slaves, led to it being called the 'cloth of sorrow' and it has been suggested the 'Blues' owes its name to the indigo which the slaves cultivated and in the indigo-blue cloth in which they were dressed." Jasleen Dhamija, "The Geography of Textiles." In *Textiles from India: The Global Trade.* Ed. Rosemary Crill (Calcutta: Seagull Books, 2006), 265.
75. I interviewed all of Dasih's known former students. None had studied all five characters of her family's Palimanan style. All had undergone some form of an initiatic bath (*mandikan kembang*), but had not performed the extensive fasts nor visited the holy shrines (*ziarah*) incumbent upon pedigreed *dalang*-in-training.
76. Robson, trans. *Deśawarnana (Nāgarakrtāgama).*
77. Literally, a house of spiritual retreat. The designated Arabic and Persian terms for *tekke* are *zawiya* and *khanaqah*, respectively.
78. The term *suluk* has a very different meaning in Javanese mystical discourse, where it refers to a polemical exchange between a *shaykh* and his student. In Arabic, *suluk* means "wayfaring."
79. Jean-Louis Bacqué-Grammont, Semavi Eyice, Nathalie Clayer, and Thierry Zarcone, eds., *Anatolia Moderna II Yeni Anadolu: Derviches et*

Cimetieres Ottomans (Paris/Istanbul: Librairie d'Amérique et d'Orient/ Institut Français d'Etudes Anatoliennes d'Istanbul, 1991); M. Baha Tanman, "Settings for the Veneration of Saints." In *The Dervish Lodge: Architecture, Art, and Sufism in Ottoman Turkey*. Ed. Raymond Lifchez (Berkeley: University of California Press, 1992), 130–171; Hans-Peter Laqueur, "Dervish Gravestones." In *The Dervish Lodge: Architecture, Art, and Sufism in Ottoman Turkey*. Ed. Raymond Lifchez (Berkeley: University of California Press, 1992), 284–295.

80. Hamid Algar, "Amāma." In *Encyclopedia Iranica*, 1:9. Ed. Ehsan Yarshater (New York: Columbia University Press, 1982), 920. The fur brimless hat, *kalpak*, *fez*, and turban were banished following World War I in Turkey and Iran by Mustafa Kemal Atatürk (the founder and first president of the Turkish Republic), who proclaimed the Hat Law of 1925. The *kalpak* worn today in Central Asia are usually constructed from wool or felt, while in Iran they are made from felt or sheepskin. According to Hamid Algar (personal communication), those made of sheepskin are still worn in Northeastern Iran and not considered problematic. The issue that conservative Muslims have with the sobrah may be that shorn human hair is considered unclean.

81. Schimmel, *Mystical Dimensions of Islam*, 14; Ladan Akbarnia with Francesca Leoni, *Light of the Sufis: The Mystical Arts of Islam* (Houston: Museum of Fine Arts, 2010), 2, 23.

82. Nawi, personal communication, June 25, 2006.

83. Benedict R. O'G. Anderson, "Idea of Power in Javanese Culture." In *Language and Power: Exploring Political Cultures in Indonesia* (Ithaca: Cornell University Press, 1990).

84. Whether the axes of the pillars of Islam are vertical, for example, *shalat* (prayer), or horizontal, for example, *zakat* (almsgiving), they always exist in relationship to God; that is, everything belongs to, and is an extension of, Allah.

85. Other terms for the third eye are *baduk* (Cirebon Javanese), *topeng*, and *tarang* (Sundanese). The third eye is widely understood as panreligious tantrism of the chakra. With the growth of spiritual theism over the centuries, it took on a transcendental quality of inner consciousness contrasted with the physical realm. It thus merges enlightenment and the external "material manifestation of the senses, a world-conquering physical strength" corresponding to a higher perceptual plane. A. David Napier, *Masks, Transformation, and Paradox* (Berkeley: University of California Press, 1986), 139.

86. Sufi binaries include remembering/forgetting, drunkenness/sobriety, right/left, horizontal/vertical, vocal/silent, and interior/exterior.

87. Ricklefs, *Mystic Synthesis in Java*, 171.

88. Sukarta Candra, personal communication, June 29, 2009.

89. Kalim, personal communication, June 26, 2006.

90. Miska Lukmanul Hakim, personal communication, June 28, 2009.

91. Dasih binti Wentar, personal communication, February 3, 1978.
92. Benedict R. O'G. Anderson, *Mythology and the Tolerance of the Javanese* (Ithaca: Cornell Modern Indonesia Project, Cornell University, 1996).
93. Some dancers, both male and female, have elected to wear white socks for a long time; however, in past generations they were not a response to piety, but instead signaled cosmopolitanism from the late Dutch era forward. They were also worn to protect the feet when performing on dirt and other inhospitable conditions.
94. Mask dancers lacking the proper lineage are referred to simply as *penari topeng* (mask dancer).

2

ISLAMIC REVIVALISM AND RELIGIOUS PIETY IN INDONESIAN CINEMA

Eric Sasono

> For Indonesian Muslim filmmakers—who are also patriots—it is his or her obligation to make film as a tool for [the nation's] struggle and medium of Islamic promulgation. From an ideological point-of-view, that task is not a difficult problem, since the philosophy of state and the nation of Indonesia has already been covered by Islamic teachings.
>
> Usmar Ismail (1965)[1]

INTRODUCTION

Islam has been the main theme of film narratives in Indonesia since 1959. The film *Titian Serambut Dibelah Tudjuh* (literally, A Hair-Width Bridge Divided Sevenfold), directed by Asrul Sani, is an example. The film tells the story[2] of a young teacher, Ibrahim, who is sent to a village to teach Islam. Arriving in the village, Ibrahim is surprised to see Islam has been abandoned by the villagers, who live a degenerate life of gambling, prostitution, and alcoholism. There is an old teacher in the village whom Ibrahim is supposed to help in teaching Islam; however, this old teacher considers Ibrahim's modernized teaching method as a heresy. Moreover, the old teacher's wife falls in love with Ibrahim, who is in love with another woman in the village. Ibrahim gets into trouble when the old teacher's wife defames him. The villagers, agitated by the old teacher, cast Ibrahim out of the village but he manages to stay after a mysterious traveler comes to the village to clear Ibrahim's name.

The film has employed for its title an idiom popular among Muslims in Indonesia. *Titian Serambut Dibelah Tudjuh* comes from a belief of Indonesian Muslims about a bridge that tests Muslims in the Afterlife.

This bridge leads into the Heaven with the flaming hell underneath. If a Muslim is proven sinless on the Judgment Day, the bridge will be an easy walkway for him/her to go through and the Heaven will welcome him/her. If the Muslim is a sinner, then he/she will see the bridge as thin as a human hair divided sevenfold and it is impossible for the sinner to walk on without falling into the hell. This title was used by Asrul Sani as an allegory to the difficult situation faced by Ibrahim to survive.

Titian Serambut Dibelah Tudjuh is a fine example to prove that Islam is the main theme in Indonesian films. In this film Islam was not depicted as a monolithic religion with complex practices and rituals to follow. The filmmaker made truth-claims by contradicting the presumed correct type of teaching (*aliran*) that the film protagonists adhered to and another type of teaching that was believed in by the antagonists. The presentation of this contradiction was important because of at least three reasons.

First, contradiction of one type of Islam to another is depicted to be taking place in specific circumstances, which becomes the context of the film plot. This context, the sociopolitical setting of the films, to some extent, was made to represent the situation of Indonesia in the period when the films were produced. It was very often that this context was an allusion to the current situation, where the filmmakers intend to criticize certain *aliran* (teachings) or Islamic groups (or in other case, the government[3]) whose attitude and behaviors were considered to denigrate Islam in general.

Second, the contradictions are portrayed to be originating from the film's protagonist who must deal with Muslim leaders in a particular context. The film protagonists were characterized with certain attitudes and behaviors that can be attributed to Islamic values, and they bring these values as the sources for improvement of community life. However, these protagonists are not easily accepted by the community and instead they are being confronted by the existing Islamic leaders and scholars (*ulama*) because their values and teaching methods are considered as heresy. In this case, two types of adherence to Islamic teachings are confronting each other, in which the filmmakers are taking the protagonists' side.

Third, the contradiction of more than one type of adherence to Islam, on the one hand, resulted in the depiction of flexibility of Islam to live in particular sociopolitical contexts and the irrelevance of just one type of Islamic teaching, on the other hand. One type of piety (usually the conventional and scriptural type of piety where the adherence toward the religion is measured by following the formal symbolistic practices of the religion) was being challenged by other types of piety (the modernized and progressive ones), which then open possibilities of creating linkage between Islamic values and contemporary issues that were being faced by Muslims in Indonesia. To put it in another way, the Islamic themes in the Indonesian films were dealing with issues that originally were foreign to Muslims to the prior generation. The "old" ways of applying the Islamic values were considered irrelevant to the current context and must be replaced with new ones that allow Muslims in Indonesia to adhere to the religion and at the same time live up to the contemporary lifestyle.[4]

In this light, these films assert that the Muslims with "modern," progressive, and more substantial type of teachings are confronting other Muslims who hold the traditional, conventional, and more formalistic teachings of Islam. In the films, the filmmakers assert that the conventional type of Islamic teaching where Islam is recognized by its formalistic symbols (such as wearing a particular model of attire, just memorizing Quran rather than implementing it in everyday life, and other formalistic deeds) should be replaced by the more substantial teaching, where Islamic values are extracted into the substance and then implemented in solving contemporary issues. Interactive teaching methods and manners in which the Islamic values are delivered to other Muslims also become important characteristics of the "modernized" Islam, because the conventional model of teaching tends to make the *ummat* or Islamic community become uninterested in Islam. The old method of teaching that insists on the pupils' memorizing the Quran whether they understand the meaning or not, and in which it is not compulsory for teachers to address the social issue contribute to the *ummat* to leave the teachings altogether. Therefore, the filmmakers suggest that Islam should be revived by new interpretations of the teachings and its methods of delivery.

The films will be discussed with attention to the characters, plotlines, the context of the stories, and representation of the contradiction of versions of Islamic values/teachings brought by the film protagonists and then how the conflict is being resolved in the films. This type of analysis will help to see the type of piety that is promoted by the filmmakers. The context (period) depicted in the film narrative is important to understand the problems that are being faced by the Muslim community. The films discussed are

1. *Al Kautsar (Syukur Nikmat)* (in Arabic, means gratitude, title of a short chapter in the Quran, 1977, directed by Chaerul Umam and written by Asrul Sani);

2. *Titian Serambut Dibelah Tujuh* (literally means, a hair-thinned bridge divided sevenfold, 1983, directed by Chaerul Umam, written by Asrul Sani);
3. *Nada dan Dakwah* (literally, tune and proselytization, 1991, directed by Chaerul Umam, and written by Asrul Sani);
4. *Perempuan Berkalung Sorban* (literally, a woman with veil, 2008, directed by Hanung Bramantyo, and written by Ginatri S. Noer); and
5. *Sang Pencerah* (The Enlightener, 2010, directed and written by Hanung Bramantyo).

THE RISE OF ISLAMIC-THEMED FILMS

The audience started paying attention to Islamic themes in films from 1977 with the release of *Al Kautsar*, a film directed by Chaerul Umam and written by Asrul Sani, one of the most important figures in Indonesian film history. The title *Al Kautsar* is taken from a famous short chapter in the Quran and this has, according to the film director Umam, attracted the Muslim audience. Umam[5] mentioned that the film stayed for five weeks in Menteng Theatre, an A-class cinema in the elite residential area of Jakarta in 1977. It was an extraordinary achievement considering this cinema regularly screened class A Hollywood films, and it was very difficult for an Indonesian film even to be scheduled there. Umam even saw many first time cinemagoers for *Al Kautsar*. They were foreign to the venue and became intimidated by the film posters of bare-chested women displayed on the walls. This type of audience, Umam claimed, made the film stay for five weeks.

Despite the broad attention that *Al Kautsar* gained, Umam said, the film was not followed up by another release of films of the same type. He said that happened because the producer of *Al Kautsar* was a newcomer who had no experience in managing film production. The large audience did not make a fortune for the producer. Instead, the mismanagement has made them bankrupt and they stopped producing any film after *Al Kautsar*. There were no other producers interested to produce film with Islamic content.[6] This has stopped public attention to Islamic content in Indonesian cinema for some time.

Other Islamic themes appeared in 1983 with the release of some notable films: *Titian Serambut Dibelah Tujuh*, which was the remake of the 1959 version (written and directed by Asrul Sani). This time, Chaerul Umam was in the director's chair. Another film was *Sunan Kalijaga* (name of the character and an Islamic proselytizer in eighteenth-century Java), an epic film of which the production bud-get is considered as the biggest in its time.[7] The reconstruction of eighteenth-century setting and one of the most important mosques in Java, Mesjid Agung Demak (Demak great mosque), has attracted media coverage during the production period. This has created good buzzes to the film, which made it the second biggest box office hit in Jakarta in the year of its release.[8] The film is also received well by the critics and nominated for some awards in the Indonesian Film Festival, including a special award as the film from an "idealistic producer."

The latest enthusiasm in film with Islamic themes occurred again in 2008 when *Ayat-ayat Cinta* (Verses of Love) directed by Hanung Bramantyo was screened. The film attracted middle-aged women from Quran classes (*ibu-ibu pengajian*); for the first time in their lives they went to a cinema joining the regular cinemagoers. *Ayat-ayat Cinta* is an adaptation of a famous novel with the same name and it stayed for almost three months in the cinema, and 3.8 million admission tickets were sold, which was the highest number of that time. The melodramatic plot of the film has made it very popular for audiences of any age who cried[9] to witness the great effort made by the film's lead character, Fakhri, in making the decision about which woman to select for marriage.

The success of *Ayat-ayat Cinta* to attract a massive audience has exceeded the filmmaker's expectations.[10] Seeing the success, some film producers jumped into the bandwagon by making films with Islam as the main theme. After *Ayat-ayat Cinta*, there are three–four Islamic themed films in the cinema (see table 2.1). Films with milder Islamic themes have also been released after *Ayat-ayat Cinta* and gained simi-lar success.

Rather than merely being meant to serve as Islamic proselytization (*dakwah*) tools, the commercial nature of the films is made apparent by observing the background of the producers. Most of the producers of the films are non-Muslims, either Catholic-Chinese or Hindu of Indian origin. Most of the directors of the film also made films devoid of Islamic themes, which makes it easy to suspect the profit motive behind the production and see these films as commercialization of religion. However, despite the commercial nature of these films, it cannot be denied that the audience showed strong religious senti-ments toward the films.

One of the sentiments toward *Ayat-ayat Cinta* was the thought that the film was able to promote the representation of peaceful Islam to the world. *Ayat-ayat Cinta* was released shortly after a Dutch pol-itician, Geert Wilder, released a film he commissioned, *Fitna*, that

Table 2.1   Recent Indonesian Islamic-theme films.

Year	Title	Director
2008	1. *Ayat-ayat Cinta* (Verses of Love)	1. Hanung Bramantyo
	2. *3 Doa 3 Cinta* (3 Wishes 3 Loves)	2. Nurman Hakim
	3. *Kun Fayakuun* (Be and Be It)	3. Guntur Novaris
	4. *Mengaku Rasul (Sesat)* (Claiming Apostle [Heretic])	4. Helfi Ch. Kardit
	5. *Syahadat Cinta* (Declaration of Love)	5. Gunawan Panggaru
	6. *Doa Yang Mengancam* (A Threatening Prayer)	6. Hanung Bramantyo
2009	1. *Perempuan Berkalung Sorban* (A Woman with Veil)	1. Hanung Bramantyo
	2. *Emak Ingin Naik Haji* (Mom Wants to Go for Hajj)	2. Aditya Gumay
	3. *Ketika Cinta Bertasbih 1* (When Love Glorifies God 1)	3. Chaerul Umam
	4. *Ketika Cinta Bertasbih 2* (When Love Glorifies God 2)	4. Chaerul Umam
2010	1. *Di Bawah Langit* (Under the Sky)	1. Gunung Nusa Pelita, Opick Tomboati
	2. *3 Hati, 2 Dunia, 1 Cinta* (3 Hearts, 2 Worlds, 1 Love)	2. Benny Setiawan
	3. *Sang Pencerah* (The Enlightened One)	3. Hanung Bramantyo
	4. *Dalam Mihrab Cinta* (In the Niche of Love)	4. Habiburrahman El Shirazzy
2011	1. *Khalifah* (name of the character, but also means a caliph, an Islamic leader)	1. Nurman Hakim
	2. *Di Bawah Lindungan Ka'bah* (Under the Protection of the *Ka'bah*)	2. Hanny Saputra
	3. *Sajadah Ka'bah* (The Praying Mat of *Ka'bah*)	3. Rhoma Irama

depicts violence committed by Muslims inspired by the Quran. The film has stirred huge controversy and was considered as bad as the publication of a cartoon of the Prophet Muhammad by a Denmark Newspaper.[11] The film was also considered as a hate speech toward Islam and Muslims. For some Indonesian audiences, *Ayat-ayat Cinta* was seen as a film that can bring a counterargument to *Fitna*.[12] The screening of *Ayat-ayat Cinta* in the Netherland is even portrayed as a deliberate effort to bring a different representation of Islam to the Dutch audience.[13] *Ayat-ayat Cinta* has started a new precedent in its capacity to build a massive sentiment for the film, which could not be found in the previous films with Islamic themes.

The sentiment for *Ayat-ayat Cinta* was somehow exceeding the film-maker's expectation. Another kind of sentiment toward the *Ayat-ayat*

Cinta was the demand for the filmmakers to adhere to some Islamic values during the production and exhibition of the film. As noted by the director, Hanung Bramantyo, in his blog,[14] there were pressures placed on him by the author of the novel and many Islamic leaders to give the major roles in the film to Muslims. Hanung mentioned that the argument behind this pressure was that the potential audience of this film (who were also exposed to the novel) expects the piety shown in the film to resemble the piety of the filmmakers, actors, and actresses in real life because they will be models for Muslims once the film becomes a success. The audience seems to have had a big hope for *Ayat-ayat Cinta* to bring a new lifestyle among the young urban Muslim related to adherence to religion and at the same time remain updated to the most current trends.

However, other audiences and the author of the novel, Habiburrahman El-Shirazzy, did not feel the same as this hopeful audience. He felt that there are many treacheries to the spirit of his novel, both in content and in the production method. For example, he feels that the actors and actress of the film, in reality, did not lead a life that good Muslims are expected to do. Habiburrahman was quoted by media stating that he will film his other novel with special intention to correct the mistakes that were made in *Ayat-ayat Cinta*.[15] For others, especially those who read the novel, the film is also a disappointment because of the gaps in the description of piety and the transformation of Fakhri. In the movie, the lead character transforms himself suddenly from being a self-confident, strong, young man into a hesitant and soft-mannered person while Fakhri in the novel was someone who makes decisions firmly with confidence because of his adherence to Islam.[16] There was an audience who felt that the film has misrepresented Islam for its massive portrayal of the "horizontal" love (love between human beings) and how women in the film put their huge efforts to gain a man's love.[17] These disappointments were taken into consideration when the next Habiburrahman novel were adapted into film.

In the adaptation of his other novel, *Ketika Cinta Bertasbih* (When Love Glorifies God, divided into two parts), Habiburrahman decided to be the producer of the film. He opened an audition for the public to act in the film. The audition was constructed and televised in an *American Idol* model, where the candidates showed their acting talents in front of a jury panel (including Habiburrahman himself). Moreover, and interestingly, the candidates must show religious capacity by reciting verses of the Quran (*mengaji*) and by answering some questions related to their adherence to Islam. One of the winners of this contest, Carissa Putri, said that she must take a special

Quran reciting course (*belajar mengaji*) to enable her to fulfill the jury's request. The demand of corresponding adherence to religion in the story of the film to the filmmakers' real life has never happened before. This is a new development in Indonesian cinema industry that was started by the release of *Ayat-ayat Cinta*.

This new development to correspond the piety depicted in the films to the filmmakers' real life happened in personal rather than in sociopolitical issues. Most of the films with Islamic themes that were released after the Suharto era dealt with personal issues, rather than social and political issues (though with some exceptions). Therefore, the types of piety that come from the films such as *Ayat-ayat Cinta* and *Ketika Cinta Bertasbih 1 & 2* are mostly related to personal life. The films such as *Ayat-ayat Cinta* and *Ketika Cinta Bertasbih* do not portray typical forms of misconduct that must be battled by Islamic leaders, such as alcoholism, prostitution, or gambling as they were usually depicted in the Indonesian films with Islamic themes in the New Order era. Instead, the main issue in *Ayat-ayat Cinta* and *Ketika Cinta Bertasbih* is love, which in the film is transformed into finding life-partners (as in the near-future marriage arrangement) because categorically love can lead Muslims into *zina* (fornication), which is strictly forbidden in Islam. The lead characters of these films are depicted performing prayers and reciting the Quran (*mengaji*). They often quote the Quran or Hadith (The Prophet Muhammad's saying as noted by his disciples) or books written by classical Islamic scholars in Arabic, but they rarely address issues related to the deprivations of the *ummat*'s life or other social and political issue. Personal issues dominate the discourse of piety in these films.

One of the concepts introduced by *Ayat-ayat Cinta* in relation to discourse on Muslim personal life is *taaruf*. *Ayat-ayat Cinta* introduces a term *taaruf* to the general public. *Taaruf* literally means "to get to know each other," but this term is put in a particular context where a man can meet a woman only in the presence of the woman's direct kin and that too can be done only in a special arrangement where marriage is planned to take place immediately after the meeting. This concept is an important one to enable young Muslims to be involved in romantic affairs within the perimeter of Islamic values. In real life, some leaders of the Islamic community promote the concept of *taaruf*. The leader of Partai Keadilan Sejahtera, Hidayat Nurwahid, has undergone *taaruf* several times to know his potential wife when he wanted to remarry after becoming a widower. He has done this in an arranged marriage and then he is dubbed by the media as "Fakhri in the real world" (Fakhri di Dunia Nyata).[18] The film has managed to induce new concepts related to certain Islamic lifestyle to the audience.

Another important discussion on a particular lifestyle brought to the public by *Ayat-ayat Cinta* is polygamous life as an Islamic solution for a love triangle, which usually becomes the main source of conflict in films. *Ayat-ayat Cinta* puts the lead character in the middle of two women he must choose to marry. In the novel, instead of being in conflict to select one of those two, Fakhri is convinced that Islam has provided a solution for him to marry both of them. In the film, Fakhri is not really confident about this solution. Instead, the film's peak point happens in Fakhri's internal psychological struggle when he is "forced" by the situation to marry both women. This is the part where the film receives huge criticism because of its weak stance on polygamous life. However, *Ayat-ayat Cinta* and then *Ketika Cinta Bertasbih* have portrayed the idea of polygamous life as something acceptable. This contrasts to the films in the 1980s, in which whenever a man leads a polygamous life, the society scoffs him.

The agenda of Islam as the source for solutions to personal lifestyle problems seems to overcome the idea of Islam as the source of progress and improvement for the *ummat*. The lead characters in *Ayat-ayat Cinta* and *Ketika Cinta Bertasbih* are not depicted as having a connection with the *ummat*. Both Fakhri and Azzam are portrayed to be busy with their personal agenda, such as maintaining their romantic affairs and building personal welfare, all inspired by Islamic teachings. These characteristics are different from the lead characters in the Islamic-themed films that are produced during the New Order era wherein they are highly involved in sociopolitical problems of the *ummat*.

ISLAMIC REVIVALISM AND PIETY

The isolation of the lead characters from the *ummat* is different from what was depicted in Indonesian films of the New Order era where they tried to bring progress and modernization to the *ummat*. The New Order was a term defined by Suharto when he stepped up on his presidency to create an impression of a total separation from the previous regime, which was called as "Old Order." Many scholars portrayed the New Order as being established by Indonesian military and supported by domesticated Muslim forces. However, the collaboration between the military and the Islamic forces did not last for long, at least in the eyes of the Muslims who felt that the New Order had left them behind. It was very common that Muslims and Islamic political forces should not maintain their political stances due to the hostile approach toward the New Order development agenda. Islam was portrayed as a religion that was obsolete and against the principles of progress and modernization. Sometimes Islam and Muslims were portrayed as "right-wing extremists" who were trying to subvert the state ideology from Pancasila into Islam.[19] During the first decade of the New Order era, Islam was considered as unsuitable to modernization and development.

The accommodation of modernization and development to Islam was promoted by an Islamic scholar and activist, Nurcholis Madjid, whose idea on "Islam Yes, Partai Islam No" has made significant change to enable Indonesian Muslims to be loyal to the national ideology while at the same time adhering to Islam. This slogan is important in relation to creating a new array of Muslims' political affiliations, and then later to their sociocultural status. Indonesian Muslims, with this new approach, could be nationalistic and Islamic at the same time. This view has given an opportunity for Indonesian Muslims, not only to see the nation-state of Indonesia as the final body politic for its people, but also to be adaptable to the state's ideology, including being supportive toward the development and modernization that have been promoted by the New Order state. This particular situation was an important feature that was addressed by the films that will be discussed below.

In the three films that were written by Asrul Sani and directed by Chaerul Umam, *Titian Serambut Dibelah Tujuh* (1983) the remake of the 1959 version, *Al Kautsar* (1977), and *Nada dan Dakwah* (1991), Islam is represented as the inspiration behind societal change and progress, while at the same time the lead characters, inspired by Islamic teachings, contradict the corrupt elites (including Islamic leaders) who have misled the *ummat*. Therefore, Islam is portrayed to be more than suitable to modernization and development. Moreover, Muslims in these films are depicted leading the community in advancing into progress and modernization, and attacking the New Order's stereotype that Islamic values are obsolete and Muslim leaders are old in their ideology and corrupt. These three films share the same characteristics, which put Islam into social-relevance especially in bringing the *ummat* from social decadence into a bright and modernized future. Rather than being a hindrance to the progress and rational thinking, which is the basic personal characteristic required by the New Order agenda, the three films portray Muslims who become the main force of progress and change, including accepting some new ideas related to modern lifestyle.

First, Asrul Sani and Chaerul Umam portray the Islamic community as being exploited and manipulated by the elites. The elites can be categorized as economic elite (local businessman) and religious elite (Islamic teacher), with the latter becoming drawn into a decadent lifestyle because of the businessman's bribe they accept. The story takes place in a relatively closed society, where the national authority and its apparatus are absent. The *ummat* live a decadent life and this is a reflection of the sociopolitical life of the period when the films were produced. The *ummat* is weak and is being made weaker by a few elites who take advantage of the situation.

In *Titian Serambut Dibelah Tujuh* (1983 version), it is not only the elite who take advantage, but there is a middleman who plays a role as the broker for deals between the economic elite and the religious leader. This broker, Arsad, does not have genuine prowess that enables him to gain a significant position in politics. Instead, he takes advantage of the ignorance of the local leaders about the public anxiousness. The anxiousness originates from a woman named Halimah who is disturbed because of the sexual attack (followed by defamation) by Arsad. In his defense to the assault accusation, Arsad defames Halimah by saying that Halimah has seduced him instead and accuses the woman of being disturbed and having commenced the misdemeanor with him in the first place. In the court proceeding, Arsad's words are weighed two times stronger than Halimah's because female witnesses in Islamic law are valued as half of male witnesses. Halimah becomes defenseless and it is concluded that the assault considered never happened. The description of Halimah's situation is a strong criticism made by Asrul Sani-Chaerul Umam of the misinterpretation of Islamic law that harms the innocents and benefits the misbehaving ones.

Besides the criticizing misinterpretation of Islamic law, Sani-Umam criticize the ignorance of the *ulama* (the Islamic leaders) about the fate of *ummat*. The gambling house in the village is the tool used to convey this criticism. The businessmen pave way for the decadent lifestyle for the *ummat* by providing a gambling house for the village. This gambling house becomes the place where the *ummat* come to escape from their deprived lives. The Islamic leaders who are supposed to alleviate poverty and bring welfare to the *ummat* become impotent and this can be seen in their attitude toward the gambling house. In both *Al Kautsar* and *Titian Serambut*, the Islamic leaders whine about the gambling house but do not do anything about it because they receive grants from the gambling house's owner to maintain their schools. This situation can be associated with the weakness of

Islamic political leaders of 1970s and 1980s who received grants from the government through the leading political party, Golongan Karya (Golkar), and stay put on the weaknesses of the *ummat*. It is also interesting to see the middleman character, Arsad, as a typical portrait of a rent-seeker in New Order politics, where most of the sources for this type of person come from political deals and brokerage in an arcane society.

In *Nada dan Dakwah* (1991), the situation is different because the society is not as close to decadence as in the other two films. There is a certain extent of external intervention to the problems that occur to the *ummat*. In *Nada dan Dakwah*, the gambling house plays an even more significant role because it is built to trap the *ummat* into debt so that the inhabitants can easily be forced to sell their land to the businessman who plans to build a factory in the village. The local Islamic leader, Haji Murad, is also in a weak position vis-à-vis the gambling house, but interestingly he goes to Jakarta to seek help from a figure who could solve this issue. Haji Murad meets Zainuddin M. Z., who in real life is a famous national Islamic figure who is known for his ability to attract thousands of audience for his public speeches. Zainuddin M. Z., one of the leaders of PPP, Partai Persatuan Pembangunan (Development and Unity Party), an Islamic oppositional party under the New Order political system, comes to the village to help Haji Murad to bring the *ummat* out of the unfortunate situation. *Nada dan Dakwah*, which is made in early 1990s, has given a sign that Islamic leaders can bring the *ummat* out of deprivation if they join their forces and eliminate their dependence on the corrupt elites.

More than asserting independence from local corrupt, elites *Nada dan Dakwah* stresses the importance of the Islamic leaders' role against the global capitalist force by depicting the film's antagonist as a businessman who cooperates with a foreign investor from South Korea. It is very interesting to see that the businessman in this film is addressed as "local comprador" by the film's lead character, Zainuddin M. Z. Indonesian intellectuals of early 1990s commonly used the term local comprador especially with the growing popularity of underdevelopment and dependency theories that originated from the intellectuals of Latin and South America. One of the intellectuals who cowrote a book on underdevelopment and dependency theories was Adi Sasono,[20] alumni of Bandung Institute of Technology, who was also an important person behind the establishment of ICMI (*Ikatan Cendekiawan Muslim Indonesia* or Indonesian Muslims Intellectuals Association), a Muslim organization that was once considered as a vehicle for President Suharto to maintain his power after he performed his hajj pilgrimage. In relation to the use of this term, Chaerul Umam admitted that "local comprador" refers to discourse that was asserted by Mr. Sasono's book and it was suggested by Asrul Sani[21] to raise Muslims' awareness of global economic independency.

The idea of global economic independency has opened a possibility of adherence to Islam as a source for fighting the global capitalist system, regardless of how weak the concept was applied in the film. Sani-Umam in *Nada dan Dakwah* did not clarify on which level the economic independence should be achieved beside a rather utopian portrayal of the farmers' ability to increase their produce and become more efficient in doing their farming. However, it is interesting to note that the source of inspiration for this idea came from the Latin American approach on underdevelopment, rather than the international caliphate system or pan-Islamism, which was popular among Muslim activists in the early twentieth century.

Second, there is a correlation between the *ummat*'s decadence and the declining relevance of the Islamic values in the *ummat*'s quotidian life. Islam is "dead" because the old Islamic teachers stick to traditional methods of teaching, which emphasize memorizing the Quran and other formalistic symbolism, such as wearing Islamic garb and sarong, rather than extracting the core values of Islam and seeking their relevance to current community life. Asrul Sani and Chaerul Umam show that this traditional and formalistic way of presenting Islam to the *ummat* has made Islam lose its significance in the society.

Therefore, the new modernized method of teaching brought by the young teachers (who come to the village as outsiders) is important to be depicted. This portrayal of old traditional/scripturalist Muslims in opposition to modernized/substantialist Muslims is typical of the scenarios written by Asrul Sani, who believes Islam promotes logical thinking and is suitable to be the base of modernization.[22] This can be seen in *Al Kautsar* and *Titian Serambut Dibelah Tujuh* where the core of the conflict is in the Quran-teaching classes (*pengajian*) where the young teachers bring a dynamic and interactive approach to the class while the old teachers stick to dictation and memorization of the Quran. Soon this new method is considered as disrespectful toward the *ulama* and, therefore, heretical.

If *Al Kautsar* and *Titian Serambut* emphasize on modernization and rational thinking, *Nada dan Dakwah* places special attention on Islamic values in relation to contemporary economic situations. It pays noteworthy attention to the economic role of Islam, where the new methods of Islamic teaching promoted in the film are related directly to the empowerment of the villagers who live as small-scale farmers striving to increase their produce. The *pengajian* that are conducted in *Nada dan Dakwah* are not limited to religious knowledge but also new techniques of farming, which are useful for the farmers and help to change their production methods. Instructing on these new techniques are important for the farmers to overcome their problems. One of the trainers led by Zainuddin M. Z.[23]—a very popular real-life Islamic proselytizer (*dai*) who played himself in the film—made this claim. In the *pengajian*, Zainuddin proclaims, whenever Islam needs to adopt "secular" knowledge and science to improve the quality of *ummat*'s life, then it is necessary for the said knowledge and science to be Islamic in nature. This viewpoint was already brought by *Al Kautsar*, but the statement from Zainuddin resembles the situation of 1990s when the attention to science and technology became significant among the Islamic community in Indonesia.

Paying special attention to science and technology was growing in 1990s, especially with the increase of many Muslim scholars and academics with backgrounds in engineering and natural sciences. These scholars and academics later played important roles in substituting for the *ulama* from religious schools background, especially in the establishment of ICMI, which was lead by B. J. Habibie, the minister of science and technology in Suharto era. B. J. Habibie held many degrees in engineering from a German university.

The awareness in technology and science as part of the religious teachings comes with another awareness in the teaching method. Zainuddin M. Z. is famous for his ability to attract thousands of audience in his congregation but, interestingly, rather than using his "magical words" to gather huge a crowd as he is usually portrayed, Zainuddin teaches the villagers in small groups of six people to raise their political consciousness against the hidden motive of the local businessman. In these small groups, Zainuddin can do almost one-on-one discussion and address individual problems and give solutions to personal issues. This method is important in the particular context of Islamic movements in the late 1980s and early 1990s. During that period, some Islamic movements changed their method in delivering religious teachings from mass congregation (*tabligh*) into smaller group discussion, known as *usroh*, and later *halaqoh*. The *halaqoh* is a method used by the urban young intellectual Muslims for developing their cadres in Islamic movements, especially in 1999 when they established their own political party, *Partai Keadilan* or Justice Party. Chaerul Umam strongly suggested that the Quran teaching classes use that *halaqoh* approach rather than mass congregation because he just recently joined a *halaqoh* himself and believes in the approach.[24] In this *halaqoh*, there is no separation between Islamic values and political/economical awareness as it is depicted in the film. Piety, in this regard, should not be applied exclusively in pure worship to God (*ibadah*), but should be broadened into politics, economy, and other worldly issues.

In this vein, Islam as teachings is portrayed to be flexible both in covering the issues faced by the *ummat*—including some "worldly issues" such as farming techniques—as well as in its teaching methods. If it is necessary, Islamic teachings can address structural issues that are faced by the *ummat*, who must deal with a local businessman backed by a South Korean financial firm. In this light, *Nada dan Dakwah* is the strongest and the only film that portrays the problem of the *ummat* facing the "structural adjustment" brought by global capital flows at the village level of Indonesia. The search for Islamic values suitable to the current situation in this regard is not limited to overcoming moralistic deeds (such as gambling, prostitution, and alcoholism) but also covers the role of the political economy of Islam to fight against global capitalism.

Third, the protagonists of the three films are young urban-modernist Muslims who come as the saviors of the villagers from its local corrupt elites. These protagonists are educated in the modern institutions and maintain their Islamic credentials by being knowledgeable in Islamic values and practices. These young urban Muslims aspire to bring progress and betterment to the *ummat*'s life rather than following mere Islamic traditions or being a secular modernist who will not be accepted by the *ummat*.

The young urban Muslims in these films are used by Asrul Sani to represent modernized Indonesian Muslims, who must give their helping hands to the disadvantaged Muslims in the villages. Sani believes that the identity of a Muslim in Indonesia is constituted by several elements at the same time: rational and modern thinking (as opposed to belief in superstition and myths), adherence to the substance of Islamic values (as opposed to formalistic symbols), and devoting his/her time and resources for the *ummat* (as opposed to utilization of knowledge in religion to manipulate *ummat* for personal benefit).[25] These characteristics have been the criteria of the Muslim par excellence in Sani-Umam's films.

This portrayal of the Muslim par excellence in Sani-Umam's films is important to see the proposition they make in their films. Islam is portrayed as "dead," in terms of becoming irrelevant to the *ummat*'s life, and the *ulama* who should help the *ummat* take personal advantage of the situation (with the exception of *Nada dan Dakwah* where the Islamic teacher becomes the catalyst for improvement of the *ummat*'s life, especially by utilizing his network to the national Islamic figures). The modernized Muslim who comes from outside the village is needed in order to help the *ummat* to overcome their problems. In this case, Sani-Umam shows that urban-modernized Muslims who believe in substantial forms of Islam (typical portrait of Muhammadiyah activist) play important role in alleviating the *ummat* from deprivation and also bring them progress and modernization.

Besides the young urban intellectuals who provide new ideas, another important characteristic of problem solving in the films is an epiphany that can make people "convert" into the pious mass.[26] Sani-Umam uses this epiphany to show the strength of Islam as a set of teachings that can provide both spiritual and worldly satisfaction to its followers. However, it can be argued that by solving the problem that way, Sani-Umam shows that the conflict resolution in local level does not need any political authority or state-sanctioned security forces. Some of the antagonist characters in the three films come back to their faith (*tobat*) and make efforts to take the *ummat's* side. In *Nada dan Dakwah*, the police come to the village very late after the protagonists control the thugs who work for the local businessman. Sani-Umam shows the relative independence of Muslims from state intervention in taking care of their business.

Sani-Umam's depiction of Islam in their three films cannot be separated from their background. Umam is the chairperson of Lembaga Seni Budaya Muhammadiyah (Muhammadiyah Art and Cultural Organization). Muhammadiyah is known for its interest toward modernization of the Islamic world. One of the biggest agenda of Muhammadiyah is education (together with economic empowerment and health improvement) for urban low-class Muslims, which is constructed based on a modern, Westernized-style educational system. Besides some portions on religious teachings, the Muhammadiyah schools usually teach modern knowledge and sciences and adjust the entire teaching method and curriculum to the national "secular" education system.[27] These characteristics of the Muhammadiyah agenda can be seen in the three Sani-Umam's film.

The case is different with Asrul Sani who is the founder of Lesbumi (Lembaga Seni Budaya Muslimin Indonesia or Indonesian Art and Culture Organization), a culture and art organization under the wing of Nahdlatul Ulama (NU), the traditionalist Muslim organization. However, his involvement in Lesbumi was merely an effort to avoid attack from the leftist artist during the 1960s,[28] while he was inclined more toward modernization. Sani is an important literary figure and playwright in Indonesia and known for his stance on modernism in his poetry, plays, and films. Sani is famous for two manifestos he wrote to defend the position of Indonesian artists of his generation in relation to the history of art and culture. In a very confident and rationalistic approach, Sani emphasized the importance of Indonesian artists to seek references from all over the world, retract the essence, and find his/her personal styles. This, in Sani's view, did not make an artist treacherous to Indonesian culture because for any Indonesian artist it is acceptable to be inspired by any schools, thoughts, or works of the world's artists since Indonesians are "the heirs to the world culture" (*ahli waris kebudayaan dunia*).[29] This background explains Asrul Sani's inclination to show modernized-progressive Muslims in his films rather than casting conventional-traditionalist Muslims as heroes.

The decision to portray modernized-progressive Muslims in the films by Asrul Sani and Chaerul Umam has gained very good appraisals from the media. The media responded relatively in positive manner toward Sani-Umam films. They described *Al Kautsar* as bringing a fresh perspective toward the industry (*Pos Kota Minggu* and *Merdeka Minggu*), especially in its religious content and high production values and the good storyline. *Titian Serambut Dibelah Tujuh* also received high praises from film critics, journalists, and the media for its religious content, especially in its modern approach to Islam. In its review of *Titian Serambut*, *Suara Karya Minggu* (July 4, 1982) paid attention to the religious content of the film, which is the outcome of good observation (from the filmmakers) of the surroundings. The reviewer also praised the message of the film: inviting Muslims not to limit their piety to religious rituals alone (prayers, etc.), because it takes more than following formalistic deeds to be pious (6). Film critic and journalist Marselli of *Kompas* newspaper (March 27, 1983) praised Al Kautsar as Chaerul Umam's best film to the date. A senior journalist H. S. Djurtatap in his review (*Pelita* April 9, 1983) stressed how Islam is more than a ritual (offering prayer and reciting Quran) but is also about the attitude to be persistent in his/her efforts, kind to other people, and firm in action (8). The modernist and substantial approach of Islam is considered as the breakthrough in Indonesian cinema at that time as well as bringing a new perspective on Islam as suitable to modernization and progress.

THE RECENT FILMS WITH ISLAMIC REVIVALISM THEME

After the Suharto era, modernization and progress appear in some films with Islamic themes. They also contextualize the story by portraying the "dead" Islam and then bring some heroes who can revive Islam in its new form. Like Sani-Umam films, the "demise" of Islam also occurs in the hand of traditionalist-formalist Muslims scholars as it is portrayed in the film titled *Perempuan Berkalung Sorban* (A Woman with Veil, 2008) and *Sang Pencerah* (The Enlightener, 2010), which were directed by Hanung Bramantyo who made the *Ayat-ayat Cinta*. These two films were made by Hanung to make amends to his image as a filmmaker who can only tell melodramatic story and does not take Islam seriously in other aspects of life.

Hanung, who went to a Muhammadiyah high school in Yogyakarta, felt that he had to mend his previous profile as a filmmaker who could make only *Ayat-ayat Cinta*, which is regarded as justifying the polygamous lifestyle. Hanung, based on his firsthand experience during the tour of *Ayat-ayat Cinta* to the Muslim community, where he had to speak to them about the film, concluded that many lay Muslims are not aware that their leaders are manipulating and taking advantage of them.[30] Based on that, Hanung feels that he must make a film that defends women's position in Islam and comes with an idea to make a film based on a novel written in 1980s by a Muslim feminist, Abidah El Khaliqiy, named *Perempuan Berkalung Sorban*. He asked a female scriptwriter Ginatri S. Noer to adapt the novel into a film to keep the women's perspective of the story.[31] The film was screened in 2009 and caused a stir among the Muslim leaders in Indonesia.

Perempuan Berkalung Sorban tells the story of Annisa (Arab word for woman), a woman who lives with her parents who own and run a *pesantren salafi* (a very conservative Islamic boarding school that carries out strict gender separation and teaches only classical Islamic texts or *kitab kuning*). Annisa is very keen to continue her education in a modern educational institution, while her parents are against the idea and state that according to Islam, the ultimate achievement of a woman is to become a good housewife for her husband. Annisa's uncle, Khudori, who also lives with Annisa's family in the *pesantren*, supports her idea but he does not have any say on this issue. For Annisa, Khudori is the only person she knows who supports her dream to go to higher education. This makes her sympathy toward him grow stronger than it can be allowed. Annisa and Khudori then fall in love with each other.

Love affairs between uncle and niece is not forbidden but considered as inappropriate in the boarding school and this makes the couple separate. Khudori is sent to Egypt to study in Al Azhar University. Annisa's heart is broken, and so is her dream of education. Her parents then arrange a marriage for her to Samsudin, the son of a rich *ulama* who can support Annisa's *pesantren*, which has experienced a financial crisis. Annisa then marries Samsudin and later finds out that he is abusive to women and cheats on her behind her back. One day, a pregnant woman comes to Annisa's door and claims that Samsudin has married her discreetly.[32] Then Annisa must accept the fact that her husband has taken a second wife, and there is nothing she can do about it.

After living a very miserable life, Annisa's hope begins to rise when Khudori comes back from Egypt. Despite her status as Samsudin's wife, Annisa does not hide her affection toward Khudori when they meet. On one occasion, Annisa and Khudori are suspected committing *zina* (illegal fornication) and almost stoned to death before Annisa's mother rescues them. Samsudin then divorces Annisa who marries Khudori afterward. The couple live a happy life for a short time because Khudori is killed in a traffic accident, probably murdered, soon. Once again, Annisa lives in misery until she finds out that she is able to help women through a legal aid office that is especially established for that purpose.

Along the story, Annisa's father keeps scorning Annisa and cannot accept her as his daughter, not until she delivers her son from Khudori. Almost at the same time Annisa's father becomes aware of Samsudin's misbehavior, including his drinking problem and his habit of being abusive to his wife. Annisa's father then decides to stop accepting financial support from Samsudin's father and grants Annisa his forgiveness. Annisa then manages to open and run a library in her father's *pesantren*, which consists of books written by Indonesian intellectuals and literary figures, and teaches writing courses to the female students. The "victory" of Annisa against her father's belief is shown in the opening of the library, symbolizing the opening of the *pesantren* toward the modernization of its intellectual life.

Regardless of its proposal on the modernization of the *pesantren*, the film has triggered a huge controversy since the criticism against the traditional *ulama*, which is represented by Annisa's father, is evident and strong. The *ulama* and *pesantren* leaders in this film are portrayed as incapable of appreciating women's life or being manipulative of women. These *ulama* are also depicted as narrow-minded people when it comes to education for women. The criticism against this film is mostly directed to the portrayal of the *ulama*, which is considered as a serious misrepresentation of Islam and the role of *ulama* in Islam. This accusation of misinterpretation is considered as an intentional blasphemy conducted by Hanung, especially because of his use of some cinematic tools in the film: the books shown in the film.

Annisa is seen in the film carrying a book entitled *Bumi Manusia* (The Earth of Mankind),[33] which is written by one who was once affiliated with the Indonesian Communist Party (Partai Komunis Indonesia or PKI), Pramoedya Ananta Toer.[34] This portrayal has made the traditionalist Muslims consider the criticism against them depicted in the film. They considered it as being based on thought originating from one of their archenemies, the Indonesian Communist Party. The film is set in the 1980s, during the New Order era, when the book was still forbidden, which means imprisonment for anybody who carries it in public. If Annisa who lives in 1980s carried this book openly in public, it means a political statement for ideological inclination rather than just an intellectual enrichment. This has added suspicion toward Hanung Bramantyo who has stated his obsession on the event of September 30, 1965 and that he has made some films based on that.[35]

Perempuan Berkalung Sorban is the second film that features the main character as a woman who opposes the decision of the Islamic authority of the community where she lives.[36] However, this is the first time the marriage between Islam and feminism is portrayed in a film and engenders criticism against the traditionalist Muslim. The Indonesian Ulama Council (Majelis Ulama Indonesia or MUI, association of Islamic scholars established during the Suharto era) criticizes the film as misrepresenting the *ulama* and leading the *ummat* into heresy. Imam Besar (the Lead Imam) of the Istiqlal Mosque (the biggest Mosque in Indonesia), Yahya Yakub, who is also the deputy of fatwa commission of MUI, says the film must be retracted from public viewing due to two reasons: first it delivers a bad image of Islam and, second. it misrepresents *pesantren* (the Islamic boarding schools).

On the other hand, the feminist movement and "progressive" Muslims think that the film is really brave in uncovering one of the unquestioned misdeeds that has been conducted by traditional *ulama*, which is to disregard woman and establish that denigration on the Islamic teachings. A woman Muslim scholar who is also an expert consultant at the Ministry of the Religious Affairs, Musdah Mulia, responding to the comment made by the Imam, said the film should not be retracted from the public screening since it "portrays the true reality that happens to Indonesian women." Moreover, Musdah said, "Muslims should not be easily angry if they receive any criticism on their discriminative practices to women that are done in the name of their religion. Muslims must be honest and admit that there are *ulama* and public figures who teach wrong views on rights and obligations of women in Islam."[37] The minister of women empowerment,

Meutia Hatta, even mentioned that the film is a very good one, and can "correct the wrong (impression) about women (and Islam in Indonesia), therefore Indonesian women will be able to compete in the international level."[38] The defenders of this film have highlighted the importance of the film in bringing a new perspective to women's issues and Islam.

Regardless of the criticisms, *Perempuan Berkalung Sorban* is an interesting example of the affinity of Islam to women's movements. Annisa promotes the idea of women's self-determination as part of Islamic teachings. Furthermore, based on her personal experience with her husband who mistreated and abused her, Annisa becomes an activist assisting women with their problems related to domestic violence. In this light, *Perempuan Berkalung Sorban* has provided an idea that adherence to Islam is interpreted as a source of activism for women's rights. With regard to revivalism, this type of Islam is successful in replacing the "dead Islam" that is represented in the viewpoints of Annisa's father who opposes the idea of women's self-determination.

Another important film by Hanung Bramantyo *Sang Pencerah* (The Enlightener, 2010) brings forward the idea of freedom of religion. *Sang Pencerah* is a biopic of Ahmad Dahlan, the founder of Muhammadiyah. Muhammadiyah is the first Islamic reformist organization in Indonesia, and currently the second largest Muslim organization in Indonesia. In the context of modern vis-à-vis traditionalist Muslim, this film should be a perfect vehicle for addressing the issue on revivalism of Islam, the subject discussed by Asrul Sani-Chaerul Umam as mentioned above. However, rather than discussing the longstanding feud between Muhammadiyah and NU regarding substantial-modernist approach versus formalist-traditionalist, the film is more interested in discussing the attack toward the Islamic minority group that occurred recently in the 2000s.

The issue of the attack on the minority group was put in the context of 1900s, during the Dutch colonialism in Indonesia. The film revolves around the life of Ahmad Dahlan starting from his youth when he witnesses the wrongdoings conducted by the *ummat*, until his adult life when he initiates a modernized school system for Muslims, which could be seen as an alternative to traditional Islamic schools (*pesantren*), on one side, and the Dutch educational system on the other. Dahlan expands his endeavor by establishing a modern organization, inspired by Budi Utomo, the first organization that was established in Java with the spirit of "Javanese nationalism." Regardless of the spirit of emancipation that was brought by the modern organization in the early 1900s in Java,[39] *Sang Pencerah* portrays, in allusion, the late 2000s, wherein some *ulama* dominated the interpretation of Islam, which engenders physical attack on a minority Muslim group. The spirit of *Sang Pencerah*, according to Hanung, is to suggest that Muslims as the majority must protect any minorities who live in Indonesia.[40]

The film's main theme of the attack on the minority group is portrayed through Ahmad Dahlan's endeavor, which is not the renewal of Islamic education system or economic empowerment of the *ummat*, but the insistence on the proper direction to the Kabah in Mecca in *sholat* (prayer) that is conducted by Muslims. Dahlan, after returning from Hajj in Mecca, criticizes the *ulama* in Java for their mistake in establishing the direction of Kabah for their mosques. The direction of Kabah is important for a Muslims in regard to the direction of the regular *sholat*. Dahlan insists that the direction of Kabah that was set by the traditionalist *ulama* in their mosques is wrong and that it must be reconfigured. The *ulama*, as represented by the Great Imam (*Imam Besar*), rejects Dahlan's idea, and considers the suggestion as sacrilegious because of the disbelief toward the ancestors who established the direction. This cause has damaged Dahlan's reputation among the *ulama*.

Dahlan is being set aside despite his status as a hajji, which is supposed to give him a place in the Great Mosque (*Masjid Besar*). Then he decides to build his own *langgar* (small mosque) near his house to be the place for his followers to learn about Islam and to do the regular five daily prayers. The *langgar* is built heading in the direction of Kabah according to Dahlan's calculation. This creates discomfort to the elite traditional *ulama* that then sent one of their charges to reprimand Dahlan about his deed. This *ulama* says that Dahlan's action might confuse the *ummat*. Dahlan is unmoved by the reprimand and continues his prayers and teaching in the *langgar* until one day the *ummat*, witnessed by some *ulama*, could not restrain themselves any longer and come to the *langgar* to destroy it. Dahlan and his followers try to stop the mob from destroying the *langgar* but they fail. In a very dramatic presentation, Hanung has made the destruction of the *langgar* as the peak dramatic point of the film to make it the most significant cause of Dahlan's endeavor in reforming Islam in his hometown. If the story is put in the context of Muhammadiyah-NU (or Muslim modernist-traditionalist) conflict, this portrayal could put traditionalist Muslims into the role of perpetrators of the violence.

To avoid accusing the traditionalist Muslim as violent perpetrators, Hanung puts the blame on Syekh Siti Djenar, a Sufi (ascetic spiritualist) who lived in Java in seventeenth century and was given a death sentence by mainstream Islamic scholars of his time for his belief in the concept of the unison of himself with God. In *Sang Pencerah*, the *ummat* is portrayed as being derailed from Islamic values by Syekh Siti Djenar, who teaches them to worship the spirits that live in big trees and boulders. This description of Siti Djenar's teaching is inadequate, and portraying it as a mainstream teaching which the majority of lay Muslims in Java followed is historically erroneous. It seems that Hanung was taking a shortcut to use Syekh Siti Djenar for reference to create a stereotypical portrayal of the common Muslim to represent the *ummat* in Indonesia who he describes as ignorant and gullible. Syekh Siti Djenar's profile as a "heretic *sufi*" who was sentenced to death by mainstream *ulama* is an easy target to create an antagonistic feature of the *ummat* as his followers. This is an important ground to give explanation to the *ummat*'s behavior at the peak of the film's plot where the *ummat* acts violently against Ahmad Dahlan.

After the attack on his *langgar*, Dahlan comes into a cul-de-sac situation when *Imam Besar* insists that Dahlan must stop his campaign for the new direction of the Kabah. Dahlan also insists that he will reestablish the *langgar*. In this critical situation, the king of Yogyakarta (The Sultan) steps in to be the mediator between the two. The king then decides that both Dahlan and Imam Besar can keep their belief on the direction of Kabah, based on the Quran text that states "wherever you direct your face, Allah always acknowledge your prayers." In this situation, *Sang Pencerah* promotes the status quo (which impedes the attack on Dahlan's faction) and the need of political authority to overcome a division between two Muslim community leaders.

This is the big difference between *Sang Pencerah* and the three Sani-Umam's films mentioned above, and *Perempuan Berkalung Sorban*. Ahmad Dahlan as prominent figure in the modernization of Islam is portrayed to be prioritizing a physical symbol (the direction of Kabah) over sociopolitical issues that revolve around the *ummat* such as economic issues related to the obligation to give offering to the "spirit" and the need of modern education for the *ummat*. The attention to various interpretations of Islam seems to be more important for Hanung rather than addressing the sociopolitical or economical agenda of the *ummat*.

In addressing the conflict of interpretation of Islam, Hanung proposes the importance of political authority to solve the contradiction among the Muslim community leaders. The two Islamic community leaders in the film cannot meet half way to find a solution for their disagreement on the direction of Kabah. In this deadlock, Sultan intervenes and decides for them something that is clearly stated in the Quran. This is contradictory to Asrul Sani-Chaerul Umam films where Muslims are described to be able to solve their problem without the intervention of political authority. Moreover, the sultan (political authority) is portrayed as the religious authority that is more knowledgeable and wiser than the Islamic community leaders, including Dahlan himself. It is arguable whether Hanung in real life wanted to suggest to the political authority to act firmer on the attackers of people because of varying interpretations of Islam, which keeps happening in several areas to various minority groups in the country.

Conflicts related to interpretations of Islam have come into attention, including the recent attack on the Ahmadiyah group prior to the production of *Sang Pencerah*. Ahmadiyah is alleged to be sacrilegious by mainstream Muslims (especially the Sunni) because of their claim that their leader Mirza Ghulam Ahmad is a new prophet after Muhammad, who, in Islam, is believed to be the "seal of the prophets." Ahmadiyah movement has been the target of many attacks, not only in Indonesia, but also in the country of its origin, Pakistan. In Indonesia, Ahmadiyah, according to the Minister of Religious Affairs Maftuh Basyuni consists of two different groups that are not related to one another: Lahore group and Qadiani group (Tempo February 26, 2006), and the Qadiani one is considered as deviating from Islam. The Minister of State Cabinet Sudi Silalahi stated that Ahmadiah Qadiani's teaching is not suitable to Islam (Kompas Agustus 8, 2005). MUI has a stronger point on Ahmadiyah. They proposed two options: Ahmadiyah must announce that they are a different religion from Islam,[41] or they must be banned to avoid further harassment from a radical Islamic group.[42] These comments from the authority (both religious and political authority) on Ahmadiyah group are considered to be paving the way to where Ahmadiyah position's is not defendable vis-à-vis the attacks against them because of their sacrilegious belief. Hanung uses Ahmad Dahlan's situation as an allusion to the minority groups in Indonesia, especially the Ahmadiyah.[43]

However, Muhammadiyah, which has been supporting the production of *Sang Pencerah* since the beginning, does not see any problem with the depiction of the attack on the minority group. The leader of Muhammadiyah, Din Syamsudin, said that Muhammadiyah was involved in supervising the story and did not see any problem with that.[44] He also endorsed *Sang Pencerah* and instructed the students of Muhammadiyah schools throughout the country to see the film. However, in comparison to approximately 30 million members of the organization, the number of audience is much smaller than expected. The number of audience for this film is around 1,206,000 as estimated by www.filmindonesia.or.id. Interestingly, during the shooting of the film, Lukman Sardi, the actor who plays Ahmad Dahlan, converted to Christianity. The film crew hid this fact from the media and the public to avoid any denigration from Muhammadiyah's side, especially if they knew that a Christian played the role of the founder of Muhammadiyyah. The film crew managed to keep the secret, until it was leaked shortly after the screening. Some media that did not like the stance of *Sang Pencerah* in defending the Ahmadiyah minority group attacked the film for this. However, Hanung Bramantyo managed to persuade the chairman of Muhammadiyah, Din Syamsuddin, not to stop the campaign on the film by telling a lie to Mr. Syamsuddin that the news about the conversion was not true.[45]

Sang Pencerah received a good review[46] including one from a board member of ICMI, Asep Saefudin (PhD)[47] who writes for *Antara*. A student of Sunan Kalijaga University, Ahmad Mutaqqin, commented how the film should be seen as a reminder for Muhammadiyah. According to him, "the movie is actually a big critique of leaders, members and constituents of the Muhammadiyah who are now narrow minded, intolerant, have poor social respect, are rigid and allergic to progress. The movie is questioning Muhammadiyah's readiness to enter in its second century."[48] Muhammadiyah did not respond openly to this criticism. They are happy with the portrayal of the founder of the organization in the film.

CONCLUSION

Both *Perempuan Berkalung Sorban* and *Sang Pencerah* share the same concerns with the Sani-Umam's three films in defining the dead Islam, which is the result of the *ulama* manipulating the religion for personal benefits. Self-criticism toward Islam, or how its elites interpret it, is one of the most important features in the revivalism of Islam, which means to reestablish the role of Islamic core values in the contemporary context. This manipulation has brought about deprivation of the *ummat* in one way or another, which becomes the main concern of the film's lead characters. Filmmakers propose a particular aspect of Islam that must be improved in order to alleviate the *ummat*'s condition. In this sequence, Islam is being presented to be relevant for the *ummat* in Indonesia.

However, different from Sani-Umam's films, the two films by Hanung Bramantyo triggered controversy among Muslims. Criticism, including from the Majelis Ulama Indonesia, toward another Hanung film was strong.[49] *Perempuan Berkalung Sorban* was criticized for its depiction of *ulama* as hindrances to women's progress in Islam. *Sang*

Pencerah received milder complaints from radical groups, probably because of the subtle allegory of the radical Muslims group's attack on the Muslim minority group that is portrayed in the film. *Sang Pencerah* does not portray a particular Islamic teaching or group or people that can be related to the ones that exist in real life, which makes it relatively free from harsh criticism such as the one in *Perempaun Berkalung Sorban*. It seems that the forbearance of the Muslims groups toward self-criticism is getting weaker in the post-Suharto era and it is interesting how filmmakers addressed such issues despite criticism against them.

The Islamic themes in Indonesian films have shown how film narratives can be utilized to portray various types of piety, which is not only related to pure worship (*ibadah murni*) but also the functionality of religion in sociopolitical life. In the three films of Asrul Sani and Chaerul Umam social structure and political awareness play important roles in defining a Muslim par excellence. Islam is suitable to modernization and societal change and, moreover, it is necessary for a Muslim to be able to contextualize Islamic values and teachings in order to make Islam "alive" and relevant to the *ummat*. Adherence toward Islam means to apply the contextualization of the religion to make the *ummat* understand that the religion will serve their needs. Otherwise, Islam will be dead in the hands of the corrupt *ulama* who manipulate religion for personal advantages.

Hanung Bramantyo's films entailing revivalism of Islam have shown the same agenda with different causes. In the case of *Perempuan Berkalung Sorban*, the narrative discusses the idea of women's rights and advocates for women against domestic violence. In this film, the importance of books as a tool for supporting progress is also shown. Taking sources from many "secular books," including one of Pramoedya Ananta Toer's books, the lead character of the film tries to correct the perception of women in Islam, especially among the people in her surroundings. To be in adherence to Islam means to respect women's rights of self-determination and to empower women to fight against domestic violence.

Sang Pencerah assesses the minority situation in Indonesia and puts them into the protagonist position. Regardless of the symbolic cause that is being defended by the minority group, the film has its stance in portraying the human rights violation that was conducted by majority groups in Indonesia. Self-criticism toward the religious practices in *Sang Pencerah* is directed to two main issues: the offering made to the "spirits" that live in trees and boulders (which is influenced by heretical teachings of Syekh Siti Djenar) and the wrong direction of Kabah in the old mosques. These two propositions, in comparison to other prepositions in the films with "Islamic revivalism" themes discussed in this chapter, can be considered as simple. The issues portrayed in Hanung Bramantyo's films are simple ones, while in Asrul Sani-Chaerul Umam's films, they are much more complex with regard to the relevance of Islamic values in the wider sociopolitical context.

The various depictions of piety in the films discussed in this chapter have shown the flexibility of Islam in Indonesia as it is addressed to the mass audience. Islam in these films is depicted as the source of inspiration for Muslims to face the contemporary life. Rather than to see the contemporary life as a nuisance that must be avoided, the description of Muslims par excellence in these films welcome the nation's current sociopolitical life and try to propose solutions for the *ummat* that needs guidance from their leaders. Islam in these films is portrayed as the source of modernization; inspiration for progress; resistance against global capitalism and defense tool against human rights violation, which fits into Usmar Ismail's vision that he states in his speech and is quoted in the beginning of this chapter.

NOTES

1. "Bagi sineas-sineas Muslim Indonesia, yang seharusnya diutamakan adalah juga patriot bangsa, adalah menjadi kewajiban untuk menjadikan film media perjuangan dan media dakwah Islamiah. Ditilik dari sudut ideologi, pekerjaan itu bukanlah merupakan suatu problem yang sukar, justru karena filsafat negara dan bangsa Indonesia sudah dicakup oleh ajaran-ajaran Islam." A speech delivered by Usmar Ismail in Conference held by PII (Pelajar Islam Indonesia or Islamic Student Association), Yogyakarta. This speech is reprinted in the book *Usmar Ismail Mengupas Film* (Usmar Ismail Analyzing Films) (Jakarta: Sinar Harapan, 1983).

2. No copy of the film survived. The synopsis here is taken from J. B. Kristanto, *Katalog Film Indonesia 1926–2007* (Indonesian Film Catalogue 1926–2007) (Jakarta: Nalar, 2007). However, the remake version (1983) of the film with the same title has survived and is still accessible at Sinematek, the Indonesian film archive. The synopsis here is taken from Kristanto's book.

3. Strong criticism against the government can be seen in *Tjoet Nja' Dhien* (1988, the name of the character, a female Aceh leader), a film about Acehnese female leader who fought against the Dutch occupation of the province in the early twentieth century. In the film Tjoet Nja' repeatedly mentioned the Dutch as *kape Belanda* (the infidel Dutch) and stated that Aceh can be governed only by Acehnese. That statement is an allusion to the excessive control from central government toward Aceh Province.

4. The contradiction of one type of Islam to another has been the main interest of scholars in their study of Islam in Indonesia. The division of "traditionalist" and "modernist" and other variants has been developed by many scholars such as Lukens-Bull (2005) and Daniels (2009).

5. In an interview on January 15, 2010.

6. Ibid.

7. Newspapers such as *Pelita* and *Berita Yudha* mentioned that the budget for this film was 700 million rupiah. See "Melongok Shooting 'Sunan Kalijaga' Penyebaran Agama Islam yang Luwes di Pulau Jawa" (A Glance on "Sunan Kalijaga" Shooting: A Flexible Islamic Proselytization in Java), *Pelita*, July 6, 1983, and "Film 'Sunan Kalijaga' Menelan Biaya Besar" ("Sunan Kalijaga" Swallowed Huge Cost), *Berita Yudha Minggu*, July 24, 1983.

8. Around 575,631 tickets were sold, the second largest ticket sales in Jakarta, according to data released by PT Perfin, a government-owned company that monitored ticket sales in Jakarta. Quoted from Kristanto, *Katalog Film Indonesia 1926–2007*, 251.

9. Based on personal observation during the screening of *Verses of Love*, and noted in a review of the film, published in *Bentara* section of Indonesian newspaper, *Kompas*, "Pertemuan Baru Islam dan Cinta" (A New Encounter of Islam and Romance), June 28, 2008.

10. A conversation with the film director, Hanung Bramantyo, who expected 1.5 million audience maximum for *Ayat-ayat Cinta*, June 2009.

11. "Dutch Film against Islam Is Released on Internet." *New York Times*; http://www.nytimes.com/2008/03/28/world/europe/28dutch.html. Accessed August 27, 2012.

12. "Fitna versus Ayat-ayat Cinta" (Fitna versus Love Verses); http://sigombak.blogspot.com/2008/04/fitna-versus-ayat-ayat-cinta.html. Accessed August 27, 2012, or this Melawan "'Fitna' dengan 'Ayat-ayat Cinta'" (To Fight "Finta" with "Love Verses"); http://atmoon.multiply.com/journal/item/199. Accessed August 27, 2012. The politician from Justice and Prosperous Party, Hidayat Nurwahid, who also chairs the People's Assembly, even stated clearly that "(Geert) Wilder Must Watch Ayat-ayat Cinta"; http://indonesia.faithfreedom.org/forum/hidayat-nurwahid-wilders-harus-menonton-ayat-ayat-cinta-t23929/. Accessed August 27, 2012.

13. See "Belanda: Film Fitna VS Ayat-ayat Cinta" (The Netherlands: Film Fitna Vs Love Verses); http://beritamuslim.blogspot.com/2008/10/belanda-film-fitna-vs-ayat-ayat-cinta.html. Accessed August 27, 2012.

14. Named as "Jagad Pakeliran"; http://hanungbramantyo.multiply.com. Accessed April 14, 2012.

15. In www.eramuslim.com, an online media known for its strong stance on Islamic values, Habiburrahman stated that when it is filmed, his second novel, *Ketika Cinta Bertasbih*, "will be, by the God's-will, guarded according to the shariah"; http://www.eramuslim.com/berita/bincang/habiburrahman-el-shirazy-film-kcb-insyaallah-pengawalan-syariahnya-ketat\.htm. Accessed April 14, 2012.

16. Writer Asma Nadia is one who feels disappointed about the film. She expressed her disappointment in her blog. Her disapproval to the film adaptation of *Ayat-ayat Cinta* is reposted in the forum available at http://forum.dudung.net/index.php?topic=2812.285. Accessed April 14, 2012. See also a note from a Muslim activist in "Merindukan Islaminya Film Islam" (Missing the Islamic Characteristics of Islamic Films); http://majalah.hidayatullah.com/?p=1242. Accessed April 14, 2012.

17. Ibid., "Merindukan Islaminya Film Islam."

18. "Perjodohan Ala Islam (1) Sosok Fahri di Dunia Nyata" (Finding Life Partner, Islamic Way (1), Figure of Fakhri in the Real World); http://news.detik.com/read/2008/04/21/092749/926457/10/sosok-fahri-di-dunia-nyata. Accessed August 24, 2012.

19. On the debate of Islam and Pancasila, see Douglas Ramage, *Politics in Indonesia, Democracy, Islam and the Ideology of Tolerance* (London and New York: Routledge, 1995) and Usmar Ismail, *Islam, Politics and Ideology in Indonesia: A Study of A Process of Muslim Acceptance of The Pancasila* (1995), a dissertation submitted to the Faculty of Graduate Studies and Research in partial fulfillment of the requirement for the degree of Doctor of Philosophy, McGill University, Canada.

20. He does not have any family relation to the author of this chapter.

21. Interview with Chaerul Umam, January 15, 2010.

22. The same motif also appears in a film that is written and directed by Sani, *Para Perintis Kemerdekaan* (Pioneers of Independence, 1977).

23. The late Zainuddin M. Z. was once dubbed as *Dai Sejuta Ummat* (The Caller of One Million People) for his ability to perform charismatic speech. He is granted Citra Award (the highest Indonesian award for achievement in film) for his role in that film, but he refused to accept it.

24. Interview, January 15, 2010.

25. Besides some of Sani's literary works and essays, which are collected in *Surat-surat dari Gelanggang* (Letter from the Gelanggang) (Pustaka Jaya, 1999), this also can be seen in his film *Para Perintis Kemerdekaan* (1977).

26. This also occurs in Sani's other films. In *Para Perintis Kemerdekaan* (Pioneers of Freedom); the problem is solved when the lead character becomes suddenly aware of her being and then cancels her plan to declaim her attachment to Islam. In *Apa Jang Kau Tjari Palupi?* (What Are You Looking For, Palupi?), the lead character also undergoes a situation close to epiphany where she becomes aware that her endeavor has ended in vain.

27. On Muhammadiyah educational program and its relation to modernity, please see Muhammad Fuad, "Islam, Modernity and Muhammadiyah Education Program." *Inter-Asia Cultural Studies* 5, 3 (2004): 400–414.

28. Personal conversation with Misbach Yusa Biran, close friend of Asrul Sani and also the first chairperson of Lesbumi (Jakarta Chapter), November 9, 2009.

29. More on Sani can be found in *Surat-surat Kepercayaan*, a collection of essay of Asrul Sani and Asrul Sani 70 Tahun, compilation of writings on Asrul Sani. On the "heirs to the world culture", see Jennifer Lyndsay and Maya H.T Liem, *Heirs to The World Culture, Being Indonesian 1950–1965*. This work investigate Sani's thought on Indonesian as part of the "world culture" and how it meant to artists who worked under particular circumstances of the Cold War and hostile feud that was initiated by the attack from the leftist artists and literary personae to other Indonesian artists.

30. Interview with Hanung Bramantyo, February 10, 2012. Hanung, who is married to Zaskia Adya Mecca, a female film star who recently began wearing a veil (*jilbab*), was offended by the *ulama*'s behavior when, during the tour of the film in the *ulama*'s *pesantren*, he was asked, "Does your wife have a sister? I want to take a third wife." For Hanung, that question is a very disrespectful one toward a woman.

31. It is important to note that the author of this chapter was the noncredited script consultant during the adaptation process of this novel into the film script. However, the inputs to this script were given in writing, as comments annotated into the scenario in a Microsoft Word document. He also had two meetings with the scriptwriter. The scriptwriter of the scenario is still responsible for the final draft.

32. Discreet marriage, without the awareness of the first wife, is made possible under the local implementation of Islamic law because of the administrative informality of the marriage.

33. The book was forbidden by the government the 1980s, the period the film is set in.

34. Pramoedya Ananta Toer was not a member of PKI or its affiliated organization but he wrote for *Lentera*, the cultural section of *Bintang Timur Daily*, newspaper that was affiliated with the communist party.

35. Hanung was born on October 1, 1975, and he has been curious to see that one day before his birthday celebration, people put up a half-pole flag (as a sign of mourning for the commemoration of September 30, 1965, killings) and pull it full pole on the next day (October 1, which is celebrated as the day of *Kesaktian Pancasila* in the New Order era as a symbol of victory of Pancasila, the five principles of the state, against the "traitors" who wanted to replace it. Based on that "curiosity," Hanung makes some films with questions related to 1965 events: *Lentera Merah* (2006, The Red Lantern) and *Legenda Sundel Bolong* (2007, The Legend of Haunted Bitch). (Personal communications, Hanung Bramantyo).

36. The first film with a Muslim woman as the lead character is *Para Perintis Kemerdekaan*; see note 8.

37. "Umat Islam sebaiknya tidak gampang marah bila mendapat kritik atas praktek diskriminasi perempuan yang mengatasnamakan agama. Umat Islam harus jujur dan mengakui selama ini memang ada tokoh agama atau ulama yang sering mengajarkan pandangan yang salah tentang hak dan kewajiban

perempuan Islam." See "Perempuan Berkalung Sorban: Musdah Mulia: Tak Perlu Ditarik, Jangan Gampang Marah Kalau Dikritik" (Woman with Veil Does Not Need to Be Retracted. Don't Be Easily Anger Whenever Criticized); http://news.detik.com/read/2009/02/06/174610 /1080758 /10/musdah-mulia-tak-perlu-ditarik-jangan-gampang-marah-kalau -dikritik. (Accessed April 14, 2012).

38. "Meutia Hatta Kepincut Karya Hanung" (Meutia Hatta Is Attracted by Hanung's Work), http://entertainment.kompas.com/ read/2009/01/27/e132341/meutia.hatta.kepincut.karya.hanung. Accessed April 14, 2012.

39. Organizations that were established in early 1900s in Indonesia such as Budi Utomo and Syarikat Islam brought the idea of emancipation of the native Indonesian (*Bumiputera*) to the Dutch colonialist, and issues such as equality before the law and economic rights dominate their agenda. For further study on Budi Utomo, see Akira Nagazumi, *The Dawn of Indonesian Nationalism, Boedi Oetomo 1908–1918* (Tokyo: Institute of Developing Economies, 1972).

40. Interview with Hanung Bramantyo, September 7, 2012.

41. "MUI: Ahmadiyah Harus Dikategorikan Non Muslim" (MUI: Ahmadiyah Should Be Considered Infidel); http://www.tribunnews .com/2011/02/17/mui-ahmadiyah-harus-dikategorikan-non-muslim. Accessed August 27, 2012.

42. "MUI Urges Government to Ban Ahmadiyah"; http://www.thejakartapost .com/news/2011/03/08/mui-urges-government-ban-ahmadiyah. html. Accessed August 27, 2012.

43. Interview with Hanung Bramantyo, September 7, 2012.

44. Interview, August 30, 2012.

45. Hanung Bramantyo, interview, February 10, 2012.

46. For example, the *Jakarta Post* called this film "An Enlightening Movie"; http://www.thejakartapost.com/news/2010/09/19/an-enlightening -movie.html. Accessed August 27, 2012.

47. "Resensi: Sang Pencerah, Mengenal Pendiri Muhammadiyah" (Review: The Enlightener, Knowing the Founder of Muhammadiyah); http://www .antaranews.com/berita/1284715324/resensi-sang-pencerah-mengenal -pendiri-muhammadiyah. Accessed August 27, 2012.

48. Mutaqin (2010), "Spirit Progressive and Moderation of 'Sang Pencerah'"; http://www.thejakartapost.com/news/2010/10/23/spirit-progressiv e-and-moderation-'sang-pencerah'.html. Accessed August 27, 2012.

49. The biggest controversy comes from another Hanung's film? (*Question Mark*), which features a woman who converted to Christianity after a divorce, while her six-year-old son remained a Muslim, and a phrase from a book that is uttered as a soliloquy in the film: "all roads leads to God"; this is considered as implying relativism in religions, which is sacrilegious.

3

EMBODYING THE DIVINE AND THE BODY POLITIC: *MAK YONG* PERFORMANCE IN RURAL KELANTAN, MALAYSIA

Patricia A. Hardwick

Mak yong is a form of Malay drama that is associated with the cultural zone of the former Pattani Sultanate that spans the southern Thai provinces of Yala, Narathiwat, and Pattani, and the northern Malaysian states of Kelantan, Terengganu, and Kedah. *Mak yong* is traditionally performed in an archaic form of Kelantanese, or Pattani Malay, a regional dialect of Malay. *Mak yong* performers are predominantly women, donning both male and female roles. Parti Islam Se-Malaysia, or PAS—the Islamic party that controls Kelantan—has enforced an official ban on *mak yong* in the Malaysian state since 1991. PAS officials argue that *mak yong* has its origin in pre-Islamic belief, encourages the worship of entities besides Allah, and objectifies women.

The twenty-one-year PAS ban on *mak yong* has altered, but not obliterated Kelantanese *mak yong* performance. Kelantanese performers continue to incorporate *mak yong* into the elastic genre of *main 'teri*, a ritual healing performance.[1] *Mak yong-main 'teri* is used to treat spiritual and social diseases unresponsive to cosmopolitan Western medicine. Although often maligned by PAS officials, the majority of rural *mak yong* performers view themselves as dedicated Muslims, and their art as a sacred healing gift. Exposed to social and political movements that emphasize the systematic omission and destruction of aspects of Malay culture that are deemed to have pre-Islamic origins, many traditional practitioners are consciously questioning and adapting their understanding and practice of traditional Kelantanese arts like shadow puppetry, or *wayang kulit, main 'teri,* and *mak yong.*[2]

This chapter will begin by exploring how Malaysian politics and the PAS ban have affected *mak yong* performance, and then move on to examining how rural Kelantanese *mak yong* performers conceptualize the body as a divine kingdom ruled by Dewa Muda, the personification of youth and youthful desire. Finally, I will investigate how individual *mak yong* practitioners understand their art as an expression of personal piety, how they employ metaphor to heal their patients, and how individual practitioners have been adapting their performances and reinterpreting their art according to the rapidly changing socio-political environment of rural Kelantan.

SETTING THE STAGE: *MAK YONG*, MALAY NATIONALISM, AND ISLAM

Although documented in academic literature as a rural dance drama that is often incorporated into healing performances (Ghulam-Sarwar 1976; Laderman 1991), *mak yong* has long been an art that has inspired the imagination of Malaysia's political elite. In the 1960s, Tan Sri Mubin Sheppard, a British colonial-officer-turned Malay nationalist scholar, began to write about *mak yong* (1960, 1967, 1969, 1972, 1974, 1983). Sheppard's highly romanticized writings represent *mak yong* as an ancient and rarefied palace art, and link *mak yong* to the worship of *Mak Hiang*, the spirit of the rice or *semangat padi*, identified with Dewi Sri, a Javanese goddess associated with the harvest (Sheppard 1972:58; 1983:33; Ghulam-Sarwar 1982:108). *Mak yong* enjoyed a brief period of Kelantanese royal sponsorship during the reign of Sultan Muhammad IV (1900–1920) and Sultan Ismail (1920–1944) (Ghulam-Sarwar 1976:5; Mohd Anis Md Nor 2005); however, royal support ended with the onset of World War II.

Mubin Sheppard's representation of *mak yong* as a classical dance drama that entertained Pattani and Kelatanese sultans from time immemorial appealed to budding Malay nationalist sympathies in the infant nation of Malaysia and was incorporated into national interpretations of heritage in the 1970s. Sheppard's construction of *mak yong* as a venerable court tradition appears in most Malaysian popular publications about *mak yong*, and even continues to be embraced by several Malay nationalist scholars (Mohamed Ghouse 1995). Ghulam-Sarwar Yousof, a Malaysian theater scholar who has done extensive research on *mak yong* over the past forty years, has attempted to debunk the nationalist construction of *mak yong* as an ancient Malay dance drama confined to the courts of Pattani and Kelantan, and to emphasize its village origins and role in ritual performance (1976, 1992, 2004).

Eddin Khoo, a Malaysian poet, writer, translator, independent art curator, and founder of PUSAKA—an organization dedicated to the documentation of traditional Kelantanese performing arts—cites Malay nationalist politics as having played an important role in the economic and social disenfranchisement of traditional Kelantanese artists. In a panel entitled "Censorship and the Eradication of a Culture" given at a seminar called *Freedom of Expression in the Arts* held on December 14, 2002, and sponsored by the National Human Rights Society of Malaysia (HAKAM), Khoo describes the appropriation of *mak yong* and *wayang kulit* by the Malaysian federal government in the 1970s as a symbol of Malay culture for the Malaysian nation. In the statement cited below Khoo also alludes to political battles between UMNO, the dominant party in the political coalition making up the federal government of Malaysia, and PAS for the Malay vote, as each party attempts to ingratiate itself to the large bloc of Malay Muslim voters by emphasizing its credentials as the more Islamic government. Khoo states that the current economic and social marginalization of traditional Kelantanese performers

> has been driven by the ideological race in Islam, part of the race for Malay supremacy between two parties that have been very competitive.
>
> This ideology subscribes to[,] and it demands, an attempt to create a pristine unadulterated pure Malay world view [*sic*]. I do not mean something that has been established or decided, but something that changes with the political exigencies of the day. The assault on traditional art forms, on their autonomy, did not start with PAS. In the 1970s we had the National Cultural Congress, which followed the riots of 1969 and NEP. (New Economic Policy)
>
> This was when bureaucrats and politicians, along with intellectuals[,] came together and decided to define Malay culture, which was to be presented to the country as national culture. This is when *Wayang Kulit*, *Mak Yong* were incorporated. However, the country is very diverse, so when one talks about Malay society or Malay art forms, what sort of traditions is one intending to present to the rest of the country—north, south, east, west? The *Mak Yong* and *Wayang Kulit* became very easy to present because they were seen as authentically Malay in expression. (Khoo quoted in Khoo, Tikamdas, and Wong 2003:31)

The validity of *mak yong* as a symbol of Malay culture, and its current ban in its home state of Kelantan for religious reasons, continues to be debated in Malaysia within the public forum of newspapers and websites. These discussions are often between political commentators who know little about the art form. Members of UMNO have been trying to wrest the rule of Kelantan away from PAS for the past twenty-one years. Grasping for the political upper hand, UMNO party members often invoke the Kelantanese PAS government ban on *mak yong* as a symbol of the restrictive nature of an Islamic fundamentalism that they claim is promoted by PAS. In turn, PAS party members argue that the continued existence of *mak yong* in its traditional form is a threat to the idealized Islamic state it desires to construct in Kelantan.

The PAS Ban and the Problematics of Female Performance in Kelantan

PAS party leaders claim that they rule according to legal theories derived from the Qur'an and Sunnah and take issue with any form of entertainment that they believe may cause moral peril. According to them, traditional Kelantanese performing arts, such as shadow puppetry and *mak yong,* have their origin in pre-Islamic beliefs and rituals, and are thus not suitable to be performed or viewed by Muslims (McIntyre 2007). *Mak yong*'s links to ritual and pre-Islamic religious systems have inspired Islamic religious conservatives to declare the art form *syirik,* or polytheistic. Practitioners of the Kelantanese performing arts are charismatic individuals and were traditionally itinerant performers, a lifestyle that often resulted in serial marriages. PAS authorities of the early 1990s developed a perception of traditional performers as advocates of licentious behavior, which led to the ban of traditional performances under a clause prohibiting acts of vice (Khoo, Tikamdas, and Wong, 2003:32).

> In 1990 after 12 years of Barisan Nasional (BN) rule in the state, the Kelantanese overwhelmingly voted for a PAS-led government. PAS were then a part of the APU (Angkatan Perpaduan Ummah) with Semangat 46, but as it later became clear they were always the party leading the alliance. They came to power basically on the platform of Islamising society, of leading Kelantan into a pure Islamic form of government...But one of the things that was most surprising was the decision to ban traditional performances. When they decided to ban these performances, the state government had no clause under which to place the ban, so the ban actually comes under acts of vice. Prostitution, gambling, and *Wayang Kulit* all come in together. (Khoo quoted in Khoo, Tikamdas, and Wong 2003:31–32.

PAS party members find problematic the prominent roles that women play as *mak yong* actresses. Traditionally, Kelantanese women have engaged in small businesses outside the home, and often many women are the sole support of their families. In this context, PAS policies have led to the creation of local council bylaws in the capital city of Kota Bharu that legislate that working Muslim women must wear the *hijab*, or headscarf, and *tutup aurat*, which includes covering all parts of the female body except the hands and face. As recently as October 20, 2011, PAS representative Ahmad Baihaki Atiqullah recommended that volunteer squads be organized to observe women workers in businesses with the intention of prosecuting women who did not adhere to the legislation requiring modest dress in the workplace (Syed Azhar 2011). The penalty for flouting PAS-legislated modest dress for women workers is a fine of RM500 (ibid.).

Changing perceptions of appropriate roles of women in society and female modesty is not something exclusive to the Kelantanese context, but is occurring throughout Muslim Southeast Asia as Middle Eastern political Islamic movements become increasingly influential in the region. In her ethnography *Women, The Recited Qur'an, and Islamic Music in Indonesia*, ethnomusicologist Anne K. Rasmussen examines the important role of women in Indonesian Islam (2010). In her last chapter, "Rethinking Women, Music, and Islam," Rasmussen notes how the modern reform of Indonesian Islamic practices has reframed female public performance from everyday, to problematic, as women's voices and bodies are redefined from *biasa saja*, or ordinary, to *aurat*, or something shameful to be concealed. Rasmussen notes that in Indonesia "the presence of active Muslim women is part and parcel of local 'traditionalist' practice ... it is more often the 'traditional' camp that is tolerant, moderate, and more likely to lean toward egalitarianism, particularly in regard to women's public works and public performance" (239). Rasmussen goes on to state: "The notion that Islam as it is practiced in the Arab world is better than that which is practiced in Indonesia is a common rationale for the proscription of aspects of Indonesian culture that have been part and parcel of Islamic life for centuries, for example women's participation and agency, local languages and customs, and performance genres, including music, dance and theater, that may be seen as local or Islamic or both" (240).

Similar social dynamics exist in present-day Kelantan, as the PAS ban on *mak yong* performance has made it impossible for traditionally trained *mak yong* actresses to continue their careers as itinerant performers. PAS policies discourage women from performing even approved genre like *dikir barat*, arguing that the act of performance places them before the male gaze, and can lead to impure thoughts by male audience. The mere appearance of a *mak yong* actress on a public stage in urban Kelantan, even one wearing a modest *hijab* beneath her princely crown, has been redefined in less than a generation. It has shifted from the performance of a traditional entertainer that once graced the court of kings, to a risqué display of a woman of questionable moral character engaging in a licentious and perhaps even morally corrupting performance.

Ironically, the prominent role that women have played in *mak yong* performances for the past one hundred years can be traced to a reevaluation of the form in response to the Islamic social mores of the Kelantanese royal court of the early twentieth century. The performance of the refined male lead, or *pak yong*, by women was an innovation introduced to *mak yong* in 1912 during the period of royal sponsorship (Ghulam-Sarwar 1976; Mohd Anis Md Nor 2005). In 1923, Long Abdul Ghaffar, the youngest son of Sultan Muhammad II of Kelantan, created Kampung Temenggung, a village that became the center of traditional Kelantanese performing arts (ibid.). According to the late Ali bin Ibrahim, a student of a former Kelantanese court performer, court performers were chosen from among the best of the village players, and village performances of *mak yong* continued during the period of royal patronage. Malaysian ethnochoreologist Mohd Anis Md Nor argues that it was during this brief period of royal sponsorship when female *mak yong* performers assumed the lead roles that *mak yong* dances became more feminine and articulate (2005).

Contemporary *mak yong* performers attribute the early twentieth-century shift from male to female performers to their predecessors' desire to follow Islamic custom, as it is considered inappropriate for a nonrelated male to touch a female, even within the context of a dramatic performance. This was solved by the expansion of female participation in *mak yong* to all major refined leads. Thus, male participation in *mak yong* was restricted to the role of unrefined characters like clowns, or *peran*, and musicians. While early twentieth-century interpretations of Islamic practice in Kelantan actually expanded the role of women in *mak yong* dramatic performances in the Kelantanese court, the contemporary PAS interpretation of Islam discourages all female public performance.

MANDALA IN MOTION

A *mak yong* performance begins with a series of dances and songs that introduce its stock characters: a divine king, his wives, his two servant-clowns, his maidservants. The *pak yong,* or divine king, is the lead refined male role performed by the most proficient actress of the troupe. The *mak yong*, the queen or princess, is the lead refined female role, also performed by an accomplished actress. The *peran tua*, or elder clown, is an unrefined male role played by an older male actor. The *peran tua* functions as a guardian and advisor to the *pak yong*, as he possesses the knowledge of the invocations needed to address spiritual beings, know sacred places, offer sacrifices, and perform rituals (Ghulam-Sarwar 1976). The *peran muda*, or the younger clown, is an unrefined supporting male role portrayed by a younger male actor who acts as a comic partner to elder clown. The *inang*, or female maidservants, are unrefined female roles that can be played by actresses or actors dressed as coarse female figures.

The movement vocabulary of formal *mak yong* dance is strongly linked to a traditional Kelantanese conception of the physical body and the metaphysical self (Hardwick 2005, 2009). A *mak yong* actress performing the role of a *pak yong* embodies the refined masculinity of a divine king and the quotidian femininity of a Kelantanese villager. This outer perception belies an inner conception held by traditional performers that the body is neither wholly male nor wholly female, but rather split between genders: the right masculine, the left feminine, each guarded by its own angel.

An emphasis on the body as a microcosm of a universal macrocosm (Kessler 1977; Laderman 1991) is steeped in the metaphysical traditions of much of insular Southeast Asia (Bateson and Mead 1942; Kessler 1977; Geertz 1980; Hobart 2003; Headly 2004; Harnish and Rasmussen 2011). Speaking of the performance traditions of the Javanese court, Harnish and Rasmussen note: "In Hindu-Buddhist ideology, a *mandala* is a visualization or physical manifestation of the center of the cosmos and represents a microcosm of the world ... Hindu-Buddhist aesthetics woven into a Sufi covering appear to underlie many of the gamelan and dance traditions of the court to the present day" (2011:18). In the dance vocabulary of Kelantanese *mak yong*, the refined movements of its female practitioners are miniaturizations of the cosmic forces that create, sustain, and destroy life. During a traditional *mak yong* performance, dancers create delicate movements with their hands that symbolize the four humors of earth, air, wind, and fire; the conception of human life, the spiritual force that animates all of creation, the spinning of the earth on its axis, and the oneness and unity of God (Hardwick 2005, 2009).

The *titik bermula*, the movement performed at the beginning as well as the end of a performance, has both a literal and figurative meaning. It was designated by the *mak yong* performer Ali bin Ibrahim, also known as Pak Ali, as one of the *ibu tari*, a movement that provides the foundation for *mak yong* dance. It is considered the official opening movement of the dance of the *Menghadap Rebab*, and it is repeated before the beginning of each new verse. This movement also appears in all subsequent *mak yong* dances. While performing the movement of *titik bermula*, the thumb of the dancer's hand is held tightly against the knuckle of the index finger. The index finger of the dancer is positioned at a 90-degree angle to the palm of the hand, while the middle finger, ring finger, and pinkie of the hand fan outward from the palm of the hand. There are no bends in the joints of the fingers, and the hand is locked in this position while the wrist rotates in an outward circle. While performing this movement, the hands of the *pak yong* are positioned a shoulder-width apart and are held slightly above shoulder-level in line with the *pak yong*'s eyes. The hands of the other female cast members are also positioned shoulder-width apart, but are slightly lower, coming no higher than the height of their shoulders (figure 3.1).

Mustafa bin Ibrahim, a native of Tumpat and an avid observer of traditional Kelantanese performing arts, explained that the *titik bermula* hand position was understood by many performers and observers of *mak yong* to be a physical representation of the name of Allah written in Arabic, with each finger corresponding to a letter in Arabic script. Pak Mustafa elaborated that in the position of *titik bermula* the pinkie finger corresponds with the Arabic letter *alif*. The ring finger corresponds

Figure 3.1 Nisah binti Mamat (Kak Nisah) demonstrates the movement of *titik bermula* to her niece Norhidayu binti Zainuddin in rural Kelantan. *Photo*: Patricia Hardwick 2004.

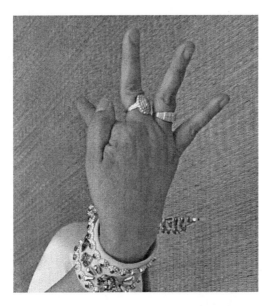

Figure 3.2   A detail of the right hand of Fatimah binti Abdullah (Kak Asmah) in the position of *titik bermula*. *Photo*: Patricia Hardwick 2004.

with the Arabic letter *lam*. The middle finger also corresponds with the Arabic letter *lam*. The index finger and the thumb together correspond with the letter *ha*. All the fingers of the hand together represent the word Allah, the name of God, as it is written in Arabic. This movement thus emphasizes that Allah is the point of beginning for all things in creation. Its constant apperance and repetition throughout the *Menghadap Rebab* and other *mak yong* dances provides performers and informed audience members a physiological reminder of the ominpresence, unity, and greatness of Allah as all aspects of *mak yong* dance begin and end with this movement (figure 3.2).

The hand position of *empat* or four is also classified by Pak Ali as an *ibu tari*. Like *titik bermula*, the hand position of four appears in all *mak yong* dances. Performers often transition from *titik bermula* to the position of *empat* as they sing songs that are performed during emotionally charged scenes within a *mak yong* performance. In the position of *empat*, the hands of the dancer are raised so that her palms face the audience. The index finger, middle finger, ring finger, and pinkie point upward and are held closely together. The thumb is tucked in close to the palm at the knuckle and flexes outward from a position near the center of the palm. The wrists of the performers are locked, extended so that the fingers curl back slightly toward the performers' forearms (figure 3.3).

Figure 3.3   Rohimah binti Zakaria (Mek Imah) demonstrates the position of *empat* as she performs the role of *pak yong* during a *mak yong* performance in rural Kelantan. *Photo*: Patricia Hardwick 2006.

According to *mak yong* performer Fatimah binti Abdullah, also known as Kak Asmah, the position of *empat* represents the four humors of earth, fire, water, and wind. In a traditional Kelantanese worldview, these four humors are the basis for all things within creation and they compose the human body. Illness occurs when one of these elements is out of balance with another. Fatimah binti Abdullah and her brother Saari bin Abdullah stressed that the four elements also correspond to the four corners of the *panggung*, the traditional four-sided open-air stage. Kak Asmah further elaborated that in the position of *empat*, the index finger represents earth, the middle finger represents water, the ring finger represents fire, and the pinkie represents wind. While the hands are held in the position of four, the arms of the dancer are held in a position referred to by Kak Asmah as the *saluran emas*, or the golden channel.

Although most *mak yong* practitioners acknowledge that each finger can represent the four humors of earth, water, fire, and wind, the symbolism attributed to this hand position is multilayered and provides insight into the complexity of the Kelantanese performing arts. Wan Midin bin Wan Majid, also known as Pak Wan Midin, is a former shadow puppeteer and celebrated *mak yong* actor. Pak Wan Midin noted that the curling back of the four raised fingers toward the wrist in the position of *empat* is difficult to accomplish, but is traditionally regarded as a particularly beautiful execution of form in *mak yong* dance. Pak Wan Midin referred to dancers who could execute this movement as having the hands of Sri Rama, as the human dancer's hands when held in this position are thought to resemble the delicate carved leather hands of the *wayang kulit Siam* shadow puppet Maharaja Sri Rama from the *wayang kulit* epic of the *Ramayana* (figure 3.4).

Figure 3.4   Photo of the *wayang kulit Siam* puppet *Maharaja Sri Rama* taken in a *kelir*. *Photo*: Patricia Hardwick 2006.

Pak Wan Midin and Pak Ali emphasize that while the hand position *empat* may seem simple, the symbolism of this *ibu tari* is complex and multivalent. The four raised fingers reference the four essential elements that compose the human body as the delicate curvature of the wrist and fingers symbolizes the idealized refined masculinity of Sri Rama. The often involuntary fluttering of the four fingers in this position is simultaneously interpreted as a mark of a performer's skill and refinement, a representation of the human heartbeat, and an embodied response to the internal wind raised within the practitioner during performance as their hands flutter like the leaves of a tree stirred by wind. While acknowledging all of the aforementioned symbolism of the *ibu tari empat*, Pak Wan Midin and Pak Ali also emphasize an interpretation of *mak yong* dance that prioritizes the importance of five in Islamic numerology. Thus, Pak Wan Midin and Pak Ali note that each of the five fingers of the hand in this position are interpreted as corresponding to the five daily Muslim prayer times of *fajar, zuhur, asar, maghrib*, and *isyak*, and the five pillars of Islam: *syahadat*, the testimony of the faith; *solat*, daily prayer; *zakat*, payment of alms to the poor; *saum*, fasting; and *Haj* or pilgrimage to Mecca.

In the following passage taken from one of my many interviews with Pak Ali, he describes how the performance of the *ibu tari* of *mak yong* dance relates to his understanding of personal piety. To Pak Ali, a performance of the *titik bermula* reflects his conception of himself as a Muslim who believes that there is no other God but Allah. As his hand position transforms from the *titik bermula* into the hand position of *empat*, his four fingers are extended, signifing the four humors of the human body. In the position of *empat*, Pak Ali opens and closes his fingers in a scissor-like motion. The movement of his five fingers representing to Pak Ali the five daily prayers required of faithful Muslims. As the five fingers flutter, Pak Ali notes that *mak yong* practioners recite prayers for a safe performance, with their extended fingers representing an extension of this recitation.

> Pak Ali: *Mak yong*'s dancing, its dancing and singing are like this. It shows us as Muslims that there is only one Allah, there is no other but him. We extend our four fingers, we regard them as earth, water, fire, and wind. If we open our fingers—our five fingers, that is five times a day, a night [a reference to the five Islamic prayers of the day] that is all…The five fingers open, five times a day, a night. For us Muslims that is all, it [the extended arm] cannot fall below the level of the chest, and it is not good for it to be raised above the level of the shoulder. The position of the right arm is the same as the left. If one recites there, one recites whatever they have learned, one will recite, when one recites, the fingers, they recite as well. (Ali bin Ibrahim, August 28, 2005)[3]

While many *mak yong* movements are invested with important religious and cosmological symbolism, some could also be described as
mimetic. These mimetic gestures represent snakes, flowers, swinging
sarong cradles, the arranging of betel leaves, and the curving of sinu-
ous pea vines. Such movements are representative of things in the
actual world; however, they are also often interpreted by traditional
performers as metaphorical references for fertility, birth, the bond
between a mother and her child, marriage, and the transitory nature
of human life (Hardwick 2005, 2009).

THE BODY AS A STATE, CASTLE, AND DEMI-GOD

In his essay "Conflict and Sovereignty in Kelantanese Malay Spirit
Seances," Clive Kessler examines one of the principal metaphors of
main 'teri, the *balai,* a model palace placed outside the performance
space until the end of the event (1977). According to Kessler the *balai*
simultaneously represents the social-political realm and an individual
patient's body. "For Kelantanese the person is, at least metaphorically,
a miniature state, an arena of contending forces, some dominant,
others usually subordinate but always having the potential to mount
insurrection and foment strife. The Englishman's home is reputedly
his castle; the Kelantanese is himself his own realm, his mind its palace,
his embattled reason its precarious sovereign" (321). Kessler regards
the *balai* as a fourfold analogy between the person, the idea of a state
represented by the *balai,* the state as an institution, and the cosmos.
Kessler reasons that it is the *bomoh,* or ritual specialist, who negotiates
an internal battle waged through a political metaphor to restore the
body of a patient to health.

I have found that in *mak yong-main 'teri* healing performances,
the political metaphor of the individual-as-state does not end with
Kessler's assessment of the *balai,* as a fourfold analogy between the
person, the idea of the state, the state as an institution, and the cosmos
(1977), but rather extends even further to traditional insular Southeast
Asian ideas about the divine sovereign as a physical manifestation of
the state. In *Negara: The Theatre State in Nineteenth-Century Bali,*
Clifford Geertz defines his doctrine of the exemplary center: "The
theory that the court-and-capital is at once a microcosm of the supernatural order—'an image of…the universe on a smaller scale'—and
the material embodiment of political order. It is not just the nucleus,
the engine, or the pivot of the state, it *is* the state" (1980:13). Geertz
explains that at the center of this state is the divine sovereign: "The
exemplary center within the exemplary center, the icon king depicted
outwardly for his subjects what he depicted inwardly to himself: the

equanimous beauty of divinity" (130). In the metaphysics of *mak yong-main 'teri,* the exemplary center is the *balai,* the individual-as-state so aptly described by Kessler (1977). However, as Geertz explains, the exemplary center within the exemplary center is the iconic divine king. In the metaphysical tradition of *mak yong-main 'teri,* at the center of the *balai,* the metaphorical state-as-self, sits the iconic figure of the crown prince, Dewa Muda, the young demi-god. The character of Dewa Muda is a symbol of the human infant, and he simultaneously represents the divine beauty and infantile passion that can be found in each individual.

DEWA MUDA AND THE FOUR JEMAGE

Most ritual performances of *mak yong* include the performance of an episode or episodes from the tale of *Dewa Muda* that *mak yong-main 'teri* practitioners deem the most beneficial to a patient. The pattern of separation, liminality, and reincorporation repeats throughout each important episode of the epic of *Dewa Muda,* underscoring the importance of the tale structure for the transformation of the health of a patient. Kelantanese healers explain that the character Dewa Muda, and by extension each individual human being, has three siblings: Abe Sejambul Lebat, Abe Kuda Hijau Jelmu Dewa, and Dewa Pechil. Dewa Muda and his three siblings are collectively referred to as the four *jemage,* or birth siblings. The embryo within the maternal womb is an incarnation of Dewa Muda. Dewa Muda's birth siblings assist in the gestation and development of the fetus, and each birth sibling is respected for its role in bringing forth human life.

Abe Sejambul Lebat, an infant's placenta, is referred to as the child's spiritual elder sibling. Traditional healers often call upon the spirit of a patient's placenta to help them heal the patient during a *mak yong-main 'teri.* In the tale of *Dewa Muda,* it is Abe Sejambul Lebat that restores Dewa Muda's broken kite, allowing him to soar to the Heavenly Kingdom to meet with the sky princess, Puteri Ratna Mas. Oral formulas recited during the performance of a *mak yong-main 'teri* describe Dewa Muda's golden kite with terms that metaphorically link it with the body of the patient. Ghulam-Sarwar Yousof argues that "[t]he golden kite of Dewa Muda then, is no less that [*sic*] the human soul, or more precisely the soul of the shaman in flight...it is in fact the soaring soul of the individual, every individual, or rather, everyman. Whether it is the literal human image or the image of the individual desiring liberation is up to interpretation" (2004:226). Performing the episode of the tale of *Dewa Muda* that deals with the restoration of Dewa Muda's kite and his flight into the heavens symbolizes the physical and psychological rebirth of a patient. This episode is often used to treat elderly individuals, or patients suffering from a long-term illness.

Abe Kuda Hijau Jelmu Dewa, Elder Brother Green Horse the Demi-God Incarnate, is understood by Kelantense healers to be the amniotic sac. In the tale of *Dewa Muda,* it is the green flying horse that brings back Dewa Muda to the Heavenly Kingdom after his resurrection from a death-like state. During birth, Kuda Hijau Jelmu Dewa as the amniotic sac becomes a child's noble steed as it conveys the infant into the world. Pak Ali drew a parallel between Kuda Hijau Jelmu Dewa and Buraq, the white-winged horse-like creature that conveyed the prophet Muhammed through the seven heavens to meet with Allah.

Dewa Pechil, a spirit-like being composed from human tissue, was created by Mok-Cik Dewa from the expelled amniotic fluid that surrounded Dewa Muda in the womb. In Malay, *pencil* means to isolate, stray away from others, or separate from society (Laderman 1991). The story of *Dewa Pechil* is one of banishment, and is only resolved when Dewa Pechil returns to the secondary forest, where he was created, to establish a spirit kingdom where his rule lasts forever. Hence, the story of *Dewa Pechil* can be performed for patients who feel that they have been maltreated and shunned by society.

Pak Ali explained that within a healing context, the story of *Dewa Pechil* is most often performed to *lepas niat,* or to release a vow made by an ill person to perform *mak yong* if they have been cured of their illness. When I asked Pak Ali if the story of *Dewa Pechil* was currently performed for healing purposes, he replied:

Pak Ali: Rarely, not very often. Only if people ask for it. The sick person asks "I want to play the story of *Dewa Pechil.*" If we pay tribute to *mak yong,* if we pay tribute to *mak yong,* if we pay tribute. A sick person, they promise, say I am the *Tok Bomoh* [the senior shaman], when they go to perform [the healing ceremony] the *bomoh* [shaman] invites the *Tok 'Teri* to go and heal. Say I am a *Tok Bomoh.* If I feel that my illness has been halted, that I am truly healed, I appear like other people, I can do a good deed, a pious duty. I want to give an offering to *mak yong.* When we give an offering to *mak yong,* we play [the story of] *Dewa Muda.* The last night of our offering we perform [the story of] *Dewa Pechil* because we want to beat the sick person. [In the play Mok Ibu Ayu beats Dewa Pechil with a cane bundle as she banishes him after forcing him to divorce her daughter]. We are not beating Dewa Pechil, but the sickness from the body... The sick person makes a vow.

A sick person vows, "If I am cured of this illness that has plagued me for the last one or two years, if I am healed, I will perform *mak yong*, I will release my vow with *mak yong*." That is the vow associated with Dewa Pechil. We must suggest it with a complete *balai* [a miniature palace hall made of forest materials that symbolizes the body and soul of the patient] lah...When Dewa Pechil enters into, we say enters into our soul. Dewa Muda also is deep within our soul as well. That is why when we *main 'teri* it is always the story of *Dewa Pechil*, the story of *Dewa Muda*. Because the human soul is disturbed. (Ali bin Ibrahim, August 2, 2005)[4]

As Pak Ali explains in the passage above, the goal of ritual perfor-mances of *mak yong* is the restoration of physical and emotional har-mony. These performances are understood to weld broken bodies and fractured souls back together through the performance of an epic tale. The tale of *Dewa Muda* centers around his infatuation and attempts at reunification with the sky princess Puteri Ratna Mas and draws on a story indigenous to northern Malaysia and southern Thailand. On a metaphorical level, Dewa Muda and Puteri Ratna Mas represent two aspects of a human soul, one female and the other male. They are two parts of one whole, separated by causes beyond their control. The couple is drawn to one another despite distance or hardship. Healing versions of *mak yong* culminate in the reunification of these characters through marriage. To Kelantanese healers, the reunification of these mythic characters through a dramatic enactment of their marriage is a powerful symbol of the restoration of internal harmony within an individual who is suffering from an illness of repressed desire.

In the version of the *mak yong* story of *Dewa Muda* that fol-lows the origins of four *jemage*, Dewa Muda and Puteri Ratna Mas marry at the end of the tale, their marriage symbolizing the restora-tion of a patient to wholeness. In this version of *Dewa Muda*, Puteri Ratna Mas and Dewa Muda are half-siblings. A demi-god descends to earth and observes Dewa Muda's mother-to-be, the Princess of the Half-Concealed Moon bathing. The demi-god is so taken by the beauty of the Princess of the Half-Concealed Moon that he ejaculates on a betel nut. The Princess of the Half-Concealed Moon then eats half of this betel nut, and throws the other half up to the sky where it is eaten by a sky giantess. In consuming the betel nut, the Princess of the Half-Concealed Moon becomes pregnant with the male lead character Dewa Muda, while the sky giantess becomes pregnant with the female lead character Puteri Ratna Mas.

On January 26, 2006, Pak Ali requested his student MD. Gel bin Mat Dali, known as Pak Agel, and his mother the late Supiah binti

Mat Ali, known as Mok Supiah, come to the house of Pak Wan Midin
for an evening of *mak yong* storytelling. After *isyak*, the last prayer of
the day, Pak Wan Midin, Pak Ali, Pak Agel, and Mok Supiah sat with
me on the floor of the *panggung* Pak Wan Midin had constructed and
discussed the tale of *Dewa Muda* and its importance for healing. Part
of the conversation between the last few great *mak yong* performers left in Kelantan included a discussion regarding the marriage of
Dewa Muda to Puteri Ratna Mas and the connection of the epic of
Dewa Muda to Islam. As Ghulam-Sarwar Yousof has observed, "*Mak
Yong* is often-times described as having derived directly from Adam
(Nabi Adam), the primeval human progenitor...[t]his results in its
being interpreted in symbolic and mystical terms often couched in
Sufi vocabulary" (1992:23).

   In an excerpt from this conversation (cited below), Pak Agel and
Pak Wan Midin emphasized that the tale of *Dewa Muda* performed
according to the origins of the four *jemage* was a story that originated
with mankind itself, from the time of Adam and his wife Hawa (Eve).
Kelantanese *mak yong* performers view Puteri Ratna Mas and Dewa
Muda as metaphors for the feminine and masculine aspects of a single
human soul. According to Islamic tradition, Adam and Hawa, like
Dewa Muda and Puteri Ratna Mas, were once one, Adam created by
Allah from dust, Hawa by Allah from one of Adam's ribs. Puteri Ratna
Mas and Dewa Muda marry in the healing version of Dewa Muda,
just as the Qur'an reveals that Adam and Hawa married one another.
According to the Qur'an, the union of Adam and Hawa produced
children, and their grandchildren married one another as cousins and
created the human race. Thus, Pak Wan Midin and Pak Agel emphasize, *Dewa Muda* is actually the story of the creation of mankind told
through *mak yong* performance.

   Pak Agel, Pak Wan Midin, and Mok Supiah assert that the *mak
yong* tale of *Dewa Mu*da comes to them through oral tradition, and it
is impossible to name its author. In this way, the story of *Dewa Muda*
is unlike Islamic writings authored by Sunni *ulama* that work within a
particular tradition or *madhhab* that start with one of the classic jurists
like Hanafi, Maliki, or Hanbali. Pak Agel, Pak Wan Midin, and Mok
Supiah are united in declaring that *mak yong* cannot and does not take
the place of Islam. Rather, the stories of the traditional Kelantanese
performing arts merely provide insight into the human condition. Pak
Wan Midin summarizes this discussion by explaining that *mak yong*
is but an allegory for the history of the human body and the history of humanity. Adam was created by Allah, Hawa was created by
Allah from part of Adam's body, Adam and Hawa were married, their

children divided and multiplied. This is what he describes as one betel nut, cut into two, divided into four.

> *Pak Agel*: If we play following the [version of *Dewa Muda*] in which they [Puteri Ratna Mas and Dewa Muda] can marry, we play following the origins of the four *jemage*. We play following the origins of these four *jemage*. Originating from lineage, the descendancy of Adam before us, he was one person with our grandmother Hawa [Eve] then...
>
> *Pak Wan Midin*: From the one man, Adam, came into being Hawa. Then they married and had children, Adam and Hawa. Why can we marry brother and sister? But they also did not marry between brother and sister. They married cousins, cousins, cousins, cousins. They became divided.
>
> *Pak Agel*: That is how the story of *Dewa Muda* is told; it is associated with the soul of a person.
>
> *Pak Wan Midin*: Meaning, it is up to the story, you cannot say that we just comment or take it here and there. We take it from the beginning, from Adam and Hawa. That is it. From one Adam was made Hawa. Only then did they have children.
>
> *Pak Agel*: One person asks who composed this story, who is the creator of this tale? We cannot say. Because the performance of this *mak yong* play [*Dewa Muda*] is the most important.
>
> *Pak Wan Midin*: This is what we call history. The history of man we say, told through a *mak yong* story.
>
> *Pak Agel*: The relationship: if in the language of the learned people of the book they are called,—
>
> *Mok Supiah*: Ulamak [Islamic scholars].
>
> *Pak Agel*: These *ulamak* they write many things. This *ulamak* does it like this, this *ulamak* does it like that. But we do know who the *ulamak mak yong* is...
>
> *Pak Wan Midin*: This thing that is *mak yong*, these things related to the performing arts, if we want to place them in the place of religion, we cannot!
>
> *Pak Agel*: We cannot!
>
> *Pak Wan Midin*: If it is our religion we can say, who wrote this book. We can say who published it.
>
> *Pak Agel*: There is Hanafi, there is Hambali, there is Maliki.
>
> *Pak Wan Midin*: There is Hambali, there is Maliki. But this thing that is *mak yong*—
>
> *Mok Supiah*: We cannot say.
>
> *Pak Wan Midin*: We can only ask any of our respected teachers, and they will also say it is history. The history of mankind placed into performance. That is all that they can say. Because this *mak yong* is also our history. Our body, one body, Adam came out, Hawa came

out, they married, they are divided. That is what people call the one betel nut, cut in two, divided into four. (Mohamed Agel bin Mat Dali, Supiah binti Mat Ali, Wan Midin bin Wan Majid, January 26, 2006)[5]

Personal Piety and the Performance of *Mak Yong*

Mak yong practitioners regard *mak yong* as a precious heritage, a gift that has been carefully managed, and painstakingly passed to them by their teachers and ancestors. For many *mak yong* performers, their performances are essential to healing others and maintaining their own personal wellness. During their performances they can release *angin*, internal "winds" or desires, that if allowed to stagnate can lead to illness. In the time before Westernized medical care was accessible to people living in rural Kelantan, traditional forms of healing like *mak yong-main 'teri* were the only recourse of medical treatment for ailing villagers. *Mak yong-main 'teri* currently functions in rural Kelantan as a complement to Western medical practice. While Western medicine focuses upon the physical diseases of an individual patient's body, *mak yong*, performed in the context of *main 'teri,* focuses on the illnesses that do not respond well to Western treatments: diseases of the mind, spirit, and soul.

Piety is an important aspect of healing for traditional performers, and prayer is understood by *mak yong* practitioners to be important for the body and the soul. Many performers, like the late Zainab binti Yaccob, affectionately known as Mok Jennab, pray before beginning their performances, noting that it is not their power, but the power of Allah that safeguards them, enables them to remember the stories of their ancestors, and makes them great performers. Mok Jennab would perform her opening prayer in the position of *bersedia*, or readiness, noting that this cross-legged sitting position mirrored the position of an infant in the womb. She viewed her performance of the *Menghadap Rebab*, the opening song and dance sequence of *mak yong*, as a physical prayer that reenacted the formation of an infant in the womb and the miracle of birth.

> Mok Jennab: Oh Allah, oh my God, it is not our power, but the power of Allah that enables us to be great performers. This is not to say that we perform for the fun of it. To play this [*mak yong*] we ask for our safety, we ask for our old stories from our ancestors that lived before us. We sit like this as we did before when we asked, when we desired to come out of our place of origins, out of our mother's womb. (Jennab binti Yaccob, July 28, 2005)[6]

When *mak yong* is performed within the elastic genre of a *main 'teri* healing ritual, a *Tok 'Teri* enters into an altered state to heal their patients. One of the physical motions that signal an onset of the state of trance is the spinning of the head. *Mak yong-main 'teri* performer, the late Saari bin Abdullah, insisted that the state of trance entered into by a *Tok 'Teri* during a healing performance was achieved entirely through the repeated recitation of the name of God. Once in an altered state the *Tok 'Teri* would be able to open a dialogue with parts of the patient's body, using metaphorical language to access the needs of a patient.

> Pak Saari: *Main puteri* [an alternative name for *main 'teri*] is a form of healing that we request from Allah the Most Compassionate, the Most Merciful. It is not something that we ask for from the Devil. So whatever they perform, they are not careless. Their head may spin, they go into trance, they have a recitation, they must say "Allah, Allah, Allah, Allah." They cannot be careless. Because in order to heal people, they have to ask Allah. Through him, with his help, that person can heal. It is not his [the performer's] power, but the power of Allah. So the people that *main puteri*, those that do it properly, they are not careless with themselves...They are within themselves. They are conscious. They cannot become unconscious. Because it is only acting, acting, they are acting with the parts of the body. They are opening a dialogue with the parts of the body...Like the guardian Awang Mahak, what is it? The hair on the body. Its part is the body hair. Awang Mahak, Awang Jidin. Awang Jidin, if I am not mistaken is the ear, Awang Jidin. (Saari bin Abdullah, June 12, 2005)[7]

While traditional performers like Mok Jennab and Pak Saari emphasize the importance of personal piety for their performances, the current religious and political environment in Kelantan has also encouraged many Kelantanese traditional performers to reassess how they view their art. As a youth in the early 1960s, Wan Midin bin Wan Majid studied to be a shadow puppeteer in the classical style of *wayang kulit Siam* with Awang Lah, a famous *dalang*, or shadow puppeteer, from Tumpat. Although Pak Wan Midin was a talented puppeteer, with a beautiful singing voice, he made the decision to stop performing *wayang kulit*, or shadow puppetry, in 1965. Pak Wan Midin explains why he felt that the traditional concept of a *dalang* as a master of his own universe of puppets, the lamp his sun, the shadow puppet world his creation, could not be resolved with his understanding of himself as a devout Muslim.

> Pak Wan Midin: This *mak yong*, our *mak yong-puteri*, we play it with what is deep within ourselves. *Wayang kulit* is [physically] external.

That is why it is external to our heart. It is external to us. So, this *wayang kulit* as it relates to us, as we ourselves are made by another, we are made by another. Another person made us, another person made us, but now we go and make puppets. It changes around the meaning. If I perform *wayang kulit*, that is, it doesn't touch my inner being. It is not like *mak yong*. With our *mak yong* we perform with wind...God is the one that made us, he animates us, infuses our bodies with breath, and places our eyes, and gives us life, enough, isn't it? He gives us food and drink.

In the end now what God has done for us, why then do we want to go and do that [referring to creating puppets and performing *wayang kulit*]. Because God created human beings, then we go and create puppets?

According to a person that follows Islam, a Muslim, like myself, Pak Wan Midin, this I cannot do. Every type of performance that I want to participate in, all types of performances, I go and reconcile it first, I go and speak with a religious scholar first. I went to go and speak with a religious scholar to investigate which was correct, and which was not correct. So what the religious scholar says we have to understand. He took out his holy book, and he read about the time of the Prophet, and what knowledge he gave to us, so that we would know. I asked him [about performing *wayang kulit*], but he said I cannot...So my heart feels that I no longer desire it, I throw it away. (Wan Midin bin Wan Majid, September 8, 2005)[8]

Pak Wan Midin felt that the traditional parallels drawn between the omnipotent *dalang* who creates, controls, and gives voice to the shadowy puppet world, and the omnipotent God who creates, controls, and gives voice to humanity were heretical to his understanding of himself as a simple man who submits to the will of Allah. Rather than becoming an anointed *dalang*, Pak Wan Midin left *wayang kulit*, directing his considerable talent as a performer into the art of *mak yong* and *main 'teri*. Pak Wan Midin, a faithful Muslim, does not feel that performing *mak yong-main 'teri* is heretical as he performs with the natural parts of his being created by God.

Audience reception of *Mak Yong-Main 'Teri* performances in rural Kelantan

The *mak yong-main 'teri* performances that I observed and documented in 2005–2006 were held either in the front room of a patient's home, or in a *panggung*, a temporary roofed structure, built in a yard adjacent to the house. Larger performances held outside of the house required a permit, granted at the discretion of local authorities. *Mak yong-main 'teri* events attracted a significant local audience of men, women, and children. When a *mak yong-main 'teri* was held inside a house, nonfamily members would crowd around doorways, windows, and other open areas of the home to view the performance. A *mak yong-main 'teri* that took place in a *panggung* outside the house provided local villagers with an unobstructed 360-degree view of the event. The events of a particular *mak yong-main 'teri* that take place in a village are often recounted and speculated upon by local residents in informal postperformance conversations that take place on front porches, at local coffee stalls, and in sundry shops scattered throughout the village landscape.

Villagers in Pasir Mas, Tumpat, and Pasir Puteh that I interviewed after *mak yong-main 'teri* performances cited numerous reasons for their attendance. Some attended due to a personal interest in the health of the patient, while others attended because they felt that they engaged vicariously with the healing events. Many observers were drawn to the performances for their sheer entertainment value. When I conducted postperformance interviews, many audience members requested copies of my video documentation as they desired to replay and comment upon the events of individual *mak yong-main 'teri* performances within the privacy of their own homes. Inexpensive video compact discs of *main 'teri* healing rituals were also available for purchase for home viewing in the Kota Bharu night market. Several older villagers revealed during postperformance interviews that they felt that viewing such recordings had a therapeutic effect, and was much less expensive than sponsoring their own healing ceremony.

Two individuals whom I interviewed stated that they intentionally avoided *mak yong-main 'teri* performances, not because they found them objectionable, but rather because they found them overwhelmingly compelling. One elderly lady, the wife of a musician, explained that she had a personal interest in *mak yong-main 'teri*, but stated that she did not dare attend an event as she feared that the performance would make her go into trance. She reasoned that she did not want to impose upon the family sponsoring the healing performance, as time would be taken away from the patient to tend to her should she become entranced. An older male villager I interviewed revealed that he too chose to avoid performances after an experience in which he found himself clinging to a tree and fighting against the music of a *mak yong-main 'teri* to prevent from being entering into a trance.

CONCLUSION

The 1991 PAS ban on *Mak Yong* performance has led to traditional *mak yong* performers increasingly incorporating *mak yong* into *main 'teri* healing performances, creating a genre that is often referred to by its practiners as *mak yong-main 'teri*, or *mak yong-'teri*. In the 1960s and 1970s, *mak yong* and *main 'teri* were recognized as two distinct genera of Kelantanese village performance, and *mak yong* was freely performed as village entertainment. The work of Carol Laderman (1991), Clive Kessler (1977), and Ghulam-Sarwar Yousof (1976) documents only the occasional performance of a *mak yong* tale in *main 'teri* healing events in the 1960s and 1970s. Except the rare performances commissioned by scholars and universities for the documentation of *mak yong* as a performing art, performances of *mak yong* independent of a *main 'teri* healing ritual are virtually nonexistent in present-day Kelantanese village life.

The political context in which *mak yong-main 'teri* exists and the religious debates it inspires can tell us much about Malaysian nationalism or the way in which contemporary Kelantanese religious scholars drawing upon their education in elite Middle Eastern universities are attempting to change a traditional Kelantanese understanding of Islam. However, I found that these debates told me little about the art of *mak yong* as it was understood by its traditional Kelantanese performers. When I began my work with *mak yong* practitioners, I found that their opinions regarding their art form had been largely unrepresented, their voices silenced in the cacophony of cultural critique by religious experts and political rivals. This controversy surrounding *mak yong* at the state and national levels is well known to Kelantanese performers. The issues, as they are presented by self-proclaimed experts in the state or national media, often do not resonate with traditionally trained *mak yong-main 'teri* practitioners who live and perform their art in rural Kelantan.

I found that contemporary *mak yong* practitioners understand their performance of *mak yong* in terms very different from those promoted on the nationalist stage or played out in the theater of state politics. Traditionally trained Kelantanese *mak yong* performers identify themselves as dedicated Muslims, and they view their performances of *mak yong* in a healing context to be an act of mercy for their patients. They attribute the power to heal to Allah; their performances, they argue, merely provide a means by which the grace of God may touch the human soul. When religious scholars claim *mak yong-main 'teri* contributes to the promotion of polytheism, the performers answer that these scholars do not possess a true understanding of their art. They emphasize that the tales they perform and the characters that they embody are not actual supernatural entities that they worship, rather, they are metaphors used by healers to describe the human body and plunge into the depths of the human soul. *Mak yong* artists note that *mak yong* may provide insight into the history of man through an art form, but they insist that it can never take the place of religion.

The understanding of contemporary Kelantanese *mak yong-main 'teri* practitioners differs considerably from that documented by Carol Laderman in her book *Taming the Wind of Desire Psychology, Medicine, and Aesthetics in Malay Shamanistic Performance* (1991). The philosophy of *main 'teri* documented by Carol Laderman places more emphasis on supernatural agents as a cause of illness, while contemporary Kelantanese practitioners openly speak of these supernatural beings as metaphors for physical, social, or emotional illness. Contemporary Kelantanese practitioners also emphasize their personal faith as Muslims and explain in depth their personal evaluations regarding what aspects of their performing arts traditions they view as problematic to their faith. Some of the differences between my observations in Kelantan from 2005 to the present and Carol Laderman's findings in Terengganu in 1975 may be due to regional and individual variations in the tradition. However, I believe that many of these differences illustrate the way in which the tradition itself is actively being reevaluated by its practitioners in response to rapid social and political change.

Raymond Firth refers to *main 'teri* as a "cathartic mechanism" (1967:212) while Douglas Raybeck argues that *main 'teri* functions to relieve social stress, in that blame for deviant behavior may be displaced onto supernatural beings (241). My research demonstrates that *mak yong-main 'teri* practitioners, confronted with changing interpretations of appropriate Islamic practice, are actively adapting how they think and speak about the microcosm of the body, the origins of illness, and their healing performances. Part of this process includes reframing longstanding concepts of supernatural beings as agents of disease. Contemporary Kelantanese healers openly discuss the supernatural beings addressed, described, and confronted in *mak yong-main 'teri* healing rituals as symbols of an internalized physical or social dysfunction that materializes in the body of a patient. Further research will demonstrate whether the recasting of traditional supernatural beliefs as modern metaphors for social dis-ease is particular to a contemporary Kelantanese cultural context, or if the reframing of the supernatural as a metaphor for social and physical disorder can be found in other cultures where traditional belief systems are undergoing rapid change.

NOTES

1. Most Kelantanese *mak yong-main 'teri* performers prefer the term *main 'teri* to describe their ritual healing performances; however, much of the academic literature on the subject references these performances using the term *main puteri* or *main peteri* (Laderman 1991:7). The use of the term *main 'teri* is currently preferred by many performers as the term *main puteri*, or playing the princess, implies a significant female role in the performances. Although there has been a long history of female participation in *main 'teri*, in most contemporary Kelantanese performances, the role of the *Tok 'Teri* is almost exclusively performed by a male practitioner. The term *'teri* is also often interpreted by performers as a shortened form of the Malay word *pateri*, meaning to weld. This definition fits performers' understanding of their art as a means to repair broken bodies and make whole fractured souls.

2. Portions of this chapter derive from my dissertation: please see Hardwick (2009) for a more comprehensive discussion of this subject.

3. The original Malay transcriptions of the statements of the individual performers quoted are included in this and all subsequent notes.
   Pak Ali: Mok yong menyanyi ada dia menyanyi dia menari macam ni. Ini dia menujukan kita oghe Islam Allah yang satu, tak dok hok lain kalu dia. Buka empat jari dia kira tanah, air, api, angin dia. Kalu dia buka jari-jari— lima jari, lima waktu sehari semale itu saja... Lima jari buka nih, lima waktu sehari, semalam. Kita oghe Islam itu aje, dia tak akan tak akan lepas labu susu nih tak baik sakat ni arah bahu. Kanan serupa kiri pun. Kalu dia ucap situ dia baca dia tu apa-apa hal pelajaran dia, dia akan baca pun dia baca, jari-jari ni pun, dia baca juga. (Ali bin Ibrahim, August 28, 2005)

4. Pak Ali: Tak, jarang sangat. Melainkan dia orang minta. Orang sakit minta "Ambo ni nok main cerita Dewa Pechil." Kalu kita bersembah mak yong, kalu bersembah mak yong, kalu bersembah. Oghe sakit, dia janji, ambo ni tok bomoh—
   Apabila gi main bomoh ajak Tok 'Teri ni gi bomoh. Ambo Tok bomoh.
   Kalu bansa ambo ni berhenti sakit, segar megah serupa oghe ramai-ramai buleh wat amal ibadat. Ambo nok semah mak yong. Apabila semah mak yong, main Dewa Muda. Male last nok semah main Dewa Pechil sebat nok katok oghe sakit tu. Bukan katok Dewa Pechil, katok penyakit dale tubuh... Orang sakit niat,
   sesatu oghe sakit niat, "Kalu sekira ambo ni sembuh sakit lama setahun dua tahun sakit, kalu ambo sembuh ambo nok main mak yong nok pelepas niat dengan mak yong." Itu lah niat kiat Dewa Pechil, kena cadang dengan balai cukup lah....
   Apa...apa bila Dewa Pechil termasuk dale, kita kata dale jiwa kita,
   Dewa Muda mendalami jiwa kita juga. Sebab itu main puteri selalu cerita Dewa Pechil selalu cerita Dewa Muda. Sebab usik jiwa seoghe manusia. (Ali bin Ibrahim, August 2, 2005)

5. Pak Agel: Kalau kita main ikut boleh bernikah ni, kita main ikut asal jemage empat.

Main asal ikut jemage empat ini. Asal titih jemage Ade dulu, dia jadi seoghe-oghe dia denge Tok Hawa gak...

Pak Wan Midin: Daripada Ade seoghe, lepas jadikan Hawa. Kemudian berkahwin dapat anak, Ade denge Hawa. Mengapa kita boleh kahwin adik-beradik?

Tapi dia tidak berkahwin juga adik-beradik. Dia kahwin sepupu sepupu sepupu, sepupu. Dia jadi pecah-pecah.

Pak Agel: Itulah mengisahkan cerita Dewa Muda yang kata, berkaite dengan jiwa seseoghe.

Pak Wan Midin: Maknanya, tersila ceritanya pun, bukan kata kita saja kita komek- komek, ambik-ambik. Daripada asal kita ambik, daripada Ade denge Hawa.

Tu saja. Satu Ade dijadikan Hawa. Baru dapat anak.

Pak Agel: Seorghe tanya cerita ni siapa dia tukang kare, siapa dia tukang dongeng?

Kita tak boleh nak royak. Sebab permainan mak yong ni hok utama.

Pak Wan Midin: Itu dipanggil sejarah. Sejarah manusia lah kita kata, dibawakan oleh cerita mak yong.

Pak Agel: Kaitannya, kalau bahasa orang alim kitab dia panggil,—

Mok Supiah: Ulamak.

Pak Agel: Ulamak ni dia cetak mace-mace. Ulamak ni buat mace ni, ulamak ni buat mace ni. Tapi ulamak mak yong ni kita tidak tahu tersih awal-awal siapa dia....

Pak Wan Midin: Benda hok mak yong, benda hok mene, kita nak teke tempat ugama, Tak leh!

Pak Agel: Tak leh!

Pak Wan Midin: Kalau ugama kita boleh kata, kitab ni keluar, siapa dia.

Boleh royak orang penerbit tu.

Pak Agel: Hanafi ada, Hambali ada, Maliki ada.

Pak Wan Midin: Hambali ada, Maliki ada. Tapi benda mak yong ni—

Mok Supiah: Tak boleh nak royak.

Pak Wan Midin: Hanya kita tanya tok guru mana-mana pun dia kata sejarah. Sejarah kita manusia meletak daripada permaine. Itu saja dia boleh royak. Kerana mak yong ni pun sejarah kita. Bade kita sebade, tubik Ade, tubik Hawa, kahwin, dia pecah-pecir. Apa ni orang panggil er pinang muda sebutir, belah dua, dibagi empat. (MD Gel bin Mat Dali, Supiah binti Mat Ali, Wan Midin bin Wan Majid, January 26, 2006)

6. Mok Jennab: Ya Allah, Ya Tuhe ku, aku ni nok mintok doa bui lanjutkan umur, tak dok sapo bata tak dok sapo bui jatuh membahyo lah ... Ya Allah, Ya Tuhan ku buke kuaso kami, kuaso Allah bui ko kami pandai ni, buke kato nok suko-suko, main ni, main mintok selamat diri pado cerito dulu, jame titih oghe dulu. Kito duduk ni, mace, dulu kito mintok. Nok keluar dari pado asal. Kanduge ibu kito tu (Jennab binti Yaccob, July 28, 2005).

7. Pak Saari: Main puteri ini adalah dia perubataan yang memohon kepada Allah Subahana Wa Ta'ala. Dia bukan memohon kepada syaitan. Jadi apa yang dia main dia tak boleh lalai. Kepala yang dia berpusing, dia lupa-lupa, dia ada satu bacaan dia mesti kata "Allah, Allah, Allah, Allah." Dia tak boleh lalai.

Sebab dia mengubati orang, dia memohon kepada Allah. Melalui dia, dengan pemohonan dia tu, orang itu boleh sembuh. Tapi bukan kuasa dia, kuasa Allah.

Jadi orang main puteri, yang betul-betul punya, dia tidak melalaikan diri dia....

Dalam diri dia. Dia sedar. Dia tak boleh kata tak sedar. Sebab lakonan dia tu saja, lakonan dia tu kalau, lakonan dia dalam anggota dia. Dia berbicara dengan anggota dia...Anggota luar pun. Macam penggawa Awang Mahak. Awang Mahak ke apa itu, bulu roma. Anggota dia bulu roma. Awang Mahak, Awang Jidin. Awang Jidin tak silap saya telinga. Awang Jidin. (Saari bin Abdullah, June 12, 2005)

8. Pak Wan Midin: Mak yong ni, mak yong-puteri kita main kita punya dalam, wayang kulit di luar...

Sebabnya luar pada hati. Luar pada diri kita. Jadi wayang kulit ni sebagai kita ni, sebagai kita sendiri orang lain yang buat kepada kita, orang lain buat. Ya ... orang lain buat kita, orang yang ada buat kita tapi sekarang kita gi buat pantung. Berganti-ganti maknya. Kita ni main wayang kulit supaya tidak sersentuh dengan diri kita. Tak seperti mak yong. Mak yong kita main angin ... Tuhan yang jadikan kita, bergerak-bergerai, bernyawa dan bubuh mata hidup cukup bukan? Degang makan minum dia bagi.

Habis sekarang dah tuhan buat kat kita, mengapa pulak kita pergi buat benda ni?...Sebab Tuhan cipta pada manusia, kita gi cipta kepada pantung.

Bagi orang Islam, muslim macam Pak Wan Midin ni tak boleh, sebab seuma mainan yang saya nak main, semua permainan saya pergi rujuk pergi cakap kepada orang alim dulu. Pergi tanya orang alim dulu bahas kita yang mana betul, yang mana tak betul. Jadi orang alim cakap kita kena faham. Dia keular kitab ke, dia baca apa pun masa Nabi dulu, apa dia bagi tahu kat kita, dah kita orang tahu. Kita tanya dia, tapi dia kata tak boleh ... Tapi rasa hati kita, tak nak, kita buang. (Wan Midin bin Wan Majid, September 8, 2005)

4

"ISLAMIC" TV DRAMAS, MALAY YOUTH, AND PIOUS VISIONS FOR MALAYSIA

Timothy P. Daniels

INTRODUCTION

Islamic proselytizers—Muslim nongovernmental organizations, the Islamic Party of Malaysia (PAS, Parti Islam SeMalaysia), and the UMNO (United Malays National Organization)-led federal government—have exerted a major influence on the public sphere over the past three decades. Their *dakwah* (proselytizing) movements and campaigns infused the public sphere and everyday life with diffuse images and expressions of piety. These diverse efforts precipitated the emergence of a "Muslim cultural sphere"—artistic and cultural discussions and expressions of "religiously inflected voices and visions"—within the broader public sphere (Nieuwkerk 2011:4). Religious-oriented websites, magazines, singing (*nasyid*) groups, and radio and television programs constitute this expanding Muslim cultural sphere in Malaysia. *Nasyid* boy bands, prevalent in Malaysia and Indonesia (see Barendregt 2011), were joined by Maher Zain, a Swedish ethnic-Lebanese singer who became a popular heartthrob in Malaysia with the release of his first compact disc *Thank You Allah* in 2009. His CD, containing pious Islamic messages cast in a variety of global pop styles, was widely distributed in Malaysia and he appeared in several live performances and magazines. Even Dato' Siti Nurhaliza, the most prominent Malay pop star of this era, released her most religious compact disc *Tahajjud Cinta* in 2009, featuring her singing the ninety-nine names of Allah and praises for Prophet Muhammad. Several seasons of *Tanah Kubur* (Gravesite), a dramatic series depicting misfortune and punishment in the grave for "sinful" acts, aired on satellite television. In 2010, the *Imam Muda* (Young Imam) television series aired that featured young men performing religious tasks in competition for a scholarship to an Islamic university in Saudi Arabia and a post as an imam in a Malaysian mosque.

Also appearing in this vibrant Muslim cultural sphere in May 2009 was a new and highly popular genre, the "Islamic" TV drama series, with the airing of *Nur Kasih* on TV3. *Nur Kasih*, written by Mira Mustaffa and directed by Kabir Bhatia and Faizal Ishak, remade some of the older TV drama themes within a robustly enchanted world. This "Islamic" drama series not only featured Malays, like the "corporate" and *kampung* (village) dramas (Thompson 2007:164), but also displayed extensive expressions and embodiment of Islamic norms, values, and motives. Scenes of prayer in mosques and homes, depictions of the holy land in the Middle East, men and women in Muslim attire, and religiously oriented dialogue and behavior saturated the twenty-six episodes of this series. *Nur Kasih*, a saga of a rural Malay Islamic teacher and his two sons' romantic relationships, was immensely popular in the Malay community, especially among the youth. Reportedly, nearly 4 million viewers tuned in to watch each weekly episode and 5 million for the final episode, while the series attracted 19 million viewers overall (*Utusan Malaysia* November 29, 2009; *Dramatic Durian* 2011). Two years later, May 2011, *Nur Kasih the Movie* was released in theaters picking up the story where the TV drama series left off. During June and July 2011 two new Islamic TV drama series aired on TV3, *Stanza Cinta* and *Tahajjud Cinta*, comprising thirteen episodes each. These three stories are different in many respects but they share the characteristic of profuse expression and embodiment of Islamic ideas and practices.

In this chapter, I interpret these three stories in relation to the broader cultural, historical, and sociopolitical context. I treat TV dramas and films as a "contested terrain that reproduces existing social struggles and transcodes the political discourses of the era" (Kellner 2009:2). "Transcode" refers to how specific political discourses and feelings are "translated, or encoded, into media texts" (2). In order to better comprehend the contours of the contested terrain, I contrast the political discourses transcoded in these three stories with those in several of Yasmin Ahmad's controversial films that embodied a different vision of Malaysian society. Moreover, I will perform a "diagnostic critique" that uses films and TV dramas "to analyze and interpret the events, hopes, fears, discourses, ideologies, and sociopolitical conflicts of the era" (34). Douglas Kellner describes this approach as involving "a dialectic of text and context, using texts to read social realities and events, and using social and historical context to help situate and interpret key films" (34–35). I extend this approach to include the voices and views of members of the local audience, and thereby triangulate between text, context, and audience perspectives. This extended approach required more extensive ethnographic research, including discussions, interviews, and participant-observation among audience members. I draw upon interviews conducted with Malay "youth"[1] and adults pertaining to TV dramas, films, and popular culture over seven months during 2010 and 2011, and with Malaysians from various backgrounds during earlier periods of ethnographic research. For the recent popular culture survey, I approached forty-eight young Malay men and women in restaurants, transportation hubs, and university campuses who consented to be interviewed. My interlocutors were primarily middle class, from rural and urban backgrounds, and not affiliated with political parties.

Including the voices and views of local audience members is important for several reasons. First, it tempers assumptions about the effects of the representations and codes in the text upon the audiences' thoughts and feelings. Audience members may frame, dismiss, or contest cinematic representations and codes in a variety of ways. Second, it serves as a check on elitist readings of texts. More privileged analysts, for instance, may read the texts as swaying, even duping, or indoctrinating the less privileged, whereas subordinates may be using or reading texts to fight dominant groups. They may also be requesting or demanding certain sorts of texts. Elitist readings tend to elide audiences' agency. Third, it facilitates a lessening of the unequal relationships between observers and local subjects, which has plagued the history of social sciences. I attempt to use audience member's views to coproduce my readings of these TV dramas and films.

Karin van Nieuwkerk (2011:10) argues that parallel developments in several Middle Eastern case studies suggest the emergence of a "post-Islamist cultural sphere" in which younger generations of Muslims are creating pious art that turns away from and reformulates rigid doctrinal views. She states that more liberal attitudes toward art, the development of a middle and upper-middle class market-oriented Islam, moderate religious ideologies, and the influence of media and the global transnational sphere indicate the emergence of this post-Islamist cultural sphere. While there has surely been the development of a market-oriented Islam and growing influence of media and the global cultural sphere (see Sloane-White 1999; Fischer 2008), Malaysian Muslim attitudes toward art and religious ideologies have remained largely conservative. Moreover, the Islamic TV dramas and film, and the emergent Muslim cultural sphere they participate in, do not constitute a counter- or oppositional public contesting a secular or Islamic state. Instead, I interpret that they contest discourses of ethnic and religious pluralism and liberal Islam, while not unambiguously endorsing the particular discourses of either UMNO or PAS. Rather than a post-Islamist cultural sphere, I argue, they indicate a "postdivision" cultural sphere, one in which Muslims, united in their piety, maintain dominance, uphold the faith, and solve social problems.

First, I will contrast these stories to the ones Yasmin Ahmad told, demonstrating the contrast between the discourses they encoded and embodied and how Malay youth read them, and how they relate to ongoing struggles in Malaysian society. Then I will turn to the ideas and feelings transcoded pertaining to class, rural/urban divisions, age, gender, and sexuality in these three Islamic dramas, and further discuss what this postdivision cultural sphere means for sociopolitical processes in Malaysia.

YASMIN AHMAD'S FILMS, PLURALISM, AND LIBERAL ISLAMIC PIETY

Yasmin Ahmad, the late Malaysian filmmaker, achieved international recognition for her work and received several film festival awards. However, her reception at home in Malaysia was mixed as her films broached sensitive matters concerning interethnic and interreligious relations among members of Malaysia's diverse society. Intergroup tensions have a long history resting in British colonial hierarchies and race-making and postcolonial communalism and institutionalized racial differentiation (Andaya and Andaya 2001; Lee 1986; Milner 1998; Reid 2001; Daniels 2005; Frisk 2009; Ting 2011). Although many outside observers perceive Malaysia as a peaceful and model plural society, ever since the racial riot of May 13, 1969, social struggles rage on erupting into intermittent acts of violence along ethnic and religious lines. Yasmin Ahmad's films and Islamic TV dramas advance and encode contested sociopolitical positions and agendas pertaining to ongoing social struggles.

Yasmin Ahmad's *Sepet* (Chinese Eyes, 2004), a romantic drama, features a Chinese boy (Ah Loong or Jason) and Malay schoolgirl (Orked) falling in love and struggling to be with each other despite social and cultural obstacles. Early in the film, Orked (Sharifah Amani), her mother (Ida Nerina), and girlfriend depart for the market, none of them wearing a headscarf as prescribed by normative Islamic piety in Malaysia. Orked, like her mother, wears a *baju kurung* (long skirt and matching tunic) and her friend wears jeans. Orked and Jason (Ng Choo Seong) meet and experience mutual attraction at Jason's stall in a street market where he sells "pirated" VCDs, and later they begin dating. They continue their budding romance—going to restaurants, taking pictures together, and holding hands—despite opposition in their respective ethnic communities. Jason fears that his parents will be angry if they find out so he tries to keep his romantic relationship hidden from them. Orked's open-minded family appears to accept her new romance and her mother and live-in maid consider Jason to be handsome. However, Orked has a heated argument with two of her Malay friends at school who disapprove of her dating a Chinese boy. She stands up to them criticizing the gender bias that disciplines Malay women and not men for engaging in romantic relationships crossing ethnic boundaries. Similarly, in a later scene, Jason exclaims to his friend that in the distant past it was easier for Chinese and Malays to intermarry but now that they are supposedly "more civilized," it is much harder to do so.[2]

Written and directed by Yasmin Ahmad, *Sepet* transcodes political discourses that challenge the special privileges and primacy of Malay Muslims and argue for an ethnic and religious pluralism in which diverse Malaysians interact and dialogue as equal belongers (see Khoo 2007). One of the controversial issues manifesting Malay privilege is the legal requirement for non-Muslims to convert to Islam to marry Malays who are defined as Muslims in the federal constitution. During the late 1990s and early 2000s many of my Chinese, Indian, Eurasian, and Melaka *Portugis* interlocutors expressed their strong opposition to this practice, and I occasionally witnessed televised debates over this issue (Daniels 2005:49, 183–208). Chinese and Indian intellectuals asserted that an easing of conversion requirements and Islamic religious norms would facilitate a more united and integrated plural society. In a scene in *Sepet*, Jason's friend articulates the frustrations of many Malaysian non-Muslims when he cautions Jason that he will have to change his religion and name and stop eating pork if he is to marry his beloved Orked.

Sepet transcodes a vision of a bottom-up multiculturalism without Malay supremacy in which diverse Malaysians can overcome their stereotypes of each other and celebrate their differences. In one scene, Jason's Chinese friend chides him for not using and telling Orked his real Chinese name, Ah Loong. Jason demands his friend not use his Chinese name in front of Orked. When she arrives, she sits between the two boys and has a friendly discussion with them. They disclose to her that Jason has an avid interest in poetry and his friend in piano playing. Orked expresses that this is surprising and not at all what she

expected from them. Jason's friend points out that the common stereotypes of Chinese and Malays are wrong. Later, in an intimate scene
when they are alone, Jason tells Orked his name is Ah Loong. Orked
responds telling him that she likes both of his names, the Chinese one
even better.

Eventually, factors outside of their control pull them apart. Before
falling for Orked, Jason gets a Chinese girl pregnant. She happens to
be the younger sister of a powerful gangster who ran the nightclub
where his mother worked. Jason is forced to return to her and sever
his ties with Orked who begins dating a Malay boy. Encoding ideas
and feelings about the unfairness of institutionalized Malay privilege,
the maid notes that Orked achieved five "A"s on her exams and won
a scholarship to study abroad, while Jason who earned seven "A"s
was not awarded anything (Khoo 2007). Jason maintains his love for
Orked and sends her flowers and a letter before she leaves for college.
Noticing that Jason is distraught, his mother comforts and informs
him that she knows about his love for Orked and does not disapprove.
She says that it was common practice for a married Chinese man to
have a relationship with a Malay woman on the side. She says she only
asks that he bring Orked home to meet her. As Orked's father (Harith
Iskander) drives them to the airport, her mother implores her to read
Jason's letter. As she reads it aloud, they both cry at his intense expression of love for her. In tears, Orked tries to call Jason who is riding
his motorcycle and later the film cuts to the tragic scene of him lying
in a puddle of blood, apparently the aftermath of a tragic accident.
Orked's father says that he does not think that Jason is "suitable" for
her, but her mother challenges his assertion informing him that this is
exactly what her father said when she wanted to marry him. This emotional exchange, equating evaluations of ethnic or religious difference
with class, status, or personality difference, transcodes hopes for a less
rigid policing of ethno-religious boundaries. *Sepet* ends in an ambigu-
ous fashion with scenes of Jason lying in the street severely injured and
later lying beside Orked in a state of marital bliss.

A touching and tragic love story, *Sepet* embodies and expresses
a liberal Islam that presents few, if any, impediments to intergroup
relations and advocates a sense of piety at odds with *dakwah* movements in Malaysia.[3] While *Sepet* shows religious quotes such as
Bismillahirrahmanirrahim (in the name of God, the most compassionate, the most merciful) on screen and has Orked's father
inquire in her absence about whether she has been keeping up her
daily prayers, it generally depicts women without headscarves and
shows Orked touching and spending time alone with Jason in rather

secluded places. *Dakwah* movements, over the past several decades, have promoted modest dress and motivated Muslim women to embody piety through wearing headscarves (Frisk 2009). Malaysian Islamic scholars, religious courts, and most pious Muslims consider Orked's behavior while dating Jason to be forbidden. However, it is the fear of this sort of rising normative Islamic piety and its influence on public life that is encoded in *Sepet*. In the mid-2000s such anxieties were widespread and intensifying with Prime Minister Mahathir Mohamad's declaration that Malaysia was already an "Islamic state," and his subsequent selection of Abdullah Ahmad Badawi, who promoted an Islamic Civilization (*Islam Hadhari*), as his successor. Many of my Malaysian non-Muslim interlocutors expressed uncertainties about the direction Malaysia was heading in and whether the vision of Malaysia as a secular nation, which they viewed as being embedded in the federal constitution, would be upheld (see Martinez 2001; Chong 2006; Chinyong 2009).

Yasmin Ahmad's *Gubra* (Anxiety, 2006), the sequel to *Sepet*, also transcodes fears of rising normative piety and embodies liberal Islam. *Gubra* picks up Orked's story a few years after her romance with Jason who we learn died in the motorcycle accident. Orked is married to an older Malay man who has an affair with another woman. In the main plot of the story, Orked meets Jason's brother, Alan (Alan Yun), who has returned to Malaysia after divorcing his Singaporean wife. Alan supports Orked as she struggles to leave her husband, and they grow closer. In a subplot, a pious *muezzin*, who recites the call to prayer at a neighborhood mosque, and his wife help a prostitute change her life and return to practicing Islam. *Gubra* not only shows religious statements on screen like *Sepet*, but it also presents more women wearing headscarves and men and women praying, performing the call to prayer, and studying recitation of the Qur'an. Nevertheless, the *muezzin* encodes a flexible piety with weak implementation of Islamic rules. Early in the film, he pets an injured dog and compassionately removes it from the road on his way to the mosque, and is shown entering the mosque and making the call to prayers without changing clothes and performing the ablutions required by normative Islamic rules to regain ritual purity after contact with a dog (cf. Khoo 2007:56). In addition, the *muezzin* and his pious wife allow prostitution to continue in the neighborhood without taking community action to end it. Moreover, liberal Islam is expressed in the attire of all the leading men and women in the story; none of them wears Islamic attire. Orked wears thin pajama pants with a skimpy, sleeveless top in public during the early part of the film. She also has a scene in the hospital, reminiscent of one with Jason in *Sepet*, in which she picks lent off the bare chest of Alan and accidentally pinches his nipple. In scenes, later in *Gubra*, Orked holds Alan's hand as they leave her cheating husband and when he escorts her into his bedroom to view the box of mementos Jason left for her.

Gubra also transcodes ethnic and religious pluralism and bottom-up multiculturalism. While driving in Alan's old truck, Orked and Alan articulate celebrations of Malaysian diversity and criticism of Malay supremacy. Orked and Alan sing a Chinese song playing on the radio, after which Orked contrasts monoculturalism in Europe with the vibrant diversity in Malaysia. She says it is so refreshing to be able to turn on the radio in Malaysia and hear Chinese and Indian music. Jason agrees but notes that non-Malays often feel that their love for Malaysia is not returned to them. Orked says many Malays are aware of this and are trying to change society. In addition, *Gubra* presents several friendly interethnic relationships other than that of Orked and Alan. Alan's mother bonds with a Malay woman visiting her husband whose hospital bed is next to Alan's father's bed. The Malay woman and her daughter, both wearing long headscarves and robes, share popular Malay cuisine (*rendang*) with Alan's parents. Alan's mother and the Malay woman warmly hug each other before they part. Orked's maid also develops a romantic relationship with a Chinese male nurse she meets at the hospital. At the end of the film, following the credits, Orked and Jason are shown lying in bed wearing wedding rings. Finally, *Gubra* expresses religious pluralism with a succession of scenes beginning with the *muezzin* performing the call to prayer and cutting to his wife with the former prostitute praying in the mosque, Alan's parents praying at their home altar, and Alan and his daughter praying in a Christian church. With this kaleidoscopic vision of religious diversity, *Gubra* contests Malay Muslim hegemony and the special status accorded to Islam.

Similarly, *Muallaf* (Convert, 2008), Yasmin Ahmad's fifth film, encodes ethnic and religious pluralism and political challenges to institutionalized distinctions that place Islam apart from and above other religions. It is a sympathetic drama about two young Malay girls, Rohani (Sharifah Amani) and Rohana (Sharifah Aleysha), who ran away from their father who drinks alcohol, frequents nightclubs, and shaves off Rohani's hair in a fit of anger. They grew up in Singapore with their educated mother, a university professor, and were forced to live with their father and mother-in-law in Kuala Lumpur after she passed away. Rohani flees to Ipoh with her younger sister after their father abuses her, but he hires a private detective and goons to track them down. Meanwhile, a Chinese schoolteacher, Brian (Brian Yap), is drawn to the rather quirky young girls, after driving the younger sister home the day she was caned by an Indian teacher frustrated with her baffling comments and recitation of pairs of numbers in class. Later, Brian and the Indian Catholic principal discover that the girls are adept in comparative religion and that the paired numbers and comments were chapters and verses of the Qur'an and quotes from other religious texts. Brian, who is going through his own personal and religious journey trying to overcome his childhood experience of abuse at the hands of his strict Catholic parents, asks to borrow the girls' Qur'an and studies it. Nevertheless, the story, though titled *Muallaf* (Convert), is not about him converting to Islam, but about the two pious Muslim girls motivating him to become a *true believer* of God. In a crucial narrative, while the girls are at a *roti canai* restaurant with Brian, they recite Sura Al-Baqara verse 62 (Q2:62):

> Those who believe (in the Qur'an)
> And those who follow the Jewish (scriptures),
> And the Christians and the Sabians,
> Any who believe in Allah
> And the Last Day,
> And work righteousness,
> Shall have their reward
> With their Lord on them
> Shall be no fear, nor shall they grieve.

Brian stops Rohana and asks her to repeat "Sabians," and she explains that they were "monotheists predating both Islam and Christianity" and that in some translations the Arabic word is interpreted as *muallaf* or convert. Transcoding liberal Islamic arguments calling for contemporary Muslims to rethink traditional interpretations, the girls agree that they should learn Arabic to better understand the verses of the Qur'an on their own. Malaysian government censors muted a few comments from this narrative before allowing the movie to open nationwide in 2009. Nevertheless, the notion that *true believers* and not Muslims alone will be rewarded by God comes across strongly here and throughout the rest of the story. Rohani counsels Brian informing him that many people move away from religion because of bad experiences they've had in the past. She demands that he speak more politely to his mother. Later, after her younger sister is captured by their father's goons, Rohani tells Brian to drive to Penang and take his mother to church on Sunday. The fact that the girls nightly forgive everyone who has harmed them impresses and motivates Brian to forgive his mother. Although Brian is shown visiting an Islamic institution, reciting the same Qur'anic verse the girls did to a comatose patient, and telling Rohani that he wants to study Arabic with her if she returns to Ipoh, we are never informed that he converts to Islam. He is depicted as someone on a journey of return to monotheistic belief, a convert (*muallaf*) to a universal monotheism.

Moreover, diverse expressions of piety are embodied in *Muallaf*. Brian's mother is constantly after him about accompanying her to church on Sundays. Immediately after witnessing Rohana being captured, Brother Anthony, the Catholic priest and school principal, runs to the chapel falling to his knees supplicating to God for the girl's safety. "In the name of God, the compassionate, the merciful" is shown on the screen at the beginning of the film in English and Mandarin. In addition, the two leading Malay actresses are shown performing prayers together wearing white prayer gowns (*telekung*) and Rohani puts on a headscarf before reciting the Qur'an to the comatose patient in the hospital. Rohani recites praises to Prophet Muhammad (*selawat*) as she rides her motorcycle and the girls recite *Ayatul Kursi*, The Throne Verse (Q2:255), and forgive people every night before going to sleep. However, these two pious Muslim girls express the same respect for all religions reading, memorizing, and reciting segments from other religious texts such as the Tao Te Ching and the Bible. Indeed, this film transcodes political discourse challenging the special status of Islam, such as laws restricting members of other religions from proselytizing to Muslims and from uttering words reserved for Islamic references (see Peletz 1993:89–90; Daniels 2005:49–50). It argues for a more horizontal rather than hierarchical relationship between Islam and other religions.

Talentime (2009), Yasmin Ahmad's final film, continues the theme of interethnic relations and ethnic and religious pluralism that runs through her films, but concentrating this time on Malay and Indian relations and representing Hinduism in Malaysia's cultural tapestry. *Talentime* signals its focus on Indians by opening the film with "In the name of God, the compassionate, the merciful" written in Tamil, the main Indian language in Malaysia. It is a dramatic story about a school's talent contest, *talentime*, and the student finalists. A romance develops between one of the finalists, Melur (Pamela Chong), a Malay Eurasian girl, and Mahesh (Mahesh Jugal Kishor), a speech-impaired Indian boy who is assigned to transport her to rehearsals for the final competition. It also depicts the racially tinged competitive relationship between two other finalists, Hafiz (Mohd Syafie Naswip) and Kahoe (Howard Hon Kahoe), which develops into a friendship in the end. Similar to

Sepet, Talentime transcodes fears of the corrosive impact of racial stereotypes and resentment, and hopes for overcoming these differences and creating a more unified multicultural society. Amidst representations of Indian culture—including ceremonies involving bathing in temples, religious and Bollywood music, clothing and dance and a cremation—a tragedy and romance play out. Early in Melur and Mahesh's budding relationship, his beloved uncle is killed on his wedding night when a quarrel broke out with Malays who were conducting funeral ceremonies. A wedding, funeral, and racial riot evokes memories of the four-day-long Kampung Medan clashes beginning March 4, 2001, in which most of the victims were poor Indian Malaysians (*Malaysiakini* March 8, 2002). In addition, Mahesh's mother's narrative about how Malays in the past tore down the temple her deceased brother built in the neighborhood articulates opposition to Malay dominance and religious intolerance. Government-enforced removal and relocation of Indian temples is a contentious issue in contemporary Malaysia (Daniels 2010:192). In 2007, the Hindu Rights Action Force (HINDRAF) protested the demolition of a Hindu temple in Kuala Lumpur and they were subjected to severe government repression (Ahmad Fauzi 2008; Nagarajan 2009). After returning home late from Melur's house, Mahesh is beaten in the street by his mother who, still mourning her brother, harbors resentment against Malays and Muslims in general. Later, Mahesh's elder sister shows their mother the e-mail her late uncle wrote to Mahesh telling him not to make the same mistake he did. His uncle was in love with a woman when he was younger but the family, including Mahesh's mother, forbade him from marrying her because she was an Indian Muslim. He told Mahesh to go after his love and not be dissuaded by the family. Mahesh follows his advice, declares his love to Melur, and in the end leaves the talent contest with her despite his mother's opposition.

Characters are also shown to be overcoming racial stereotypes in some subplots. Kahoe, a Chinese boy, resents Hafiz's high grades and claims that he cheated on the exam. The Chinese teacher investigates but finds that Hafiz earned his grade fairly. Kahoe and Hafiz have an exchange in which Kahoe declares he is better than Hafiz and that Hafiz will be successful even with second-rate grades because of institutionalized Malay privilege, but Hafiz responds stating that he works as hard as he does because he does not want to gain success through relying on preferential treatment for Malays. The Chinese teacher later chastises Kahoe telling him that Hafiz is not as stupid as he thinks and he is not as smart as he thinks. In the final competition, at the emotional climax, Kahoe comes on stage and plays the

erhu, a Chinese string instrument, accompanying Hafiz who is singing his amazing original composition. The boys hug after the performance signaling their triumphant friendship. Likewise, Datin Kalsom,
Melur's mother's friend, visits and asks if the family is worried about
what Mei Ling, their Chinese maid, touches before she comes to cook
for them. One of the young girls responds facetiously stating that Mei
Ling has a dog with lots of saliva. Datin Kalsom, who appears to not
pray, refuses to eat the snacks Mei Ling cooked, making her concerns
about *halal* food and pollution seem more about race than religion.
In a later scene as they are driving, Melur's mother informs Kalsom
that Mei Ling is a Chinese Muslim. Kalsom is astonished and asks
how she can be a Muslim with a name like Mei Ling. The young girls
rebuke her, and the Malay chauvinism she represents, stating that she
became a Muslim and not a Malay or Arab.

Finally, while *Talentime* does not entail the same concentration on
religion as *Muallaf,* it does embody liberal Islamic piety. Similar to
Sepet and *Gubra,* Melur and all the other main Muslim female characters do not wear headscarves. Hafiz wears a white Islamic cap (*songkok*)
during his final performance, and Mei Ling and some other women at
the house are shown wearing white prayer gowns following evening
prayers. However, neither Hafiz nor Mei Ling corrects Melur's behavior with Mahesh, which flouts normative Islamic piety. Hafiz is shown
sitting on the side asking Mahesh to drive safely as Melur sits behind
him on his motorcycle clutching his shoulders or waist. Likewise, Mei
Ling, who has expressed her concerns about Melur's intentions with
Mahesh, confronts them sitting together outside the house and chastises Melur for trying to be alone with the boy. Melur retorts that she
has no intention of committing a sin with Mahesh. After hearing that
Mei Ling welcomes them into the house and the couple sleeps side
by side on the floor in the middle of the living room. Encoding liberal Islamic piety, this film sends the message that it is permissible for
youth to engage in limited physical contact and private activities while
dating as long as there is no sex before marriage.

Most of the Malay youth I interviewed perceived Yasmin Ahmad's
films not as "Islamic" stories and criticized their ethnic and religious pluralism. Some youth appeared to echo the publicized adverse comments
of Islamic scholars and officials about improper elements in *Gubra* and
Muallaf (see Khoo 2007). For instance, Maryam, a twenty-five-year-old
college graduate, stated that the way *Gubra* shows a man making ritual
ablution and "then holds a dog and makes his prayer…this gives a bad
impression of the understanding of Muslims about Islam."[4] Similarly, a
young Malay couple told me it was "un-Islamic" and *haram* (forbidden)

when "the actress had her hair cut off for" the *Muallaf* film. "In real life she had to go with her hair cut off and this is *haram* from an Islamic perspective." Others mentioned the style of dating and romance as not properly Islamic. Nevertheless, most interpreted her films to be more about multiculturalism and race relations than religion. Azmi, a twenty-five-year-old college student, said: "In Yasmin Ahmad films, she looks at things from the perspective of *bangsa* [nationality] and *budaya* [culture], but we have to look at it from the perspective of *agama* [religion]...Yasmin looks from the view of *bangsa*...her films are not realistic. Her films are idealistic." They tended to reject the notions encoded in Yasmin Ahmad's films. Azma, a twenty-six-year-old college graduate, told me her films are

> sort of *Satu Malaysia* [One Malaysia] films...Islamic people don't really feel good about them...she tried to involve all the *kaum* [races] in them...Uh, they were not Islamic films, but she wanted to put Islam on the same level with other religions...her films were alright but they did not prioritize Islam...she wanted all of *Satu Malaysia* to watch them.[5]

This framing of Yasmin's films as a kind of *Satu Malaysia* (One Malaysia) representation appeared to be widely shared among Malay youth, and ironically associates her films with the hegemonic discourses she aimed to counter. Zaini and Nor, a young Malay couple, labeled her *Satu Malaysia* films as "patriotic" and felt they were "boring" repetitions of multicultural representations of Malaysian society. Perhaps what is most disturbing about Yasmin's multiculturalism for Malay youth is that it does not come paired with Malay and Muslim distinctiveness as in the hegemonic version but contests it (see Daniels 2005). This is what Nazma targets when she says, "that is another problem, a *Satu Malaysia*...there is a *Satu Malaysia* in terms of *bangsa* [nationality], but there is no *Satu Malaysia* in terms of religion, because Islam is above other religions. Maybe she thinks that to make Malaysia proud is to let other countries see that Malaysia is a harmonious country." Many of my interlocutors were concerned about what Yasmin's films meant for normative Islamic piety. Maryam expressed it this way: "It is nice showing good relations between the different ethnic groups, but it must be limited. You must be careful when mixing groups in a harmonious way that you do not make a mistake."

In sum, Yasmin Ahmad's films transcode discourses of ethnic and religious pluralism, bottom-up multiculturalism and liberal Islam that contest Malay supremacy, Islamic separatism, and conservative Islamic ideologies. They encode fears of rising normative Islamic piety and racial chauvinism and hopes for a celebration of difference and a flexible, less strict Islamic piety that will facilitate rather than hinder intergroup relations. Malay youth tend to read her films as skirting proper Islamic norms and emphasizing a form of multiculturalism that elides the special place of Islam in Malaysian society.

"Islamic" TV Dramas, Malay Hegemony, and Normative Islamic Piety

In contrast with Yasmin Ahmad's films, *Nur Kasih, Tahajjud Cinta,* and *Stanza Cinta* transcode Malay Muslim distinctiveness, exclusivity, and normative Islamic piety. Malay youth also read them as "Islamic" in the way they prioritize and express Islamic values and norms. *Nur Kasih* (Light of Love, 2009) tells the story of a rural Islamic teacher, Ustaz Hassan (Dato' Jalaluddin Hassan), struggling to instill Islamic knowledge and norms into his two sons. Ustaz Hassan and his wife, Hajjah Khadijah (Liza Othman), learn at the beginning of the series that he is terminally ill and does not have long to live. When they call their two sons, Aidil (Fizz Fairuz) and Adam (Remy Ishak), back home to be with their father before he passes, the series shows how the paths of the young men have diverged since their childhood. Aidil, the older son, who was obedient and pious as a child, is now studying at Al-Azhar University in Cairo, Egypt. He has continued to tread on a road of religious piety and advancing his Islamic knowledge. On the other hand, Adam, who was rebellious since his childhood, is studying architecture in Sydney, Australia, where he is living a wild life, drinking, using drugs, and fornicating with his Malay Eurasian girlfriend Katrina (Sharifah Sofea). In several scenes flashing back to their childhood, we are shown how Aidil always tried to protect Adam, even sacrificing himself for his brother's sake. Adam stopped praying and studying Qur'anic recitation out of spite for his father who often beat him punishing his disobedient behavior. The corporal punishment only seemed to harden his heart against his father and normative Islamic piety.

After they return home, Aidil becomes attracted to Nur Amina (Tiz Zaqyah), the eldest daughter of the village Imam, Ustaz Abu Bakar, and wants his father to have them engaged to be married. Aidil is impressed with Nur's piety and the way she teaches children in the village Islamic school. However, instead of proposing that Aidil marry Nur, Ustaz Hassan decides Adam should marry her. He declares that he wants to wed Adam with a pure pious woman like Siti Khadijah,

Prophet Muhammad's first wife, in order to save Adam and bring him back to the right path. Both sets of parents agree to this *kahwin paksa* (forced marriage). Adam consents because it is his father's last wish, and Nur, who expected to be engaged to Aidil, also consents much to Adam's chagrin. She keeps it a secret that she had a crush on Adam as a young schoolgirl; however, as an obedient daughter we are led to believe that she would have followed her parent's wishes in any event. Aidil is brokenhearted but accepts out of obedience for his parents and continues to sacrifice for Adam. Ustaz Hassan lives long enough to see Adam get married to Nur and passes away not long thereafter. The rest of the saga tells the story of the relationships between Adam, Aidil and Nur, and Adam and Katrina, who eventually are wed, and Aidil, Siti Sarah (Nur's younger sister), and Aleya, a wealthy urban woman who marries Aidil.

Nur Kasih, featuring all Malay characters living and interacting in a Malay world, transcodes discourses of Malay separateness and hegemony. Unlike Yasmin Ahmad's stories and Malay "corporate dramas" depicting diverse urban contexts, *Nur Kasih* is centered in a *kampung* in which practically all interactions are among Malays. They are shown to conduct their lives together in homes, mosques, Islamic universities, and workplaces. Even in the urban scenes, at the International Islamic University, the architectural firm where Nur and Adam work, and the government office where Aidil works, there appear to be only Malay employees. Malays fill all positions of leadership, power, and authority. The few non-Malay characters in the series embody stereotypes that reinforce Malay distinctiveness and superiority. For instance, an Indian sundry shopkeeper wearing a *dhoti* (Indian-style wrap) pulled up over his knees appears in a few scenes. He is depicted as a rather goofy character inclined toward gossiping and cackling nonsense. Nur shops at his store ignoring his gossip and keeping any interaction required for the economic exchange to the minimum. Similarly, Katrina, Adam's "Malay" Eurasian girlfriend, is labeled *putih* (white) in a derogatory fashion by Ustaz Hassan. She and her white Australian friends represent Western decadence and immorality that threaten to steer Adam further away from normative Islamic piety. Ustaz Hassan's emotional uttering of *putih* and images of Adam's "sinful" behavior in Australia, encode Malay fears of the increasing influence of globalization upon Malay Muslim society and culture. This opposition of Malayness and whiteness also enhances the moral urgency of Ustaz Hassan's mission to save Adam by marrying him to a pious Malay woman.

Moreover, unlike the "*kampung* stories" popular in the 1990s that encoded discourses of development-oriented "New Malays" through contrasting rural poverty with urban success (Thompson 2007:173–174), *Nur Kasih* represents the countryside as a moral center of Islam and Malay customs (*adat*). Rather than images of the struggling rural poor, this show casts stable Malay families in large traditional houses surrounded by plush green fields. Malay youth are shown giving salaams (Islamic greetings of peace) to their parents and wives to their husbands by kissing or bringing one's forehead to their hands. This customary act of deference reproduces the hierarchical order between generations and genders. Similarly, the customs of *kahwin paksa* and asking for forgiveness, especially from one's parents, reinforces the traditional parental authority in Malay families. Adam was told to ask for his father's forgiveness as a child and adult. These customary practices are intertwined with Islamic values that call for respect for one's parents and from wives toward their husbands. Moreover, in several scenes Hajjah Khadijah and Ustaz Hassan are shown teaching their sons and other youth in the village to recite Qur'an. Thus, *Nur Kasih* transcodes discourses of Malay distinctiveness and exclusivity through situating an all-Malay cast in a rural setting where they embody and perpetuate Malay *adat* and Islam across generations.

Furthermore, whether they are depicted in rural or urban settings, the Malays in *Nur Kasih* are *Muslim* Malays embodying normative Islamic piety. They wear Islamic-style clothing, robes, tunics, caps, headscarves, and occasionally turbans and facial veils (*niqab*). Men and women in the main and supporting cast are also shown performing daily prayers, supplicating to Allah for help, and teaching and reciting Qur'an. There are also several beautiful scenes of the main cast performing pilgrimages in the holy land, which projects *Muslim* Malays as not only members of the global Muslim *ummah* but exemplary members amidst violent extremists. The family loses contact with Adam and eventually believes that he was killed in a terrorist incident that took place while he was on a business trip to Mumbai, India. This organized and vicious assault on the hotel where he was staying recalls the 2008 Mumbai terrorist attacks. Representations of pious and peaceful *Muslim* Malays before a backdrop of violent extremists encode aspirations and hopes for Malays to lead the global Muslim *ummah* to peaceful resolutions of clashes with non-Muslim forces. Aidil's manner of approaching Nur and Aleya when he had a romantic interest in them also embodies piety. He did not date them and their public meetings, by chance or for business, did not entail any body contact. Adam met Nur and Aidil met Aleya in parent-chaperoned meetings. Moreover, the plot encodes fears and moral panics about rising numbers of Malays becoming *murtad* (apostates) and hopes of bringing the disobedient to normative piety. Both Adam and Katrina leave behind their "sinful" lives and become pious Muslims. A Muslim man calls Adam back to Islam when he is in prison for the drunk-driving incident that caused pregnant Katrina to lose their child. A group of pious Indonesian women called Katrina to Islam, after she hits rock bottom from a drinking and partying binge, taking her to a remote area and training her in Islamic practices. She eventually returns to Adam wearing a black robe and facial veil. For a time, Adam practices polygamy, being married to Nur and Katrina. When Adam is believed dead in India, the family contemplated Aidil marrying Nur as a second wife. *Nur Kasih* represents polygamy as an integral part of a pious Muslim way of life.

Nur Kasih the Movie (2011), also written by Mira Mustaffa and directed by Kabir Bhatia, continues the family saga six years from where the television series left off. Aidil, having lost his wife, Aleya, who was hit by a car, is a single parent of two young children. Adam and Nur run an architectural firm and Adam conducts religious classes for Malay street kids in the city. Adam tries to draw these troubled youth closer to Islam through teaching them in a relaxed fashion, accepting them into the classes as they are, without imposing normative prerequisites. Adam invites a guest *ustaz* to give a religious talk who refuses to teach them because the youth are not sitting in gender-segregated groups and the women are not wearing headscarves. Adam explains his gradual approach of calling the youth to Islam but the *ustaz* rejects his reasoning and asserts that the "ends do not justify the means." This episode encodes moderate Muslim discourses that criticize overly rigid and strict ways of implementing normative practices and rulings. It can be read as targeting the Malaysian Islamic Party and other Islamic organizations that have in the past promoted an immediate and full implementation of *shari'a*. Many moderate Muslim voices argue that people need to be educated or allowed to cultivate their personal piety before strict rules and laws are institutionalized.[6]

Adam, still shaken by his traumatic experience in Mumbai, has recurring nightmares of Nur being shot during a terrorist attack at a public market in the Middle East. He supplicates to Allah asking that anything be taken from him except Nur Amina. During their trip to Jordan, they are both injured in a train accident but survive. But when Adam returns to the scene of the accident to find Nur's ring he crashes in the desert. Two Arab boys save him from the sandstorm. Nur and Aidil eventually find Adam who is being nursed back to health by the boy's family. They take Adam to the hospital where they find out that his heart is failing and he will soon die. Nur, under the stress of large hospital bills, tries to earn money from architectural projects. A Malay developer invites her to his office for a meeting in which he asks her to design a nightclub project for his firm. After discovering that the entertainment club would entail several "sinful" activities, Nur tells him that she fears that the project does not *sesuai* or fit with her intentions. The Malay developer calls her narrow minded and claims that Malays cannot advance economically with such thinking. Nur asserts that her sustenance is determined by Allah and not by him and leaves. This episode encodes pious Muslim discourses criticizing economic development schemes that accumulate money through promoting sinful activities that don't *sesuai* with Allah's directives. It can be read as targeting the UMNO-led federal government and its plan in 2010 to expand the entertainment hub in Selangor and "New Malay" developmentalism in general.[7] Nur and Adam have to sell their house in the city and return to the village. Adam nearly dies but is saved at the last minute with the transplanted heart of one of his students, who is killed trying to defend Aidil from a gang of street thugs. Adam and Nur finally have a son and grow old together. Adam, Aidil, and Nur live a full life dedicated to charity and spreading Islamic knowledge.

In the sociopolitical context of intense ongoing debates about race, religion, and the nation, *Nur Kasih*, the series and film, encodes Malay and Muslim hegemony. Following the hotly contested twelfth National Election in 2008, which saw opposition parties win an unprecedented five states, Malay fears began to rise over their growing political divisions. Many felt that with Malays being divided between UMNO, PAS, and the Anwar Ibrahim–led People's Justice Party (PKR), non-Malays and non-Muslims would form a majority and seize control of the government. *Nur Kasih* transcodes discourses of resolving these divisions through piety rather than politics. While the film can be read as criticizing PAS and UMNO at times, it does not unambiguously embrace either of their polarizing political discourses. Moreover, Islam, long intertwined with Malay *adat*, has been the political symbol constantly at the center of contests between these two political parties (Chinyong 2009). Thus, *Nur Kasih* adopts a unifying discourse emphasizing Islam and Malay customs, a posture that resonates widely with Islamic nongovernmental organizations and Malay individuals and transcends political divisions in the Malay community.

According to Malay youth I interviewed, *Nur Kasih*, the television series was much more popular than the film. Although both featured Tiz Zaqyah and Remy Ishak as Nur Amina and Adam, who Malay youth found very attractive, they were more interested in the story of their earlier romance and family and interpersonal interactions in the series. Several Malay youth told me that *Nur Kasih* was the first Islamic drama to appeal to them. Fariza, a twenty-six-year-old college graduate, said she liked the way Aidil was always so good even though "he could not marry his love." She also appreciated the compassion and the way Adam changed in the movie, becoming more obedient and pious. Contrasting other popular Malay shows to Islamic dramas, she said that "in the Islamic ones, they change in the end, but the other ones are just for entertainment and there is no benefit." Muaz, a thirty-three-year-old unmarried man, like many other respondents, described *Nur Kasih* as a form of *dakwah*, bringing Malay youth closer to Islam. When I asked Fariza and many other Malay youth what kind of hopes they take from *Nur Kasih* for Malaysia, they said they hoped for a "more Islamic Malaysia" and to have children who are obedient like Aidil and Nur or Adam in the end. Rosnani, a nineteen-year-old college student, was one of the few to speak explicitly about hoping for Malay Muslim hegemony. She said Malay youth feel that "Malays should lead everything in the country...and no Chinese or Indians should be ministers in the government...If others like Chinese or Indians are leaders then what will happen to Islam?" she asked.

Tahajjud Cinta and *Stanza Cinta* also transcode discourses of Malay Muslim hegemony and normative Islamic piety. *Tahajjud Cinta* (Purity of Love, 2011), written by Mazela Manan and directed by Eirma Fatima, is the story of two young Malay women, Citra Maisara (Nur Fazura) and Seri (Fouziah Gous), who study Islamic law in Jordan and are committed to struggling for justice and women's rights. Citra comes from a wealthy corporate Malay family that wants her to study nonreligious topics in London, but she secretly studies Islamic law in Jordan. While Citra is overseas, she speaks fluent Arabic and is active leading women in political demonstrations for human rights and justice. Seri comes from a poor rural family that had to borrow money from the wealthy village Islamic teacher, Ustaz Shauki (Eman Manan), to send her abroad for Islamic studies. Both women embody piety wearing Middle Eastern–style black robes (*abaya*) and facial veils (*niqab*) while in Jordan and *baju kurung* and headscarves when back in Malaysia. Citra struggles with her parents, moving out of their house, to pursue her career as a *shari'a* lawyer. They eventually come around to support her when she defends her sister, Emelda (Tiz Zaqyah), who is being physically abused by her husband. Seri and Sollahudin (Remy Ishak), Ustaz Shauki's son, fall in love after she returns to the village. Seri also wants to pursue a career as a *shari'a* lawyer but is forced to teach at Ustaz Shauki's Islamic school and later to become his fourth wife. Ustaz Shauki uses Seri's father's indebtedness to manipulate him into forcing her into these positions against her will. Sollahudin and Citra try to help Seri to no avail. She is forced to marry Ustaz Shauki who abuses her. When he catches Sollahudin trying to help her, Ustaz Shauki charges them with adultery and has the community apply the Islamic penal code, *hudud*, stoning them and leaving them for dead in the ground. Citra and Sollahudin's mother save them. In the end, Ustaz Shauki is found to be a hypocrite when he is caught in the process of committing adultery with a flirtatious village woman he is supposed to be instructing. Similar to *Nur Kasih*, this story displays beautiful scenes of the Middle East with Malays leading the Muslim *ummah* against injustice and plays out in all-Malay Muslim rural and urban contexts in Malaysia.

Moreover, *Tahajjud Cinta* is also animated by Islamic values and goals, centered on Citra's struggle to protect Muslim women from abuse through the just implementation of Islamic law. She challenges abusive males, her sister's husband, and Ustaz Shauki, attempts to manipulate Islamic concepts and laws to their advantage. As such, *Tahajjud Cinta* transcodes liberal and moderate Muslim discourses, like those of Sisters in Islam (SIS), that criticizes the implementation of Islamic family laws as unfair for women. However, instead of arguing from liberal secularist or Western feminist positions, Citra contends within a normative Islamic worldview. She defeats Emelda's husband's claims, that Emelda was disobedient (*nushuz*) for leaving the house without his permission and that their parents violated his rights by coming to their daughter's aid, through using her Islamic legal expertise. Likewise, she counters and exposes Ustaz Shauki's twisting of scriptural references to serve his personal desires through reciting other verses of Qur'an that are more applicable to the case at hand. Several episodes depicting him as a skillful practitioner of yoga, which the Malaysian National Fatwa Council banned for Muslims in 2008, marks him as a deviant *ustaz* to the Malaysian Muslim audience.[8] This series transcodes fears of knowledgeable but deviant Muslim scholars using institutionalized Islamic norms to their own advantage. Nevertheless, some of my Malay interlocutors felt it was controversial to depict an *ustaz*, possessing so much scriptural knowledge, as deviant. Fadzilah, a twenty-three-year-old college student, said: "He is speaking of the teachings of Allah. Perhaps they can show him getting those teachings from another place, a different place, but not in a *pondok* [boarding] Islamic school. This is rather sensitive…that they show this *ustaz* like this…their mission may be true but their method of delivery is not good." However, most of my interlocutors liked the series and felt vindicated when Ustaz Shauki was finally exposed as a hypocrite before the entire village. Delivering its normative Islamic message at the end of the final episode, the show displays the following *hadith* on the screen in Malay:

> Rasulullah, may peace be upon him, declared: There will come a time in the end, when people look for worldly gain through selling religion. They will present themselves to others as wearing clothes made from sheepskin faking selfless sacrifice of worldly comforts to gain the sympathy of many people and their speech will be sweeter than sugar while their hearts are like those of wolves. [My translation]

Stanza Cinta (Love Stanza, 2011) also encodes and delivers messages of normative piety and Malay Muslim distinctiveness and hegemony. Based on a novel and script written by Nurull Halawati and directed by Along Kamaludin, *Stanza Cinta* is a romantic drama focusing on Amni Sorfina (Nur Fathia), a pious Malay university student, and her relationships with two men, Irfan (Aaron Aziz) and Taufik (Fizz Fairuz). Unlike the other two Islamic dramas, this story takes place in predominantly urban contexts, since Amni and Irfan reside in the city. However, similar to *Nur Kasih*, urban scenes in *Stanza Cinta*, whether in hospitals, universities, night clubs, homes, mosques, or on the street, are represented as all-Malay settings involving interactions among themselves. Thus, Malays inhabit all positions of authority in these social situations. Irfan and Taufik are contrasting characters just like Adam and Aidil in *Nur Kasih*: one is pious and the other naughty. Irfan is from a wealthy nonreligious urban family. He frequents night clubs and is a womanizer. However, after he meets Amni who invites him to attend religious talks at a mosque he undergoes a personal transformation turning his life toward piety. In the process, he also leads his parents and younger sister to become pious. Likewise, Amni makes *dakwah* with her dormitory roommate, Auni, inviting her to begin performing daily prayers. By the end of the series, she embodies piety like Amni, wearing *baju kurung* and headscarves. Just as we have seen with *Nur Kasih*, *Stanza Cinta* transcodes fears of increasing numbers of *murtad* and hopes of their transformative return to the path of piety.

Irfan confesses his love to Amni, but she initially appears more interested in Taufik, a pious *nasyid* singer who travels from the village to perform in the city. Taufik plans to propose marriage to Amni; however, his mother and the parents of a village girl force him to marry their daughter. Amni convinced that Irfan has indeed changed, leaving his sinful life behind, accepts his marriage proposal. But just before they are wed, Irfan who has been sick for some time, suddenly dies. Taufik manages to get out of the forced marriage because the young girl, more interested in continuing her education, refuses to consummate the marriage.[9] In the end, Taufik and Amni come together and have the opportunity for their love stanza.

In sum, these three Islamic dramas transcode Malay Muslim separateness and hegemony projecting all-Malay inhabited and led rural and urban social milieu. They also encode discourses of normative piety with images of *Muslim* Malays embodying piety in dress, worship, social interactions, courting, and in leading the global *ummah*. *Nur Kasih* and *Stanza Cinta* encode fears of the *murtad* problem and hopes of bringing disobedient Muslims to pious lives.

My Malay interlocutors, savvy users of social media and active participants in the broader cultural sphere, read these television dramas and film as entailing special meanings. Many of them told me they were fans of Korean television series, Hollywood films, American rhythm and blues, and rock and roll. Nevertheless, their interest in, and consumption of, various genres of the national and global cultural sphere did not preclude their enthusiasm for images of Malay customs and religious virtue. Some Malay youth voiced concerns about the gaps between public piety and personal practice represented in the series and real life.[10] Azmi felt scenes showing women in the supporting cast, such as Nur Amina's younger sister, who embodied piety in terms of wearing headscarves, spreading slander and discord (*fitnah*) as realistic. He felt these gaps in piety are ever present in Malaysian society. However, Fadzilah felt it was distasteful and inappropriate to cast women wearing headscarves in such a fashion. Azmi and some other youth also criticized actors and actresses in *Nur Kasih* for not embodying piety in their real lives the way they do in these shows.

When I asked one of my Malay interlocutors, Cahaya, a social science graduate student, whether she thought these Islamic dramas suggested UMNO's or PAS' vision and mission for Malaysia, she felt reluctant to answer on her own so she conducted a survey of her lecturers and friends. Later she reported that "they seem to have the same opinion as me that those dramas do not portray any kind of vision or mission of either UMNO or PAS." Although these stories encode some liberal and moderate Muslim criticism of political elements in the Malay Muslim community, they do not unambiguously endorse any particular political faction. Instead, in an increasingly divided political field, they encode Malay Muslim unity through piety.

CLASS AND RURAL/URBAN DIVISION

In the process of transcoding Malay Muslim unity through piety, these dramas deemphasize some intra-Malay social divisions. Class and locality differences are presented as not problematical or resolvable through piety rather than conflict. For instance, several of the romantic relationships, such as Aidil and Aleya in *Nur Kasih* and Amni and Irfan in *Stanza Cinta* cross these social divisions. Aleya and Irfan are from wealthy urban families, while Aidil and Aleya are from rural and lower class backgrounds. Aidil is shown driving his small humble car to Aleya's family's urban mansion. Amni shares a small dormitory room and gets caught hanging her laundry in front of a teacher's house. However, Aidil's and Amni's lower class backgrounds are never an issue in these relationships. Moreover piety is not solely associated with rural or urban contexts, but represented as traversing these places. Aleya's family is a pious upper class family, and Irfan's family becomes pious and is shown praying together in the house. Citra is also a pious woman from a wealthy urban family. However, Malay interlocutors, for several years, have informed me about growing tensions over class and status differences and their enhanced significance. Many reported losing good ties with friends and family due to attention paid to social standing and the drive for social mobility. They also spoke about the rising costs of marital exchanges, in particular the amount the groom's family is expected to pay to the bride's family. These stories can be read as encoding hopes and dreams for intimate social relations without disturbances caused by differences in social standing.

Furthermore, the hegemonic UMNO-BN government's "New Malay" development-oriented discourse downgraded rural Malay places associating them with "backwardness" and poverty (see Thompson 2007). These stories do not create an oppositional return-to-the-village discourse valorizing rural places and in turn denigrating urban spaces as centers of "sin" and decadence. I read them as imagining these spaces as connected through piety. Surely, the rural spaces of Nur Amina, Citra, and Taufik are centers of Malay *adat* and normative Islamic piety, but they and others, like Irfan's *ustaz*, are also shown transmitting Islamic knowledge in the city. In addition, the antagonistic men in *Tahajjud Cinta*, the targets of pious Muslims, are located in urban and rural places. Citra's sister's husband is a wealthy urban businessman with the resources to pay lawyers to represent his interests. On the other hand, Ustaz Shauki is a wealthy and influential rural Islamic schoolteacher who controlled the father of a lower class rural family. Similarly, Nur Amina rejects the Malay developer's proposal for an entertainment complex as not fitting with the sort of moral economy she wanted. The bases of these problems are not presented as located in class, but in proper Islamic piety. Thus, they are resolved not by class struggle, but through pious obedience and emphasizing normative Islamic values. Nur turns away from the developer who was thinking only of achieving worldly gain even at the moral expense of promoting forbidden activities. Citra and her family and the *shari'a* court intervene to protect a wife from an alcohol-consuming abusive husband. Likewise, villagers come together to expose and stop a deviant *ustaz* from continuing to utilize Islam to satisfy his lustful desires. In each of these stories, there is a moral victory of the pious in the end.

Generation, Gender, and Sexuality

In contrast to class and status differences, these Malay television dramas directly express intergenerational and gender tensions. As described earlier, each of these three stories involves a forced marriage (*kahwin paksa*). Malay parents force Nur and Adam to marry in *Nur Kasih*, Taufik to marry a village girl in *Stanza Cinta*, and Seri to marry Ustaz Shauki in *Tahajjud Cinta*. Adam's father decides upon his marriage in order to bring him back to Islam. However, in the other two cases, pious motives are not propelling the parents. Taufik's mother pressures him into the marriage because his deceased father made an agreement with one of his village friends to have their children wed. Seri's father feels obligated and afraid to refuse the influential *ustaz*'s proposal. Both of these fathers are shown scolding and beating their daughters into submission. They reprimand the girls for committing an act of disloyalty, amounting to treason, in refusing to accept the arranged marriage. My Malay interlocutors tell me that this custom was more common for previous generations but is still occasionally practiced in the village context. As Carsten (1997:198) states, "villagers assert that young men and women should follow their parents' wishes over the choice of spouse…An *anak dara* [virgin] should not refuse her parents' choice." Indeed, the common denominator encoded in each of these three cases is parental authority. Although most Malay youth I interviewed disagree with the custom of *kahwin paksa*, they do agree that parental approval of their spousal selection is important if not essential prior to marriage. Nowadays, they prefer to find their own candidate spouse and then seek parental approval. For instance, Cahaya told me: "As for myself, my husband decided to *lamar* [propose to] me after two months we've being a close friend. Before I accept him,

I'd brought him to meet my parents and ask their opinion. If my parents refuse, I don't mind to reject him. For me, our parents know the best for their child." Like many Malay youth, during the two months of their courting, Cahaya only met her boyfriend in public or in the presence of her relatives.

On the other hand, many Malay youth who are looking for their own spouses through dating do not embody piety in this fashion. Occasionally, the media reports Malay youth being charged for improper proximity or consorting with the opposite sex *(khalwat)* or attempting to perform sexual acts outside of marriage *(zina)*. A few Malay youth have even informed me that they have fornicated. Moreover, television and print media sensationalize numerous sad reports of abandoned babies, which have contributed to a moral panic over the premarital sexual behavior of Malay women. Malaysian government Islamic think-tanks have been busy trying to figure out what to do about this problem. Malay youth have also been engaging in dialogue about sexuality and marriage. Some pious Malay women tell me they agree with the custom of *kahwin paksa* in the sense that parents should arrange their marriages with men they don't know. They note all the moral problems with the way many Malays are dating nowadays and feel it is better to fall in love after marriage than before. These complex issues of sexuality, parental control, and normative Islamic piety are encoded in these television dramas. I read them as transcoding nightmares of sexuality out of control and hopes for adherence to Islamic courting and marriage norms *through* recognition of parental authority.

Not only do they point toward parental authority, but these stories also project highly enchanted romances. Malay characters are shown supplicating to Allah for their predetermined marriage partners *(jodoh)*. Moments of physical and emotional attraction are ensconced in deeper religious meanings. Nur's crush on Adam as a young girl finds fruition in the pious motives of his father. Nur's love for Adam endures all the trials and tribulations of him leaving her to return to his Australian girlfriend. Amni and Taufik are drawn to each other's piety and meet just by chance at a gigantic mosque. Moreover, Nur's love for Adam and Amni's for Irfan is also a form of *dakwah*, calling these wayward fornicating men back to Islam. They embed the notion of love and marriage for the sake of Allah and not for one's own worldly desires. The notion that it is not only allowed for a pious Malay virgin *(anak dara)* to marry a man who has fornicated but also part of a higher purpose represents a shift in conventional Malay thought. As Banks (1983:152) notes, "like experience should wed like experience. A man who has never married should marry a woman who has never married (an *anak dara*)." This conventional understanding is based in interpretations of verse three of Sura An-Nur (Q24:3):

> The adulterer cannot have
> Sexual relations with any but an
> Adulteress or an idolatress,
> And the adulteress, none can have
> Sexual relations with her but an
> Adulterer or an idolater;
> To the Believers such a thing
> Is forbidden.

Malay youth and adults inform me that these unbalanced matches, in terms of sexual experience, of pious virgin women with presently or formerly sinful men are a form of *dakwah*, a benefit to the Muslim community, and a way to serve Allah. Nadiah, a twenty-three-year-old college student, said: "The romance in *Nur Kasih* is Islamic; they are with each other for the sake of Allah." The enchantment of these romances make relations formerly viewed as inappropriate an expression and embodiment of piety.

As we have seen, women are projected as important agents of *dakwah* in these Islamic dramas. They actively call spouses, other relatives, friends, roommates, and business associates to normative piety. Women are also shown to be active as students in pursuing higher education and as professionals, such as architects, teachers, and lawyers. Moreover, as noted earlier, these stories encode some liberal and moderate Muslim discourses critical of the unjust treatment of women. In *Nur Kasih*, Nur's father, Ustaz Abu Bakar, asserts that a man can also be *nushuz* (disobedient), referring to Adam during the time he was still causing problems for Nur. Similarly, in *Tahajjud Cinta*, the polygamous family of the deviant *ustaz* is shown to be unhappy and unjust to the cowives. SIS has been arguing against the gender-biased charge of *nushuz* in Malaysian Islamic family law and for reform of the law and practice of polygamy.[11] Nevertheless, these Islamic dramas embody the widely shared conservative model of men as the head of families. Men are corrected and stopped from being irresponsible, untrustworthy, and cruel leaders but not uprooted from their "proper" position of leadership according to normative Islamic piety. Unlike class and locality, recognizing and correctly accounting for generation and gender differences is projected as important ingredients in pious visions for Malay society.

Conclusion

During the early twenty-first century, Yasmin Ahmad's films and Islamic television dramas are a field of contested sociopolitical discourses. Battling with the ethnic and religious pluralism, multiculturalism, and liberal Islamic piety encoded in Yasmin Ahmad's films, the newly emerging Islamic television dramas embed Malay and Muslim separateness, hegemony, and normative Islamic piety. Even the fears, hopes, dreams, and nightmares they encode appear to contrast. Whereas most Malay youth found Yasmin Ahmad's films to be controversial, they welcomed *Nur Kasih* and the two subsequent television series discussed here. Why is there such a clash between these discourses during the 2000s? Why hasn't a "liberal" or "light" post-Islamist Muslim cultural sphere taken center stage in Malaysia as in several Middle Eastern countries? Why is this Muslim cultural sphere not focusing more on contesting the Malaysian state?

First, colonial and postcolonial pattern of race-based communal identification and organization has remained dominant and widely institutionalized (Lee 1986; Daniels 2005, 2010). Second, the sociopolitical and cultural onus placed on Malay and Muslim supremacy was intensified in the post-1969 racial riot context (Mahathir 1970). Third, the Islamic revival over the past three–four decades has strengthened conservative Islamic attitudes, ideologies, normative piety, and the significance of maintaining and protecting Muslim hegemony. The UMNO-led federal government, PAS, and most Islamic non-governmental organizations have championed the Malay and Muslim struggles in their own ways. In this regard, it is important to note that Malay political parties, civil society groups, and NGOs have participated together with the state in the drive toward Islamization and political Islam (Chinyong 2009). Fourth, as Helen Ting (2011) points out, current government policies and legal provisions tend to produce more rigid ethnic boundaries even while interethnic interactions are more fluid in many contexts. Finally, the fears and hopes of the Malay Muslim population, despite increasing participation in the broader cultural sphere of global pop music, film and television series, remain strongly connected to Islamic values, notions, and motives. Thus, the critical thrust of the emerging Muslim sphere is to contest challenges to Malay and Muslim hegemony rather than to counter the state or Muslim parties and organizations they deem to be representing their interests. However, given the way these television dramas encode some discourses critical of "New Malay" developmentalism, overly rigid fundamentalism, and unjust treatment of women, there appear to be some openings for social and cultural critique within an overarching normative Islamic worldview.

Notes

1. The Malay cultural category *pemuda* or "youth" refers to a potentially extended period of adolescence between childhood and marriage. All the young Malays I surveyed for this study were unmarried except for one twenty-eight-year-old woman who was recently married.
2. This is referring to Chinese immigrants who settled on the west coast hundreds of years ago in places like Melaka where they intermarried with Malays without converting to Islam. These marriages are conventionally thought to have been between Chinese men and Malay women and their descendants are called *Babas* (males) and *Nyonyas* (females) or "Straits-born Chinese" (Daniels 2005:68). Nowadays, many normative piety-oriented Muslims resent this sort of statement that reflects nostalgically upon a period when Muslims were not observant of their religious norms.
3. Khoo (2007) argues that Yasmin Ahmad expresses a variety of Sufi Islam in her films that contests the literalist and "scripturalist" Islam advocated by the Malaysian state and held by most Malaysian Muslims.
4. Maryam and the other names I use for my interlocutors are pseudonyms.
5. Under Prime Minister Najib Abdul Razak's leadership, *Satu Malaysia* (One Malaysia) has been the UMNO-led National Front's major slogan. It is basically a repackaging of former prime minister Mahathir Mohamad's top-down multiculturalism.
6. During my research on discourses of *sharia* in 2010–2012, I found that the PAS has begun to adopt this more moderate approach arguing for education about Islamic laws with a gradual implementation.
7. A broad spectrum of Malay Muslim organizations, including PAS, Ulama Muda UMNO, and PERKASA (a Malay rights organization), and the Mufti of Perak, Tan Sri Harussani Zakaria, called for the federal government to cancel its plan for an expansion of the entertainment hub in Selangor contained within the Economic Transformation Program (*Sinarharian* October 29, 2010).
8. The Malaysian national council of Islamic authorities issued this edict asserting that yoga contains Hindu elements that could be detrimental to the faith of a Muslim. A judge in the Federal Territories *sharia* court told me that yoga must be banned for Muslims because it entails a form of meditation requiring the emptying out of the mind that no Muslim should perform. Muslims must always keep awareness of *Tauhid*, the oneness of God in their minds.
9. Having been forced into the marriage, this young village girl adopts the divorce strategy available to her. Carsten (1997:214) writes: "In fact a

bride's refusal to consummate a marriage is an accepted way of obtaining a divorce, and provides her with an alternative to refusing a match beforehand, which is generally unacceptable."

10. Lara Deeb (2006:220) discusses the gaps in public and personal piety of Shi'i women active in nongovernmental organizations. Some of them publicly embody piety in dress but in their personal lives engage in acts frowned upon publicly. On the other hand, some of these activist women don't publicly embody piety in dress but are highly pious in their personal lives.

11. The Islamic Family Law (Federal Territories) Act 1984, amended in 1992 and 1994, states that "a wife shall not be entitled to maintenance when she is *nusyuz* [*nushuz*], or unreasonably refuses to obey the lawful wishes or commands of her husband." There is no application of *nushuz* to a husband in this act. Hjh. Nik Noriani, a SIS activist, writes: "It is suggested that there is a need to re-understand the concept of *nusyuz* as disruption of marital harmony by either spouse, rather than as disobedience of the wife to the commands of the husband" (2003:38). Hjh. Nik Noriani and other Muslim feminist scholars also make several recommendations for reforming laws and practices of polygamy in Malaysia, Indonesia, Singapore, and the Philippines (23–30).

5

COMPLICATING SENSES OF MASCULINITY, FEMININITY, AND ISLAM THROUGH THE PERFORMING ARTS IN MALANG, EAST JAVA

*Christina Sunardi**

THINKING ABOUT MUSLIM MALANG AND CROSS-GENDER DANCE

As prior chapters in this compilation have demonstrated, Islam infuses many aspects of daily life, traditions of performance, and popular culture in Indonesia and in Malaysia. The Regency of Malang in East Java, where I conducted fieldwork on gamelan music, dance, and theater spanning from 2005 to 2007 was no exception. By far, most of the gamelan musicians and dancers I consulted were Muslim, albeit of different degrees of piety. Muslims sponsored performances for Muslim celebrations such as circumcisions to celebrate a boy's transition into adulthood. Performances were also sometimes held in explicitly Muslim spaces. For example, I attended a performance of *ludruk*—a type of theater that includes a series of opening acts, such as dancing, singing, and comic routines, as well as a main play or drama—at an Islamic boarding school. Furthermore, the Muslim call to prayer consistently reinforced the presence of Islam as it permeated sonic space five times a day through the loudspeakers attached to numerous mosques and prayer rooms (see also Rasmussen 2010:38–73), marking different times of the day and, to a certain extent, regulating some types of activity. In many cases, lessons, rehearsals, and performances were scheduled so as not to conflict with the call to prayer after sunset, at nightfall, and before sunrise. If a lesson, practice session, rehearsal, or performance (including performances that lasted well into the night or all night) did not end before the call to prayer at these particular times, a break was usually taken during the call (see also Sunardi 2012).[1]

Strikingly, despite the prevalence of Islam in Malang and despite Islam's prohibitions against cross-dressing as well as taking on the gendered attributes of the opposite sex (Peacock 1987:19; Oetomo 2000:51), it was not unusual for both males and females to perform east Javanese presentational dances[2] as cross-gender dances.[3] East Javanese presentational dance is characterized by male and female styles, as are dance forms associated with other cultural regions in Indonesia (e.g., Ross, present volume). Although there are quite a range of male and female Javanese dance styles depending on regional style, character portrayed, and type of dance, in general, male styles feature wider, more open stances; higher arm positions; and larger movement volumes and female styles feature more narrow stances; lower arm positions; and smaller movement volumes (see also Brakel 1993; Brakel-Papenhuyzen 1995; Hughes-Freeland 1995). There are male (*lanang*) and female (*putri*) styles of the east Javanese dances *Beskalan* and *Ngremo*—*Beskalan Lanang* (figure 5.1) and *Beskalan Putri* (figure 5.2), and *Ngremo Lanang* and *Ngremo Putri*—as well as male and female styles of east Javanese masked dance. While the gender of the dance style is not necessarily mapped to the biological sex of the dancer (see also Hughes-Freeland 2008b:163 n13), whether males and/or females perform a particular dance is, however, connected to the performance conventions of a particular context, including historical era (Sunardi 2009, in review).

Beskalan, *Ngremo*, and masked dance have been performed in various contexts in Malang. *Beskalan* and *Ngremo* usually function as opening or welcoming dances that precede various types of performance, including various types of theater, music, and/or dance. Usually an individual, group, or institution hosts such performances to celebrate particular events, including weddings, circumcisions, anniversaries, birthdays, village purification ceremonies, particular days on the Javanese calendar, Indonesian Independence Day celebrations, and inaugurations. *Beskalan*, *Ngremo*, and masked dance are also performed in the contexts of competitions and festivals. Masked dances may be performed as independent dances—often as opening or welcoming dances—or they may be performed as part of a masked dance drama called *wayang topèng*, usually for the types of events listed above (see also Onghokham 1972:113). *Beskalan*, *Ngremo*, and masked dance are also performed for other reasons. For example, I

Figure 5.1   Supriono Hadi Prasetya poses in a *Beskalan Lanang* costume, 2006. (In the context of performance, the dancer would also wear a set of bells around the right ankle, as can be seen in figure 5.2.) (Photograph by the author.)

observed *Beskalan Putri* and the masked dance *Bapang* performed as entertainment during an agricultural meeting. I also witnessed *Bapang* performed to welcome the head of the regency (*bupati*) as he visited a village.

The musicians and dancers I consulted were quite used to males performing female style dance and females performing male style dance. In some contexts and for some dances, performers assumed or expected that the dance would be performed as a cross-gender dance, so prevalent was the convention in Malang. Performers also recognized that, related to some dancers' individual personalities and/or body types, some males were better suited for female style dances and vice versa. In other words, performers recognized that the embodiment and expression of gender was not limited to biological sex.

Figure 5.2   Wahyu Winarti poses in a *Beskalan Putri* costume, 2006. (Photograph by the author.)

At the same time, assumptions and constructions of masculinity and femininity in Malang were affected by dominant Indonesian ideologies. Drawing selectively from representations of gender and gender ideologies of earlier times—including representations of masculinity and femininity rooted in pre-Islamic Javanese culture, as well as Javanese aristocratic, orthodox Muslim, and Dutch colonial ideologies—dominant Indonesian ideologies mapped gender to biological sex in a one-to-one ratio, privileged heterosexuality, and constructed manhood and womanhood in particular ways (Blackwood 2005). Since the Indonesian revolution (1945–1949), dominant discourses have encouraged males to be brave, strong, handsome, deep-voiced, and to act as leaders of their households, communities, and nation; meanwhile, a larger, more physically powerful looking male body type came to be held up as a model of manliness, replacing the cultural preference given to a more slightly built but spiritually potent and highly refined male figure.[4] Following the Indonesian revolution, dominant ideologies of female subjects have encouraged women to be refined, polite, quiet, and dedicated to the home and their social roles as wives and mothers, contrasting with the roles that women have historically played (and continue to play) as soldiers, traders, social and political organizers, and leaders, among others.[5]

In creating public cultural space for dancers to embody the gendered attributes of the opposite sex[6] through the performance of *Beskalan*, *Ngremo*, and masked dance as cross-gender dances, the dancers and musicians I consulted and observed played multiple social roles in regard to gender. On the one hand, performers were reifying dominant norms by articulating ideal constructions of "male" and "female" in terms of physical appearance, behavior, and sonic attributes through established dance styles, including musical conventions. On the other hand, they were pushing at and redefining dominant constructions of gender—also in terms of physical appearance, behavior, and musical conventions—by undermining a one-to-one mapping of biological sex and gender role (Sunardi 2009, in review). The prevalence of such gender negotiation through cross-gender dance in Malang—a place where the presence of Islam is so strong—has led me to think further about relationships between the performing arts, senses of gender, and approaches to Islam.

I wish to clarify that performers did not frequently bring up Islam as an issue with me, but instead for the most part focused on issues of performance practice, regional identity, and their memories of how dances used to be performed in the past, issues that I have been exploring elsewhere (Sunardi 2010a, 2010b, 2011, in review). Performers did, however, respond to my inquiries about Islam and sometimes did make comments about increasing orthodoxy and piety in Islamic practice, providing me an opportunity to develop in this chapter an understanding of how individual artists in Malang approached and experienced Islam in the early twenty-first century through the rubric of gender.

APPROACHING ISLAM, INDIVIDUAL AGENCY, AND SENSES OF GENDER

To explore intersections of the performing arts, senses of gender, and religion, I take a cultural approach to Islam. Like the anthropologist Timothy Daniels, I view Islam (and religion in general) as a multidimensional "system serving numerous functions, including intellectualist or explanative, emotional, cathartic, social—both unifying and conflictive—and symbolic ends" (2009:5). This "multidimensional" cultural approach to religion enables me to think through the ways performers make sense of gender and performance in relation to Islam. Similar to the ethnomusicologist Andrew Weintraub, I work to "[understand] how meanings about Islam and their musical expressions are enunciated within specific historical and socio-cultural conditions" (2011:319). In this chapter, I focus on the attitudes that individual gamelan musicians and dancers articulated within the framework of "musical expressions"—or, more broadly, "artistic expressions"—as well as the music or dance they performed. Like Timothy Daniels in the previous chapter of this volume, I recognize and emphasize the agency of the people with whom I spoke (present volume).

I build from Susan Blackburn, Bianca Smith, and Siti Syamsiyatun (2008), as well as the work of Anne Rasmussen (2010); Suzanne Brenner (1996); Tom Boellstorff (2005a); Andrew Weintraub (2011) and many others who emphasize the agency of individuals as gendered actors who shape the practice, expression, and embodiment of Islam in Indonesia as they make sense of gender in their own ways, in effect negotiating Islam and dominant gender ideologies. In their introduction to *Indonesian Islam in a New Era*, Blackburn, Smith, and Syamsiyatun emphasize the links between agency, gender, and Islam, highlighting that their edited compilation "demonstrates that by understanding the agentic role women play in Muslim societies and cultures such as Indonesia, we gain further insight into the practice of Islam more broadly, and into the creative lives of women who understand and negotiate their worlds in different ways" (2008:2). In the same vein, I am interested in how performers of different ages—female as well as male—who identified as Muslim and/or talked about their experiences living as Muslim "negotiated their worlds." I do so by exploring how such performers negotiated Islam, their lives as artists, and senses of gender in the early twenty-first century.[7]

Issues concerning Islam in Indonesia are particularly relevant in the specific sociohistorical context of the Reformation era (1998–present). The ethnomusicologists David Harnish and Anne Rasmussen observe that "debates and discussions about the place of Islam in public and private life permeate recent Indonesian history, and this debate has intensified since the fall of the autocratic President Suharto in 1998 and the ushering in of political reform (*reformasi*) and democracy" (2011:8). I contend that musicians and dancers in Malang were contributing to such debates and discussions about the place of Islam by making sense of Islam and their professions as artists in ways that allowed them to make and maintain cultural spaces in which to complicate dominant senses of gender both on- and offstage during the Reformation

era. I show that the senses of gender that performers expressed and
embodied included senses of female masculinity, or masculinity that is
expressed, embodied, and owned by females (Halberstam 1998; see
also Blackwood 2010:29; Blackwood and Weiringa 2007:9, 14–15)
as well as senses of male femininity, or femininity that is expressed,
embodied, and owned by males (Boellstorff 2004).

To emphasize that individuals expressed particular senses of
gender in particular ways in particular contexts, I draw on Evelyn
Blackwood's concept of "contingent masculinity" (2010:21). In
her analysis of *tombois* (females who live as men) in Padang, West
Sumatra, she approaches masculinity as contingent in order to highlight the importance of context in the expression and production
of gender (175). She seeks to "consider how gendered individuals,
such as tombois, may take up subject positions that move back and
forth across the ideological boundaries of normative sex/gender systems through the performance of both masculinity and femininity"
(159). She writes that "a theory of contingent masculinities takes
into account the multiple allegiances as well as anxieties that produce rich and complicated subjectivities. Tombois in Padang take
up and embody sometimes contrastive subject positions in different
contexts" (177). The emphasis on the expression of a certain gender subjectivity in a particular context that is conditioned by that
context is critical to an examination of how varying circumstances
condition performers' expressions of gender—such as the contexts
of performance and the contexts of offstage daily life. In this chapter, I explore some of the ways performers in Malang expressed and
embodied contingent masculinities as well as contingent femininities,
including contingent female masculinities and contingent male femininities. My main argument is that in complicating senses of masculinity and femininity, performers were contributing to the continuous
processes of shaping, expressing, experiencing, and/or embodying
diverse approaches to Islam.

NEGOTIATING ISLAM LOCALLY

For the performers I consulted, negotiating Islam was very much a local
matter. Performers talked about Islam largely in relation to Muslims in
their communities, positioning themselves along an Islamic spectrum
(Daniels 2009). Performers and others in Malang consistently used the
term *fanatik* to refer to Muslims who were devout and orthodox in
their approaches to Islam—including those who identified as *santri*, or
who others in their communities identified as *santri* (Geertz 1960). It

is important to bear in mind that the Indonesian term *fanatik* has some different shadings than the English word "fanatic." In their authoritative Indonesian-English dictionary, John M. Echols and Hassan Shadily define *fanatik* as "adhering strictly to a religion" (1994:162), which is consistent with the ways people used the term in Malang. While those who are religious fanatics—in the sense of being extremists—could be included in the Indonesian category *fanatik*, not everyone who is *fanatik* is an extremist. In other words, not everyone who is *fanatik* is necessarily a fanatic or fanatical. To convey the meaning of the Indonesian term as used by people I consulted in Malang, I maintain the Indonesian spelling in italics. At the other end of the spectrum from *fanatiks* were those who defined themselves as *nétral* (neutral) or *fair* (fair), terms they used to indicate what they felt was their more independent, open, and/or flexible approach to religion. The anthropologist James Peacock notes the tensions between those who approach Islam in different ways, as well as the use of the term *fanatik*: "the *santri* deride the majority as '*Islam statistik*'—that is, Muslim in name only—while they in turn are taunted as '*Islam fanatik*,' or more simply, 'Arabs'" (1981:140). Clearly, aligning oneself with a particular approach to Islam while labeling another's carried potentially divisive implications.

Some artists were concerned with Islam as a local matter because they perceived that increasing orthodoxy had a tangible impact on their professional activities—that is, their ability to earn a living as professional musicians and dancers. Some performers, including those who were themselves Muslim, connected a decline in performance activity in their neighborhoods over the years to the increasing presence of Muslims who were orthodox in their beliefs and practices. Such perspectives support the anthropologist Robert Hefner's argument that increasing orthodoxy in Islamic practice contributed to a decline in frequency of *tayuban* (or *tayub*), dance events that feature female singer-dancers who sing and dance for tips to the accompaniment of a gamelan ensemble. Hefner observed this decline in rural east Java between the late 1970s and the mid-1980s (1987a, 1987b).

The blame the performers I consulted placed upon orthodox and/ or devout Muslims for a decrease in the popularity of the performing arts, however, belied the many factors affecting changes in the performing arts, including changes in the popularity of particular genres. While older performers talked about the decline in the popularity of particular forms of theater such as masked dance drama and *ludruk*, they recognized that other genres such as hobby horse dance—called *jaranan* or other such names (see Kartomi 1973; Schrieber 1991; Van Groenendael 2008)—continued to be in demand. They also recognized that genres of popular music such as *campur sari* and *dangdut* had increased in frequency of performance over the years. Maintaining many conventions of older participatory dance events like *tayuban*, many *dangdut* performances have involved erotic professional female singer-dancers who dance with males from among the audience (Spiller 2008:195–202; 2010:37, 94–95, 134–138; Weintraub 2010:191–192). From my observations in Malang, the same argument could be made for some *campur sari* performances. Indeed, while I infrequently heard about performances of masked dance or *ludruk*, I did not have the time and energy to attend all the *jaranan* and *campur sari* performances about which I was told—performances that often included music influenced by *dangdut*. This further indicated the popularity of some genres over others in early twenty-first-century Malang as well as the continuity of past practices into the present, albeit sometimes in altered forms. In addition, since 1997 economic factors such as the devaluation of the Indonesian currency and dramatic increases in the price of oil products made it difficult for average families to afford sponsoring live performances that featured large numbers of musicians and dancers such as masked dance drama and *ludruk*.

Although Robert Hefner focuses on the impact of increasing Islamic orthodoxy and piety on ritual activity—including *tayuban*—in rural east Java, he also recognizes other complex cultural and economic factors that contributed to the decline in *tayuban* and other ritual activity he observed in the late 1970s–mid-1980s, including shifts in patterns of consumption. That is, people became more likely to display their wealth through "more privatized status goods, like radios, televisions, and motorcycles" rather than elaborate rituals (Hefner 1987a:548; see also 1987b:93–94). Acknowledging the impact of poverty, he notes too that many people simply could not afford to sponsor elaborate ritual events (1987a:548). Hefner also connects the changing attitudes that contributed to a decline in certain types of ritual celebrations to policies of the New Order government (1966–1998), as well as young people's desires to achieve modernity by aligning themselves with more orthodox manifestations of Islam and leaving behind what they saw as old-fashioned beliefs in local spirits (548).

While increasing orthodoxy and piety in Islamic practice was a strong cultural pressure in Reformation era east Java, as in New Order times, I suggest that it was not as destructive to the arts as performers and Hefner's articles might have suggested (despite Hefner's recognition of other factors) (1987a, 1987b). A host's decision about what type of performance to sponsor depended on many considerations, including the costs of the performances, how much the sponsor could afford, how much the sponsor wished to spend on sponsoring a performance, personal preferences, and the reactions of other people in a particular neighborhood. Performers' generalizations that increasing orthodoxy and piety have contributed to decreases in performing arts activity does, however, reinforce the point that negotiating Islam was very much a local matter—a locally relevant concern—for musicians and dancers.

While some artists who were Muslim situated themselves in relation to Muslims they perceived as *fanatik*, and indicated pressures they felt from Muslims who discouraged the arts, the dancer Luluk Ratna Herawati (b. 1967) recognized the support of a person she described as a *fanatik* Muslim, her father. She said that he supports her interest in dance because that is what she likes to do. Luluk's comments importantly point to the flexible and tolerant attitude of a *fanatik* Muslim, suggesting that despite the piety of more orthodox Muslims, some are nonetheless tolerant and supportive of the performing arts. Furthermore, the support that Luluk had from her father likely contributed to her own opinion as a Muslim woman about dance costumes: Luluk explained that she knows Muslims think that dance is questionable because the dancers wear strapless costumes, but she does not have a problem because she believes the costumes are still polite (personal communication [p.c. hereafter], January 4, 2006).

Muslim performers related to other Muslims in their communities in different ways, reinforcing diverse approaches to the religion. The musicians Kusnadi (b. 1944) and Achmad Suwarno (b. 1952) said that there are many Muslims in their neighborhoods who like the arts (p.c., Kusnadi, February 4, 2006; Achmad Suwarno, April 3, 2006). Speaking about his amicable relationship with other Muslims in his community, Achmad Suwarno said that he gets along well with Muslims, noting that he can participate in prayer and has a good relationship with the mosque because he repairs the *jidor*, a large drum (p.c., April 3, 2006). The vocalist and dancer Sumi'anah (b. 1955), a woman who has performed female and male style dances in the course of her career, did not have a problem being Muslim and an artist. In regard to religion, she said that one has to see the environment. She described the community in which she lived as being Muslim but not so *fanatik*, implying the religious tolerance of most of the people in her neighborhood (p.c., March 3, 2006).

The artist Lestari (b. 1954) said that everyone in his neighborhood knows that he is a *ludruk* performer who specializes in female roles, and he has never had a problem in his community. He related that when he departs to go somewhere, people sometimes ask him in a friendly and familiar manner, "aren't you performing?" (*nggak pentas a?*). Lestari took this as a gesture of support, and one that meant that his neighbors were good (*baik*) and accepting of his profession (p.c., April 30, 2006). In other words, he felt that the community in which he lived was tolerant and accepting of him performing female roles. Lestari's acceptance by other Muslims in his community may have been related to the fact that he lived as a man in his daily life and thus conformed to dominant cultural expectations for males to live as men even though he embodied femininity as a profession. Artists who were *waria* (males who live as female) did not necessarily experience the same degree of acceptance in their communities, as we will see, suggesting that generally artists involved with cross-gender dance performance were accepted as along as they did not push at ideological boundaries of gender beyond certain limits in their daily lives.

The blame that some performers placed on *fanatik* Muslims as well as performers' descriptions of many Muslims' support of the arts and artists evinces the different approaches to Islam and different senses of Islamic piety in Java, which have been described and analyzed by many scholars, including Clifford Geertz (1960); Koentjaraningrat (1985); Robert Hefner (1987a, 1987b, 2000); Mark Woodward (1989); Suzanne Brenner (1996); Andrew Beatty (1999); Timothy Daniels (2009); and others. I further explore diverse approaches to Islam and senses of piety in Javanese culture, particularly at the local community level by examining ways musicians and dancers in Malang negotiated Islam in relation to their artistic activity. Performers' approaches included separating religion and art, and specifying their personal approaches to Islam—often emphasizing flexibility and tolerance. With the intent of foregrounding local perspectives, I view these approaches as strategies that individual artists employed in order to negotiate Islamic beliefs and practices in their own ways. Performers were thereby mediating religious piety, in effect contributing to the continuous processes of shaping Islam in contemporary Java.

SEPARATING RELIGION AND ART

Some performers separated religion from art. The musician Komari (b. 1957; figure 5.3) asserted that there are separate times for prayer and for art and that "it was not art if these two activities were joined" (p.c., May 24, 2006).[8] Komari did not have any problems with being Muslim and playing music, and said that his feelings are not hurt if Muslims say that playing music is not permitted. He believes that it is up to "the one above," implying God. Komari's views on piety and the performing arts

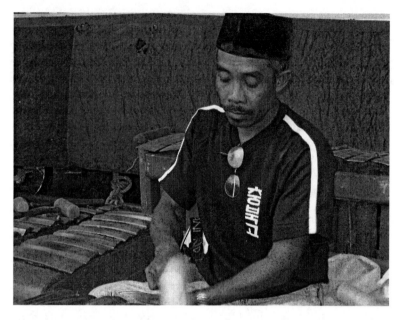

Figure 5.3 Komari plays a gamelan instrument at an afternoon *ludruk* performance, 2006. That performance, typical of *ludruk* performances in Malang, featured males who performed the female style dance *Ngremo Putri*, as well as other female roles. (Photograph by the author.)

are important because as a Muslim musician who accompanies dances performed as cross-gender dances—like other Muslim musicians who do so—he was participating in the expression and cultural production of masculinities and femininities, which complicated dominant norms.

Like Komari, Kusnadi, my principal gamelan teacher, contributed to the complication of gender in multiple ways through his profession as a musician. In accompanying female singer-dancers, he was contributing to the maintenance of social roles for females as singer-dancers despite dominant stereotypes that portray such female artists as sexually loose and greedy for money—the opposite of the "proper" and "self-sacrificing" wife and mother in dominant discourses and ideologies (Spiller 2010:86–89). Furthermore, Kusnadi contributed to the complication of gender by accompanying dances performed as cross-gender dances. For example, he contributed to the production of female masculinity when he drummed for females performing male style dances. Although he felt different when a female performed male style dance, he still believed that the drummer and the drumming should convey the maleness of the character. At the same time, he emphasized that one had to pay attention to the abilities of the dancer. Giving the example of the strong male style masked dance *Klana*, he said that the tempo should not be too fast because a female would not be able to do it (p.c., February 4, 2006). In maintaining the maleness of the character while drumming at a slower tempo, which he believed better accommodated the abilities of female dancers, Kusnadi contributed to the articulation of a complicated sense of gender—a masculinity nuanced by the female-ness of the dancer—a sense of female masculinity that was contingent upon the context of performance. He also contributed to the produc-tion of contingent male femininity when he drummed for males per-forming female style dance, such as those who performed *Ngremo Putri* in *ludruk* theater.

The dancer Warananingtyas Palupi (b. 1980) also separated artistic activity from religious life. When I asked her how she approached con-flicts between religious beliefs and her dancing, she said that she just does not think about religious restrictions. She separates religion and culture, recognizing that this is different for different people. Her younger sister, she noted as an example, is more conservative, adheres more to her reli-gious beliefs, and does not want to dance in a strapless top. Palupi also explained that she has a friend whose parents are devout Muslims and do not allow that friend to dance (p.c., November 15, 2005).

Palupi complicated senses of gender by recognizing that her per-sonality (as a woman) did not map to the representation of femininity expressed through refined female styles of dance. In talking about her own preferences for male style dance she tied aspects of dance to her character and behavior in her everyday life. Palupi said that she has a hard time with refined female style dances because they are too slow; she is not slow or relaxed (p.c., November 15–16, 2005). Although she neither described herself as a third gender, nor lived as a man in her daily life, she did attribute her affinity for male style dance to her "strong" personality, indicating her more "masculine" traits and thereby complicating dominant ideologies of womanhood. In articulating her "strength" in a "masculine" manner through the conventions of male style dance in the context of performance, Palupi produced contingent female masculinity.

Some performers justified their artistic activities as their professions, which was another way of separating religion from artistic activity. Suradi (1945–2009), a male who performed female roles in *ludruk* in the 1960s and 1970s and as a female vocalist (*pesindhèn*) in the 1960s, said that he did not feel any personal conflict between his artistic activi-ties and religious beliefs. He said that his religious beliefs and artistic activities were compatible (*cocok-cocok aja*), and that his artistic activity was his work (p.c., Suradi, May 3, 2006). Although performing was his profession and he lived as a man in his offstage life, he nonetheless subverted dominant constructions of gender that mapped femininity to female bodies. For him, applying and removing makeup were crucial processes in his transformation into and out of womanhood. He said that he started to feel like a woman when he began to do his hair and makeup and felt like a man again when his hair and makeup had been removed (p.c., May 3, 2006). He negotiated this process in and out of womanhood—a contingent male femininity—as a Muslim man by situating this process as part of his profession. He nonetheless challenged dominant ideologies that mapped femininity to female-born bodies.

Like the aforementioned artists, the vocalist and dancer Sri Handayani (b. 1982) did not have a personal problem with her religion and her profession as an artist. Responding to my question as to whether she ever felt any incompatibility with her religious beliefs, Sri explained:

> No, that is our work, you know. Why should we feel ashamed, why? It is our work, right, our work in order to eat, right? As far as religious matters, that is between us and the one above. Yes, so [work and religion] cannot be all mixed up. The important thing is that we are right, yes?—Work a job that is *halal*. (p.c., March 29, 2006)[9]

In using the word *halal*—what is permitted or allowed by Islam—Sri was evoking Islam in order to legitimize her profession as an artist, a striking assertion given the immoral, licentious stereotype of female singer-dancers in Java. Invoking Islamic discourse, she was insisting on the "rightness" of her profession.

Other female performers have drawn on religious discourse to legitimize their professions and in effect challenge dominant ideologies of womanhood. In his observations of *tayuban* in rural east Java, Robert Hefner found that just about all of the female singer-dancers identified as Muslim, and some specified that they were "good Muslims" (1987b:77). The *dangdut* singer Inul Daratista, who was at the center of national controversy in the early 2000s for a style of dancing that some Indonesians found to be too sexually provocative, positioned herself as a Muslim and insisted that her art and her religion were separate matters (Daniels 2009:88–89). Sri, the dancers that Hefner consulted, and Inul were challenging dominant Indonesian gender ideologies who insisted that women be "proper wives and mothers," making cultural space for women—including Muslim women—to publically assert other roles (e.g., as artists) and to display their sexuality.

Sri further complicated senses of gender through *Ngremo Tayub*, a substyle of *Ngremo Lanang* (male style *Ngremo*) that is almost inevitably performed by females. Sri, like other *Ngremo Tayub* dancers, complicated senses of gender by not only expressing masculinity, but also by undermining a clear separation between maleness and femaleness. She enhanced her womanly beauty while also embodying masculinity through costuming and makeup. As seen in figure 5.4, her female figure is enhanced through the cut of the top and the way she has fastened it. Sri's bare arms reinforce her womanliness and are rather erotic in a Muslim context that encourages women to cover their shoulders and, often, their arms. She puts on a wig of short hair—a "male" style haircut—and a male style head cloth. She has also used cosmetics to make her femaleness apparent. The false eyelashes, the style of the eye makeup, and the style of blush on her cheeks are recognizably feminine according to conventions of east Javanese dance makeup. Her mustache and eyebrows feature fine lines that reinforce her femininity, and she has not used a pencil to thicken the fine hairs on the side of her face to create thick, more "manly" sideburns. Her juxtaposition of masculinity and femininity when in this costume—an articulation of contingent female masculinity—is really quite striking (figure 5.4).

Figure 5.4   Sri Handayani poses in a *Ngremo Tayub* costume, 2006. (Photograph by the author.)

Sri undermined a clear separation between maleness and femaleness through *Ngremo Tayub* in other ways as well, such as by singing. *Ngremo* dancers often sing in the course of performing the
dance, whether *Ngremo Putri*, *Ngremo Lanang*, or *Ngremo Tayub*.
When women like Sri sing in the course of performing male styles
of *Ngremo*, the femaleness of their voices subverts the maleness of
the dance style, making it obvious to audiences and the other performers that the dancers are women. Yet another way Sri embodied
her femininity through male style dance was maintaining her sense of
herself as a woman. She said that she does not feel like a man when
performing, indicating that she did not feel a "complete" transformation to maleness (p.c., March 29, 2006). She was thus showing that

Figure 5.5   Sri sings at a *tayuban* dance event in typical female style dress, 2006.
(Photograph by the author.)

as a woman, she could be "manly," and thereby embodying a sense of female masculinity. Furthermore, in some performances she moved between maleness and femaleness by performing the male style dance *Ngremo Tayub*, then going offstage to change her outfit into female style dress, and then performing for the rest of the event as a vocalist and/or dancer (figure 5.5). By complicating and moving between senses of maleness and femaleness at different points of a performance, she was in effect demonstrating that the expression of gender is contingent upon circumstance. Sri, a Muslim woman, undermined a clear separation between femaleness and maleness promulgated in official ideologies through her profession as an artist, also contesting official ideologies of womanhood and "proper" roles for women.

PERSONAL APPROACHES TO ISLAM: EMPHASIZING FLEXIBILITY AND TOLERANCE

An equally important strategy that performers employed to negotiate Islam and the performing arts was specifying their personal approaches to the religion—that is, making sense of the religion in their own ways. Taking a flexible and tolerant approach to Islam and other religions was key. Some talked about the importance of not differentiating people based on religion. For example, Suradi, introduced above, said that gamelan has existed since past times, and that the art of gamelan belongs to everyone. Although there were people who differentiated others based on religion, he believed that religion was up to the individual. He did not believe that religion prohibited or forbade (*melarang*) the arts, insisting that he was "free" (*bebas*)— that is, open-minded or accepting (p.c., May 3, 2006).

Lestari, also introduced earlier, and, who like Suradi was a male who identified as Muslim and specialized in female roles in *ludruk*, similarly took a flexible approach to Islam. Lestari, too, was thus able to legitimize his identity as a Muslim man and his profession as a female impersonator. He said that he has never had a problem with religion and being a *ludruk* artist who specializes in female roles, indicating his piety by noting that he also participates in the Islamic ritual prayers (*ikut solat*). Asserting his tolerance, he said that he does not differentiate religions, maintaining that all religions are good (p.c., April 30, 2006).

As a Muslim man, Lestari recognized the femaleness of his own self—his male femininity—and also moved between maleness and femaleness in the course of preparing for the performance, during the performance, and after the performance. Strikingly, Lestari attributed his ability to perform convincingly as a woman to his ability to locate and draw on his feminine qualities, that is, the femaleness he located within his own self, in effect blurring his on- and offstage subjectivity. He explained that dancers have to find the character of *Ngremo Putri* (*Ngremo* in the female style) and its coquettishness from their own selves—that one has to search for the ways to move in order to be more beautiful, such as the way to move the neck coquettishly and to smile sweetly. He still felt like himself when he did his makeup, but when he stepped onto the stage, he felt like a woman. Sometimes that feeling did not disappear when he exited from the stage, especially if he knew that he would appear onstage again for another part of the performance, such as to sing or act in the play. When he completed performing he felt like himself again (p.c., April 30, 2006). In embodying male femininity in particular ways in particular contexts—contingent male femininity—Lestari complicated ideologies that separated maleness and femaleness into distinct gendered and sexed categories.

Lestari reinforced the femininity he embodied as a specialist of female roles onstage as well as the femaleness he located within his own self by referring to himself as a *seniwati*, the feminine form of the word *seniman*, or artist (p.c., April 30, 2006). This is analogous to a man in English referring to himself as an actress, waitress, or stewardess. In identifying himself as a *seniwati*, Lestari linked his temporary transformations to womanhood to his identity as a professional, gendered performer, further complicating what it means to be a Muslim male (and man) in contemporary east Java.

Budi Utomo (b. 1963), a dancer who specializes in masked dance, identified as Muslim but not *fanatik*.[10] He did not have any problems with religion and his artistic activities. He said that to be an artist one has to be *fair* (fair), explaining that he has performed at churches, although not yet at an Islamic boarding school. In referencing churches, Utomo was also referencing and recognizing the religious heterogeneity that characterizes Javanese society despite the large Muslim majority. He said that he does not like *fanatik* people, and that while his mother's relatives are all *fanatik*, he has not followed suit (p.c., January 6, 2006).

Utomo's flexibility toward religion has given him the flexibility in outlook to perform dances as cross-gender dances, as seen with others who perform dances as cross-gender dances. Utomo has performed female style dance in the course of his career, thereby embodying femaleness. He talked about performing female characters for masked dance in terms of necessity to the performance—saying that he performed female style dance when no one else in the all-male troupe wanted to do so (p.c., Budi Utomo, January 6, 2006). He discussed his embodiment of femaleness in terms of his competence as a dancer, attributing his ability to look like a woman onstage to spontaneity (*spontanitas*), from the movement and demeanor. Recognizing that his competence was not entirely his own, Utomo said that his ability to dance was a gift from God (p.c., January 6, 2006). Utomo was thus using religiously inspired discourse to account for and, on some level, to justify, his abilities as a dancer and his abilities to perform female style dance. One implication is that he was using religiously inspired discourse to legitimize his expression of male femininity, a sense of male femininity that was contingent upon the context of performance.

Other artists recognized that although they identified as Muslim, they found meaning in Javanese spiritual beliefs and practices, implying their flexible approach to Islam. A puppeteer, dancer, and musician, B. Supriono Hadi Prasetya (b. 1976; figure 5.1) said that even from his childhood days, he has not been satisfied with Islam because the things that he enjoyed doing were not allowed, such as drawing. At the time of the interview, he felt that he was more *abangan* (p.c., November 10, 2005) (see Geertz 1960). The musician Juma'i (b. c. 1952?) specified that he is Muslim, but "Javanese Islam" (*Islam Jawa*), similarly implying a syncretic approach to Islam that incorporates Javanese spiritual beliefs and practices (p.c., February 28, 2006).

The musician Dennis Suwarno (b. 1957) also referred to the importance that Javanese spiritual beliefs and practices (*kejawèn*) had for him, distancing his approach to religion from that of orthodox Muslims. He explained that he does not care for the way *fanatik* Muslims talk and think—like how they talk as though they know everything and how they judge people. When confronted by *fanatik* Muslims, he poses questions such as "are we born or made born?" (*apa kita dilahir or terlahir?*). The answer, he highlighted, would have different implications for the meaning of life. He said that when he asks people questions like these, they are quiet (*diam aja*)—with the implication that they are stumped, unable to think of a suitable response—and then leave him alone (p.c., August 8, 2006). By resisting what he thought were strict interpretations of Islam, Warno was insisting on his own tolerance and flexibility as well as the importance of such an approach, thereby maintaining cultural space for tolerance and flexibility, as he discussed his personal approach to religion and spirituality.

Some male artists who specialized in female roles lived as *waria*. *Waria* is currently a culturally sensitive term for males who live as female in Indonesia, although many people in Java call such males *banci*, or other less culturally sensitive terms (Boellstorff 2004, 2005b:9, 11; Oetomo 1996, 2000). Despite the recognition and support that *waria* received from local governments since the second half of the 1960s (Oetomo 2000:51) and the strides that *waria* have made in terms of visibility since the 1970s, *waria* still must contend with social—including religious—pressures to live as men (p.c., Samsuaretho and Totok, May 9 and 16, 2006; Boellstorff 2004). Samsuaretho (b. 1955), a *waria* who began to study the arts as a child and actively performed in *ludruk* theater from 1978 to 1991, is an important figure in the *ludruk* and *waria* communities in Malang and is known as "Mama Samsu." She[11] talked about *waria*'s struggles to be accepted by their families and communities, as did the *waria* Tom Boellstorff consulted (2004). Furthermore, Samsu explained that Muslims who are *fanatik* believed that having one's makeup done by a *waria* beautician or makeup artist was filthy and prohibited (p.c., May 9, 2006). One moral implication was that it was sinful.

Some attitudes have not changed much since the 1960s. In his research on *ludruk* in early 1960s Surabaya, James Peacock found that "[s]antri vehemently condemn ludruk transvestites because, they say, it is a sin for male and female elements to mix in a public performance" (1987:203). He found that in some cases, *ludruk* transvestites who came from pious Muslim families were beaten and/or driven away by their fathers (Peacock 1987:203; 1978:219). Related to such social pressures, some *ludruk* performers who specialize in female roles have female hearts, but do not live openly as *waria* (p.c., Samsuaretho and Totok, May 9, 2006). The stage was thus an important socially acceptable space for such males to fully embody womanhood, if only temporarily. In other words, for some, the full expression and embodiment of their male femininity was contingent upon the context of performance. Others, like Mama Samsu, however, expressed and embodied their senses of femininity by living as *waria*.

Mama Samsu drew on her personal approach to religion to counter negative ideas stemming from some *fanatik* Muslims. Posing the question of who was judging, humans or God, she answered that God is the one to judge, and that everyone is God's creation. Referring to many *waria*'s and *ludruk* female impersonators' experiences of being forced to live as men and marry women, but unable to satisfy their wives (implying sexually)—Samsu said that *waria* and *ludruk* female impersonators cannot help it because they were made like that by God (p.c., May 9, 2006). In other words, God made some males feminine and sexually desire male partners, not females.

When I asked Samsu what her religion was, she replied, chuckling, *nétral*—implying her independent and open-minded approach to religion. She went on to explain that at one time, she and her long-term partner Totok argued about religion. She questioned why one had to approach God through Islam, articulating her belief in a supreme God while also expressing reservation about choosing Islam as the way to practice monotheism.

> CS: As for yourself, what is your religion?
> S: Religion? I am *nétral*. That's why in the past—what year was that—Pak Tot and I got into an argument. Pak Tot entered Islam. Go ahead, [I said,] enter Islam, [but] approaching God does not [have to be] through Islam. As for me, every night that I can't sleep, yes, I ask God—after all the one who made me is God, right? If I feel that I am dirty, I bathe until I am clean and change into a clean shirt. Then I pray, God, I'm asking for this and this, what way is the path? Like that, right? (p.c., Christina Sunardi and Samsuaretho, May 9, 2006)[12]

Mama Samsu decided, however to "enter Islam" (*masuk Islam*) with Totok and they went to an Islamic boarding school (*pondok*), consulting an Islamic teacher (*kyai*). Totok, however, distanced himself from Samsu, which led to a fight that resulted in their temporary separation:

> Yes, I entered Islam with Pak Tot. I went along to a *pondok*, to a *kyai*... He [Pak Tot] didn't want to sleep with me ... He washed his own shirts. Yes, so that is why—yes, he couldn't live with me. "Someone like me can't do this," I said to him. We argued—bad—to the point that I broke up with him. To the point that we broke up. He ran off. [I said] "Take whatever you want. If you feel like you have a right to something take it." (p.c., Samsuaretho, May 9, 2006)[13]

Relating their reunification, she concluded the narrative about their argument with the point that God was the one to judge.

> In the end he got sick, asked someone for help, and I was asked to pick him up. Now, the one to judge is God, not those people. (p.c., Samsuaretho, May 9, 2006)[14]

Although at the time of the interview, Mama Samsu articulated an independent approach to God and religion, she also described the importance of respect for the context, as when serving as a beautician for a wedding. She noted that when she goes to a mosque, she makes the effort to wear a headscarf (*saya berusaha pakai jilbab*). She also said that she wears appropriate attire when she goes to a church (p.c., May 9, 2006).

Samsu's decision to wear women's attire to mosques is also significant because the issue of what *waria* should "wear when praying as Muslims" (Oetomo 2000:54)—male attire because *waria* are male, or female attire because *waria* live as female—remains unsettled within *waria* communities (54–55). By specifying women's attire to go to mosques (e.g., a headscarf) (although not necessarily specifying whether to pray), Samsu was insisting that Muslim society recognize the femininity with which she identified. In addition, she was providing an example to other *waria* who felt similarly about their femininity as well as demonstrating her own respectability.

Reinforcing her propriety, Mama Samsu spoke of her long-term relationship with Totok (saying that they had been together for twenty-six years at the time of the interview) (p.c., May 9, 2006). Samsu thereby countered negative assumptions about *waria*'s licentiousness and availability as prostitutes. In other words, Samsu implied that she was not sexually promiscuous, and her relationship with Totok was not an illicit relationship between a client and a sex worker, but a respectable long-term relationship. In fact, their fight and temporary breakup over religion seems to have strengthened their resolve to be together. For his part, Totok reinforced an open and tolerant approach to Islam—apparently having altered his prior attitude. He expressed his belief that there were males with female hearts since the times of Mohammad, thereby legitimizing the existence of multiple gendered identities and sexual preferences in a Muslim past (p.c., May 9, 2006). By establishing their views on religion as well as invoking God and Mohammad to embrace males with female hearts—and, by extension, their male lovers—Samsu and Totok drew on religion to legitimize their romantic and sexual relationship, which was nonnormative by dominant Indonesian and Islamic standards. As Samsu related, however, the process by and through which they negotiated their approach to religion and their relationship over the years has not always been easy and smooth.

The example of Samsu and her relationship with Totok provides a productive comparison to the ways Indonesian males who identify as *gay* (males who live as men and desire other males who live as men) have made sense of their sexuality, lifestyles, and Islam, as explored by Tom Boellstorff (2005a).[15] For example, *gay* Muslim men expressed different attitudes toward the sinfulness of being *gay*. While some did find being *gay* a sin, the predominant views Boellstorff found were that being *gay* was either not sinful or "a minor sin easily forgiven by God" (580). Thus similar to Samsu, many of Boellstorff's *gay* Muslim interlocutors referenced ultimate judgment by God. Also in the same vein as Samsu, "many *gay* Muslims concluded they were created *gay* by God and, thus, that they were not sinning" (580). While the categories *gay*, *waria*, and *waria*-loving men[16] are separate subjectivities—and in some cases, *gay* men and *waria* form separate communities (Oetomo 1996; 2000:53; Boellstorff 2005b:159, 175–177)—there are clearly similarities in the ways that some *gay* men, *waria*, and *waria*-loving men have made sense of themselves through their approaches to religion. In a nutshell, some *gay* men, in a similar manner as Samsu and Totok, made sense of Islam—and religion in general—in their own ways in order to legitimize gender identities and sexualities that were nonnormative by the standards of dominant Indonesian (and Islamic) gender ideology.

COMPLICATING GENDER, COMPLICATING ISLAM

In negotiating gender ideologies and Islam in Reformation era Malang, artists who identified as Muslim and/or talked about their experiences living as Muslim were contributing to the cultural production of localized expressions of the religion through performance and their offstage lives. The different approaches to Islam that performers articulated suggest underlying tensions between those who situated themselves at different ends of an Islamic spectrum (Daniels 2009) and point to strategies performers employed to negotiate these tensions in order to make sense of Islam, their professions as artists, and their lifestyles in their own ways. In so doing, musicians and dancers were complicating, challenging, subverting, and disrupting dominant "normative" and normalized senses of gender that mapped femininity to female-born bodies and masculinity to male-born bodies.

Performers made and maintained cultural space for the public articulation of diverse senses of gender—including senses of female masculinity (Halberstam 1998) and senses of male femininity (Boellstroff 2004). In some cases, the expression of female masculinity and male femininity was contingent (Blackwood 2010), affected by the circumstances of performance, rendering performance a critical site of gender politics and production. Some artists pushed at dominant constructions of gender in their offstage lives as well. That cross-gender dance practices are supported by Muslims in the larger society indicates a larger cultural need for nonnormative constructions of gender in Malang—a worthy topic for another chapter. Here I wish to conclude by reiterating the point that as performers made sense of masculinity and femininity in particular contexts, they negotiated increasing Islamic piety, exhibiting their agency and impact on the representation as well as the production of diverse, complex, shifting senses of gender and approaches to Islam in contemporary Java.

Notes

* My research was funded at various stages by a Fulbright-Hays Doctoral Dissertation Research Abroad Program Fellowship; a University of California Office of the President Pacific Rim Mini Grant; University of California, Berkeley Center for Southeast Asia Studies Grant-in-Aid Scholarships; and a University of California, Berkeley Graduate Division Travel Award. I thank Didik Nini Thowok and LPK Tari Natya Lakshita, M. Soleh Adi Pramono and Padepokan Seni Mangun Dharma (PSMD), and the Indonesian Institute of Sciences (Lembaga Ilmu Pengetahuan Indonesia [LIPI]) for sponsoring me in Indonesia. I thank the many musicians and dancers in Malang who took the time to share their perspectives, lives, and art with me. Many thanks go to Timothy Daniels for compiling this volume, for inviting me to contribute this chapter, and for his feedback and encouragement. I also thank an anonymous reader for the University of Illinois Press who directed me to productive sources. While that reviewer's comments were directed toward a different project, I have used some of the sources he or she suggested to develop my points in this chapter. Thanks are due as well to Patricia Hardwick, Laurie Ross, Eric Sasono, and the anonymous reader for Palgrave Macmillan; their comments on earlier drafts of this chapter were also very helpful. Any shortcomings, misinterpretations, or errors are entirely my own.

1. For the most part, people did not seem too concerned about scheduling events around the call to prayer at midday and in the late afternoon. One artist with whom I practiced, however, sometimes did wish to stop musical activity during these times out of respect for those who wished to pray.

2. By presentational dance, I am referring to dance in which, for the most part, the dancers are separate from the audience. In Malang, however, as in other parts of Indonesia, the distinction between dancer and audience member may be blurred when members of the audience enter into the performance space and dance with the dancers, as in some performances of *Ngremo Tayub*, a dance described later in this chapter. Thus when referring to presentational dance in Malang, I recognize that boundaries between audience and performer may be flexible in certain contexts, in effect blurring clear distinctions between presentational and participatory dance, as Henry Spiller has highlighted from his observations of dance events in West Java (2010:37).

3. Various cross-gender dance traditions also exist or have existed in other parts of Indonesia, including Cirebon (Ross, present volume), Banyumas (Lysloff 2001/2002:12–13), the Yogyakarta and Surakarta areas (Hughes-Freeland 1995:183–185; 2008a; 2008b:144, 163n13; Mrázek 2005; Ross 2005), Banyuwangi (Wolbers 1989:8; 1993:35; Sutton 1993:136), and Bali (Wolbers 1989:8; McPhee 1966:xvi, 7, 113, 170, 181, 191, 296–297; Diamond 2008; Hughes-Freeland 2008b:163n13; Downing 2009). For a compilation on cross-gender traditions in different parts of Indonesia, see Wahyudi and Simatupang (2005). In addition, James Peacock identifies transvestism in different parts of Indonesia (1978:209–211). Transvestism in Indonesia has also been referenced and/or analyzed in many other works. Due to considerations of space, I have listed just sampling of references in this note.

4. My sources for changing ideologies of masculinity and men's roles include Anderson (1965:28); Peacock (1987:204, n3; 206–207); Wieringa (2002:99); Weintraub (2004:110); Shiraishi (1997); and Spiller (2010:26). For more detailed discussions of changing ideologies of masculinity, see Sunardi (2009, in review).

5. My sources for changing ideologies of femininity and different roles women have historically taken in Java include Anderson (1965:26); Carey and Houben (1987); Sumarsam (1995:26–27); Walton (1996); Sears (1996a); Shiraishi (1997); Brenner (1998); Wieringa (2002); Blackwood (2005); and Weiss (2006). For more complete discussions of changes in gender ideology and roles females have taken, see Sunardi (2009, in review).

6. I recognize that "sex" is a complex category that is in many ways culturally constructed (Butler 1999:10–11; 1993).

7. A discussion of audience perspectives, while also important, goes beyond the scope of this chapter. For audience responses to cross-gender dancers, see Peacock (1987) and Sunardi (2009, in review).

8. "Kalau dijadikan satu itu bukan seni" (p.c., Komari, May 24, 2006).

9. "Nggak, kita kan ya 'is, perkerjaan itu, mbak. Kenapa harus opo ya, malu, kenapa? Kita kan, kerja kan, kerja to, untuk makan? Kalau, kalau urusan agama kita ya sama yang di atas 'gini. Ya, jadi nggak boleh dicampur aduk. Yang penting kita benar 'gitu aja, ya? Kerjaé halal gitu" (p.c., Sri Handayani, March 29, 2006).

10. As far as Budi Utomo communicated to me, "Budi Utomo" is his complete, given name. What is noteworthy here is that he shares a name with an organization (spelled Budi Utomo or Budi Oetomo) closely connected to the rise of Indonesian nationalism during the first part of the twentieth century. As Karen Strassler explains, "Budi Oetomo (a proto-nationalist organization founded in 1908) has an enshrined place in nationalist narratives as the origin of the nationalist movement" (2005:311, n43). At the time of my fieldwork, however, Utomo did not say why he was named this or what his name meant, and I did not think of asking him these questions. He usually went by "Cak Ut" and that was

how I addressed him. My gamelan teacher Kusnadi and other musicians of Kusnadi's group referred to him as "Utomo." I use Budi Utomo or Utomo in this chapter, rather than Cak Ut, to be more formal.

11. I use the pronoun "she" because Mama Samsu wore women's clothes and lived as a female.

12. *CS*: Kalau Mama Samsu sendiri agama apa?
    S: Agama? Saya itu nétral [says chuckling]. Makannya sama Pak Tot dulu kemarin—tahun berapa itu ya—bertongkar sama-sama Pak Tot itu. Pak Tot itu ke, masuk Islam, lho silakan, masuk Islam, pendekatan dengan Tuhan itu nggak melalui Islam. Saya itu setiap malam ndak bisa tidur ya minta kepada Tuhan, o yang, yang membuat saya kan Tuhan. Saya kalau merasakan saya itu kotor gitu, ya, muandi bersih gitu, ya wis, ganti baju bersih. Terus berdoa, Tuhan saya minta gini, gini, jalannya gi mana. Kan gitu, ya? (p.c., Christina Sunardi and Samsuaretho, May 9, 2006).

13. Iya, sama Pak Tot masuk Islam. Ikut ke pondok, ke kyai, gitu…Tidur ndak mau dengan saya [following words were not clear]. Baju dicuci sendiri. Ya makan dari di situ—iya, iya ndak bisa, ndak bisa hidup dengan saya—"orang seperti saya ndak bisa, gitu Pak Tot," saya omong gitu. Bertongkar, ramai, gitu, sampai pisah koq saya itu. Sampai pisah. Melarikan diri dia. "Bawahin apa yang kamu minta. Kamu merasa hak milikmu bawahin" (p.c., Samsuaretho, May 9, 2006).

14. "Akhirnya sakit, sakit minta tolong orang gitu saya suruh jemput, gitu. Sekarang yang nilai Tuhan, bukan orang itu" (p.c., Samsuaretho, May 9, 2006).

15. I follow Boellstorff's practice of italicizing *gay* to indicate that the Indonesian concept is not exactly the same as the English-language concept "gay" (Boellstorff 2005a:575; 2005b:8).

16. Oetomo highlights that *waria*-loving men do not identify as homosexual and "form an unmarked, nameless category" (2000:50). Totok did not name his sexual orientation or identity to me (and I did not ask). In retrospect, it seems that his and my nondiscussion of the matter reinforces the "namelessness" of *waria*-loving men as a category of sexual orientation and gendered subjectivity.

6

SOCIAL DRAMA, *DANGDUT*, AND POPULAR CULTURE*

Timothy P. Daniels

In the beginning of 2003, in the midst of a stalling reformation, a national controversy arose surrounding the new pop cultural star, Inul Daratista, and her dynamic and erotic performance style. Hailing from humble roots in East Java, she soared to national stardom upon the wings of her energetic new dance style called *goyang ngebor* or "The Drill" that she displayed on national television. On the heels of her popularity, *dangdut*—a longtime popular local cultural form among the lower social strata—broadened in its fan base encompassing the upper classes. Nevertheless, a broad array of forces aligned themselves against Inul and her new, highly visualized form of performance, attempting to restrict her appearances in local and national contexts. Indonesians were divided over what this emerging star, her body and style, meant, and for a moment they sidelined many pressing problems as the debate raged. I will attempt to capture some of the social and cultural depth of this conflict applying a revised version of Victor Turner's (1974, 1987) concept of social drama.

Victor Turner differentiated "social dramas" from more harmonious "processual units," describing their constituent phases as breach, mounting crisis, redressive actions, and reintegration. Instead of looking at these dramatic episodes as moments between largely harmonious social processes, I will examine them as parts of ongoing conflict and social contradictions that may appear as more harmonious only due to everyday theatrics of power, what Scott (1990b:426) called the "duress of the quotidian." I pay close attention to conditions at both ends of the social drama, before the breach and after the reintegration. In addition, within the drama itself, I will combine cognitive and symbolic approaches, highlighting not only multivocality and communitas, but also the depth of cultural ideas, complex concepts that are evident in opposing perspectives. I will demonstrate that multiple interpretations of Inul's body, and by extension female bodies, and of her manner of dressing and dancing evoke contrasting forms of encyclopedic knowledge. This knowledge and the emotions it engenders produce forms of communitas for opposing segments of Indonesian society, a form of normative communitas for Muslim reformers and spontaneous/existential communitas for Inul supporters. Although my interviews and discussions with local people indicate a wide range of positions on Inul's performance style and reformist Muslim attempts to censor her, this social drama featured a strong opposition between institutionalized Islamic and antistructural populist visions for Indonesian society. Before proceeding to discuss the extended temporal field of the social drama, I will place *dangdut* in its local context alongside other popular cultural forms. In the final section, I will discuss some implications of this dramatic moment for equalization.

DANGDUT AMIDST OTHER LOCAL CULTURAL FORMS

The Department of Tourism and Culture and the Yogyakarta Palace often staged *dangdut* performances for mass entertainment at public events, including the night market of the palace-sponsored *Sekaten*, as part of the celebration of Prophet Muhammad's birthday.[1] During *Sekaten* 2004, Ira Swara, one of three female hosts of a new nationally televised *dangdut* show, "DagDigDut," performed inside the elaborate walled and tented structures built in the northern palace square. Civil servants, business owners, and families and neighbors present *dangdut* throughout the region at nightclubs, amusement parks, tourism venues, and at weddings and other rites of passage. People have long been familiar with the erotic nature of *dangdut* performances in these local contexts. Whenever people have some time off, holidays and vacations, they can easily find *dangdut* shows that organizers and promoters make available for mass consumption. In fact, for *Lebaran*, one of the most meaningful and widely celebrated Muslim holidays following a month of fasting and soul-searching, *dangdut* was presented at numerous stages throughout the region. These sites included the popular tourist locations at Kaliurang and Parangtritis, Glagah, Trisik, Kulonprogo, Mangiran Bantul, Rawa Jombor Klaten—mostly mountain and beach sites—and at the privately owned amusement parks, Purawisata and Gembira Loka (KR November 24, 2003). It has become a tradition to seek out tourist and amusement sites for rest and relaxation with friends and family, and many of whom *mudik* return to their hometowns for *Lebaran*. In Grobogan, Central Java, permission to stage *dangdut* at three tourist sites for *Lebaran* was rejected by the local tourism office because they feared there would be so many people there that disturbances would take place (KR November 24, 2003).

For *Lebaran*, I went to the Gembira Loka amusement park and zoo, where, together with the Purawisata, there were five days of cultural performances featuring *dangdut* in an event titled *Pentas Dangdut Lebaran 2003*. There were two stages at Gembira Loka, one for *dangdut* and one for traditional cultural arts such as *jathilan* and *angguk putri*. The hypnotizing Javanese rhythms and singing rang out through the amusement park as fifty or sixty people stood around the fenced-in area where the spirit-possessed performers danced in trance climbing trees, fighting with swords, and opening unripe coconuts with their bare teeth. Locals know *jathilan, reog*, and their variants for these and other exciting feats, including chewing glass, which they call *atraksi* (attractions), expressing the mass appeal these old village "syncretistic" forms hold for people. People associated these cultural forms with *abangan* because of traditional *kejawen* practices, such as making offerings before performances, spirit-possession, and visiting cemeteries and sacred sources of water in search of supernatural powers, to which the performers of these forms often adhere. For many spectators, *jathilan* holds no religious meaning or novelty since they often see it in their villages as entertainment for weddings, circumcisions, and graduations because it is much cheaper than sponsoring *dangdut*. Nevertheless, they are attracted to the strong emotions such as fear and amazement it inspires. *Angguk putri*, performed on this traditional stage on a different day, is one of the local cultural forms, like *kuntulan* and *badui*, which local people associated with "*santri*" because *selawat* and other religious songs traditionally accompany these dance performances (Kuntowijoyo, Kasniyah, and Abubakar 1987; Soetrisman et al. 2003) and they *did* not involve dancing in trance. However, this *angguk putri* group, exhibiting a recent pattern of change for many of the cultural forms associated with *santri*, did have several female performers go into trance and perform *atraksi* attempting to capture more interest from the masses. Nevertheless, few people watched these shows, compared to the thousands of people amassed to see the *atraksi* in the area where the *dangdut* stage was located. This popularity of *dangdut* as a public cultural form was one of the main reasons I decided to include it in this study contrary to my initial plans.

Hundreds of young men were crowded around the front and sides of this *dangdut* stage, some shouting and spinning around swinging their shirts, some dancing with their friends, even under the direct sunlight, and some had alcohol on their breathe as they pushed forward moving closer to the performers. These men gazed at the string of female *dangdut* performers wearing tight clothes and miniskirts and stretched out their hands to the women seeking to shake their hands after they came out on the stage. The interaction between the performers and males in the audience, shaking hands and chatting, sometimes saying "naughty" things, follows a pattern of flirtation that seems to have long been a part of this pop cultural form.[2] Their songs were about love, romance, and enjoying life for the most part, and taken together with the music, exhibited this form's *orkes melayu* roots and its absorptive quality. This cultural form is similar to the Malay language in the way it is spread across the region, and like *bahasa Melayu*, which was a common market language before becoming national languages in Malaysia and Indonesia, *musik Melayu* was also *budaya rakyat*, the culture of the common people across the Malayo-Indonesian region. Malay performance arts, music and dance, have long absorbed Arab influence. However, *dangdut* appears to have emerged with its distinctive rhythms in the 1960s with several songs with Indian-style beats (Mona Lohanda 1991;139–140). It has continued to absorb Indian and Arab elements, and in the 1970s and 1980s Rhoma Irama moved *dangdut* in the direction of mixing Western beats such as rock and jazz with *dangdut* rhythms (143). In the 1990s and 2000s, *dangdut* has been absorbing cultural flows from the United States and Japan, sometimes via Korea and Taiwan, countries that have also fallen under the influence of hegemonic American images of beauty and body style (Faruk and Aprinus Salam 2003).

Each of the female performers, besides wearing revealing clothing, swung their hips and gyrated in various sexually suggestive ways precipitating excitement from the mostly male audience, which was typical for local *dangdut* performers long before Inul Daratista emerged on the national stage with her *goyang ngebor*. Performers of many traditional cultural arts, such as *dombret, ronggeng, jaipong,* and *tayub,* from various regions across Java, also employ many erotic body movements, and *campursari* and *dangdut* performers incorporate these movements into their *goyang* (see Pioquinto 1995:80–81; Faruk and Aprinus Salam 2003:100, 199; Sumbogo 2003). However, before Inul became prominent, the *goyang* of most nationally televised *dangdut* performers involved swaying the body slightly to the music, and many people even considered this inappropriate at times. They tried to make their body movements fit the music and lyrics, whereas with Inul and those following her, highly visualized dance movements dominate performances regardless of music or lyrics (Faruk and Aprinus Salam 2003:120–136). Nowadays, the "feminine aura" of *dangdut* has expanded in its expression of female sexuality. Many locals have told me that they perceive men who perform *dangdut* as being feminine, with the possible exception of the "King of *Dangdut*," Rhoma Irama, who sang many songs encouraging people to be mindful of religious values and norms. Locals considered most male *dangdut* performers to be like *waria*, third gender males, or at least "weak" men lacking in their masculinity.[3] The nature of their songs, about missing lovers or being heart broke and so forth, no doubt, contributes to this perceived contradiction of behavioral expectations for men. Yet, this symbolic association of *dangdut* with femininity has now moved further to put female sexuality on display in both local and nationally televised contests, as each of these performers on the Gembira Loka stage stuck out their buttocks or made grinding movements with their hips, at times evoking the *goyang* styles of many new national *dangdut* stars.

On another occasion, I attended a *dangdut* program called "Goyang Sehati" on the Purawisata stage during one of its "regular" Saturday night shows. Only this time, it was not the routine weekly event, as the *dangdut* program was promoted together with a *waria* beauty contest, *Waria Luwes Grandfinal 2003*. This was the fourteenth year that this entertainment promotion company has organized this contest and *dangdut* show. The *waria* beauty contest took place first with fifteen *waria* dressed in *sarong* and *kebaya* (traditional Javanese female attire) and twenty *waria* dressed in evening gowns who stepped across the stage in high-heeled shoes to the supportive shouts, screams, and applause from their friends, fellow *waria*, and hundreds of heterosexual men. There were many *waria* present from the area, including the head of the *waria* association, and some of them were wearing Islamic headscarves. In this social space, an entertainment venue, heterosexual men seemed to accept and enjoy the presence of *waria*, even dancing together in the same area in front of the stage later in the evening. I later interviewed a young headscarf-wearing *waria*, a student at UGM writing her undergraduate thesis (*skripsi*) on *waria* that I met at this Purawisata program. She told me that she is baffled by the way heterosexual men seem to accept *waria* as entertainers but look down on them and discriminate against them in the broader societal context. Indeed, Dorce, a *waria* who has had a sex-change operation, is a popular entertainer and hosts several shows on television, but *waria* still experience stigmatization as a sexual minority and find it hard to be accepted and included in society-at-large as anything other than entertainers and prostitutes. Perhaps people are willing to accept them more in a *dangdut* context, because of the sexual openness and sex trade that increasingly characterizes these entertainment venues.[4]

After the *waria* contest, the *dangdut* show began with the host introducing the first performer who was a male *dangdut* singer and the audience stayed where they were, a fair distance from the stage, for the most part as he performed. However, when the next performer, the first of a series of female singers who took the stage, a flood of men moved from the sides and back to the area in front of the stage. Following the typical script, the female artists, mostly wearing tight pants, stepped forward and shook the hands of several men and swiveled their hips and other body parts in popular *goyang* styles, while the heterosexual men, dancing beside *waria*, reveled in their sexuality.

Every television station now broadcasts *dangdut* shows featuring popular national stars, such as Nita Thalia, Ira Swara, Anissa Bahar, and Kristina, following the controversial emergence of Inul Daratista on the national stage in early 2003. Most of these shows involve predominantly female artists performing in tight-fitting attire with backup bands, background dancers, and an audience. Some are broadcast live and others recorded, and some present only *dangdut* artists while others, like Inul's *Sang Bintang* on *SCTV*, regularly include "pop" and "rock" groups as well. The female singers, at times accompanied by male singers, and mostly female background dancers, who are also generally dressed in short skirts and tops and tight-fitting attire, perform various types of sensual *goyang*. They are increasingly exploring mesmerizing feats of "physical technology," high energy grinding, and acrobatics to create a circus-like spectacle for onlookers (Simatupang 2003). Some shows even highlight women in the audience swinging their hips and grinding their bodies like the performers on stage. Other television stations broadcast them live from large entertainment centers with thousands of enthusiastic, mostly male fans, crowded around the stage performing the usual rites. *Dangdut* performances entailing the foregrounding of sex, with the female body as spectacle, long present in Central Java, has gone national (cf. Pioquinto 1995:60, 80). Many of the artists have their own distinctive styles of *goyang*, such as Inul's *goyang ngebor*, Anissa Bahar's *goyang patah-patah*, or Uut Permatasari's *goyang ngecor*[5] that are named, or Nita Thalia's, Ira Swara's, and Dewi Persik's that have not taken on names of their own but are also quite well-known.

The *goyang* named or not has become a symbolic object that has taken on a life of its own as a commodity in the world of marketing and advertising. A long list of Indonesian and foreign companies advertise their products, from motorcycles to hair shampoo, on commercials during *dangdut* programs, and some like Sarimi (instant noodle brand) have their own shows. The cost of advertising during these widely watched shows is relatively expensive and some of this money from the enhanced popularity of *dangdut* descends into the hands of the artists, many of whom have suddenly experienced radical changes in the material conditions of their lives (Tempo October 27, 2002:128; Forum March 30, 2003:52–57; Pioquinto 1995:83–86). Similar to rap music, which arose out of poor African American neighborhoods in the United States and stigmatized as low-class culture before becoming part of national pop culture, *dangdut*, long popular with *wong cilik* (J. common people), has become a national pop form popular with all social strata, rich, middle class, and poor. To understand the dynamics of the mushrooming of *dangdut* we need to look briefly at the controversy surrounding Inul Daratista.

SOCIAL DRAMA AND REFORMATION DYNAMICS

Victor Turner's social drama (1974, 1987) framework can be used fruitfully to analyze the controversial emergence of *dangdut* on the national stage as described above; yet, we must consider the social conflict before the "breach" and following the "reintegration" of the crisis. Long before the breach, during the New Order regime, former president Suharto extended his authoritarian rule over cultural forms and Islamic organization, supporting forms that trumpeted his ideology and political messages and suppressing forms and organizations that seemed opposed to his interests. *Dangdut*, among other *abangan* cultural forms, was stigmatized as low-class, unrefined culture, and was largely restricted from the national stage except for Bang Haji Rhoma Irama, who "cleaned up" this raw pop cultural form with many songs containing normative Islamic messages. Rhoma Irama obtained extensive access to the government television station, TVRI, after leaving PPP (an Islamic party) and joining Golkar, the dominant government party during the New Order era (Faruk and Aprinus Salam 2003:313–321). Cultural artists who did not join up with government-controlled organizations were not given access to television stations, which were all directly owned by the government or Suharto and his family members until the 1990s. President Suharto and Golkar used artists such as Rhoma Irama to gather public support for every general election. In 1975, the New Order regime formed a group of Islamic scholars, MUI (Majelis Ulama Indonesia), as a national council for these forces used to make authoritative Islamic rulings (*fatwa*) consistent with the perspectives and interests of the political elite (322; Hooker 2003). People came to consider MUI as an institution providing an Islamic stamp to the wishes of the New Order regime. In the latter period of Suharto's rule, he also developed relationships with ICMI (Ikatan Cendekiawan Muslim Indonesia), utilizing this modernist Muslim intellectual organization to strengthen his position with this sector of the Muslim community, as opposition to his authoritarian rule grew stronger among the masses of ordinary and middle-class Indonesians.[6] In the era of *Reformasi*, following the mass uprisings and protests that finally ousted Suharto from power, many of the groups and individuals seen as supporting the New Order regime lost much of their credibility with the people.

Moreover, following the fall of Suharto, many groups formerly supportive of the New Order regime together with several Muslim elements of the reformation movement, waged campaigns for "moral" change, not to speak of the macrostructural issues the masses felt to be most pressing. MUI, quickly reinvented as a reformist institution after Suharto fell, focused its attention on "moral" problems such as gambling, prostitution, narcotics, pornography, rather than on KKN (Corruption, Collusion, and Nepotism), which was the main focus of protesters. Along these lines, MUI issued a *fatwa* in April 2001 on pornography and pornographic activities, and in the same year, they forbade the importation and use of some Japanese products because they reportedly contained pork fat.[7] Other Islamic organizations and parties focused on the "moral" challenges posed by Christianization and Westernization and the fighting in Maluku and Poso between Muslims and Christians (322–335). MUI also issued a *fatwa* in 2003 forbidding interest from banks. These morally framed issues gained much momentum in the US-led "War on Terror," with these problems interpreted as stemming from non-Muslim, Western influence. Activist reformers attacked many nightclubs, catering to foreigners, across Indonesia. However, a backlash from other segments of Indonesian society began to take shape and grow stronger opposing the reformist discourse and approach to reformation. United States funded many "traditionalist" groups arguing against the moralizing and anti-American discourse of the reformers (see Ramage 2004). Thus, when the conflict over Inul arose, there had been a standoff for some time between Muslim reformists and their detractors, both Indonesian and Western, who had gained an upper hand with the presidential victory of Megawati Sukarnoputri.

The initial appearance of Inul on the live, nationally broadcast show, "Digoda," on Trans TV, in January 2003 (FX Rudy Gunawan 2003:3), in which she performed her exciting *goyang ngebor*, precipitated the "breach" wherein many Islamic organizations and institutions began to protest the openly sexual nature of her performances. Inul was already popular in local areas, and video compact discs of her shows were circulating across the region, exhibiting many of her scintillating movements on stage. Her presentation style combines the sexy, athletic style from the West, especially the United States, with the cute and lovely style from Japan. She says she derived inspiration for her *goyang* from watching MTV and subsequently tried to fit MTV-style dance to the music and tempo of *dangdut* (Faruk and Aprinus Salam 2003:58, 67–109). MUI of east Java, in February 2003, declared that Inul's attire and dancing fell under their ruling against pornography and requested the government to restrict her performances (30). They also threatened television stations with punishment for airing "pornography" (Forum May 11, 2003). As the "mounting crisis" proceeded, MUI in Solo and municipal authorities in Yogyakarta also made moves to restrict Inul from performing in these cities, arguing that her clothing and *goyang* did not fit with the culture of these areas and would degrade the morals of people. Rhoma Irama, the head of PAMMI (Persatuan Artis Musik Melayu Indonesia), the Indonesian Malay Music Artists' Association, also argued that Inul must be stopped from performing and immediately forbade her from using any of his songs and those of other members of PAMMI. These "normative" Islamic voices expressed concerns about Inul's explicit flouting of Islamic norms of covering required parts of the body (*aurat*) and how her sexually provocative movements would arouse the *hawa nafsu*, lustful desires, of men in the general public leading to low morality and an increase in cases of rape. Rhoma Irama declared that struggling to boycott "*dangdut* ala Inul" is *jihad* (22). Some of my local contacts agreed with this criticism of Inul and applied it to other *dangdut* artists arguing that they should be restricted; yet, allowing for *dangdut* in a changed form. One neomodernist Muslim activist told me that there is "no *dangdut* in Islam," expressing total opposition to it as a cultural form.

In the process of resolving the conflict, Inul met with Rhoma Irama to apologize for her behavior, reportedly kissing his knee and crying, but Inul rejected his demands and the requests of other religious figures arguing that her *goyang* was her unique style and refusing to change it. She said: "They can give me advice, but they can't stop me singing or dancing the way I want to. I'm a Muslim, but

I'm also an artist. I don't want to mix religion and art" (FX Rudy
Gunawan 2003:77). Rhoma Irama in turn continued to call for her
suppression and a holy war against *Inulisasi*, the spread of her type
of performances in the music world and on television. On the other
hand, the dominant mass media and masses of people, some forming
fan clubs, supported Inul. Many of my respondents have expressed
opinions that MUI and Rhoma Irama went about advising Inul in
the wrong way and that they do not have the right to tell her how to
perform. Most respondents to surveys supported Inul over Rhoma
and many of them expressed the view that Rhoma is a *munafik* or
hypocrite charging that he is guilty of the things he accuses Inul of
and that he has a large sexual libido, having married more than one
wife and having been involved in sex scandals (see Faruk and Aprinus
Salam 2003:239–245). Furthermore, most people seem to consider
dangdut to be art (*seni*) and/or entertainment (*hiburan*) and feel that
religious principles and rulings should not intrude in these domains
of cultural life. Others have expressed the view that *dangdut* is *budaya
rakyat*, people's culture, thereby opposing attempts to undermine
its connection with the people; and, for them, people who participate in a *dangdut* show dancing together form a special bond and
relationship.

Inul received immense publicity when Taufik Kiemas, the husband
of President Megawati Sukarnoputri, appeared on national television
swinging his own buttocks dancing with her. Moreover, she received
support from former president Abdurrahman Wahid who met and
held press conferences with her in which he argued that it was a case of
"human rights" and Inul's freedom of expression had to be defended
(Forum May 11, 2003:33). Some of my local contacts echoed Gus
Dur's position about human rights; even many of those who disagree
with her style of dressing and dancing think that authorities should not
force her to comply with religious rulings. In the "redressive" phase
of this social drama, the courts did not interpret Inul's performance
as "pornography" or "pornographic activity" and television stations
have not been restricted from airing her performances. Emha Ainun
Nadjib, a famous playwright, poet, and Islamic leader (see chapters 6
and 7), and other public figures began to make the call for people to
focus on more important, substantive issues rather than continuing to
bicker over Inul's butt and "body politics" (Faruk and Aprinus Salam
2003:175–180). Not only did Inul evade formal court censure, but
with "reintegration" Inul obtained two television programs, one musical show, *Sang Bintang* (The Star), and one dramatic series, *Kenapa
Harus Inul* (Why It Has to Be Inul), about her life and experiences.

In fact, *dangdut* programs and "gossip" shows about *dangdut* artists spread like wildfire as television stations and corporations hustled to capitalize on the power of the *goyang*. Before moving on to discuss this "reintegration" further, let us look more deeply at some of the key symbols, notions, and projections of desirable futures that arose and were expressed during the mounting crisis.

In the midst of this social drama, the major disputed symbol was that of Inul's body, especially her butt and hips. Inul's tight-fitting body suits and gyrating movements with her butt sticking out, often facing the audience, has generated strong responses on all sides. Most people view her body and movements as sexy and erotic and express strong feelings about it. While many of her supporters revel in the enjoyment of physical arousal and excitement, drawing attention to how large and strong her butt is, those who view her sensuality negatively, argue that her form of attire leaves the female *aurat* open, insufficiently covered, thereby arousing lower and sinful human desires, *hawa nafsu*. According to their interpretations of Islamic concepts, reformists argue that people must keep the human body and its physical desires under control, regulated along the course of permitted satisfaction prescribed through the divine guidance of the Qur'an and the traditions of Prophet Muhammad. If these desires are out of control, they are susceptible to demonic temptation that leads to more immorality and forbidden, evil activities, such as fornication and rape. In fact, reformists interpreted Inul's presentation style as "pornographic" and entailing "pornographic actions" due to the way they flout Islamic principles of proper covering for the body and openly express sexuality. From this perspective, people interpreted her *goyang* as *goyangan setan* or "Satan's Dance." Similarly, some people, arguing from the perspective of traditional customs and "Indonesian" etiquette, asserted that Inul's style of dancing, with her buttocks toward the audience, is considered extremely disrespectful in local cultures. For instance, in Java it is the norm for people to partially cover their backside with their arm and hand when turning their backs to people in social settings. Furthermore, from the perspective of traditional Javanese philosophy, the body (*tubuh*) is lower than the soul (*ruh*), brawn (*okol*) to brain (*akal*), and so forth, a cosmic hierarchy Inul inverts with her dominance of body over the soul. This perspective casts common people, *wong cilik*, as creatures living on the level of the body, while the aristocrats, intellectuals, and mystic masters live at higher spiritual levels in which they control their bodies with *akal* (Faruk and Aprinus Salam 2003:173). In addition to evoking ideas about proper body covering, control of the body, and channeling desires along permitted lines and evil forces, reformists call upon other complex concepts such as *dakwah* (Ar. Da'wa; calling to Islam), *mubaligh* (person introducing Islam), *jihad* (holy struggle), and *ummat* (Islamic community) that emphasize the imperative to properly promote Islamic standards. Clearly, the female body and Inul's dance and attire elicit encyclopedic meanings, all that people know about such matters, and not just lexical or dictionary meanings of these symbols (see Lehman 1978).

In contrast to these meanings along the ideological or normative pole, local supporters of Inul remain much closer to the "orectic" or concrete poles, largely elaborating upon the experience of sensuality, though nonetheless drawing upon encyclopedic knowledge. However, they do frame these experiences in terms of "creative dance," "art," "entertainment," with performers making a living, and "people's music and culture." This perspective often places the significance of art and entertainment as an avenue for people to free themselves from frustrations, a space to be free from the stresses and travels of everyday life. It also relates the form of *dangdut* Inul represents to the "common people," meaning average village and urban neighborhood residents of the lower classes, constructing a "grassroots" identity. Gus Dur and other intellectuals presented the more ideological interpretation supporting Inul's body and dance style, calling upon concepts of "human rights" and "freedoms" of artistic expression and so forth. These concepts provided a rhetorical and political frame for many of her supporters who were more concerned with, and focused upon enjoying life, submerged in the feast of sensuality. The sense of communitas, a diffuse feeling of equality and oneness, for these common, local supporters, did not emanate from the concepts of rights, freedoms, and liberal democracy, but from the experience of Inul's "body language" and their intense dancing, entering into trance-like states of consciousness (Faruk and Aprinus Salam 2003:187).[8] Inul facilitates potent feelings of equality through her public disregarding of normative behavior, turning her butt to the audience and performing her sensual moves in defiance of Islamic and Indonesian normative authorities. In one popular song, "*Goyang* Inul" (Inul's *Goyang*), written for Inul, she and other performers who sing it tell spectators, "adult men and women, not to be surprised or mad when Inul dances, excuse it…one thousand one kinds of problems, just forget them and look at Inul's *goyang* as medicine to make you happy, healthy, and prosperous." Most popular *dangdut* songs are about love, romance, problems in relationships, and defiantly about sensual *goyang* itself. Local participants elaborate on this deviant, antistructural behavior through drinking, taking drugs, and pulling their shirts off and screaming in front of the stages.

This contrasts with the reformists sense of communitas produced and expressed through calls to the Muslim *ummat* coming together to perform their duties of upholding proper morality, spreading Islam, and fighting against the forces of evil, men, and demons. These campaigns and the intense feelings they bring forth create a broad, powerful sense of equality of all Muslims as humble servants of God, submerged in a community of believers. Reformists often express feelings that they are acting out of the desire to change the dominant social and cultural patterns in the world that are supported by corrupt rulers and global forces. This reformist movement, led by highly structured groups, maintains a sense of normative and ideological communitas produced through its antistructural ideas envisioning a space in which all fellow believers participate in struggling to realize Islam in the world. They project desirable futures in which the Muslim majority in Indonesian society will unite behind a campaign to formally institute Islamic laws. Proper public comportment and morality, an Islamized social order, will be upheld by state-institutionalized and enforced legal rulings. Yet, in contrast to the largely existential communitas of common people who participate in *dangdut* "happenings," reformist groups have "routinized" their antistructural spirit of communitas within hierarchically organized groups and institutions that are already an integral part of the social structure. Indeed, the masses of Inul supporters project desirable futures in which everyday people will have better ways of making a living and improving their quality of life. They project visions of an Indonesian society where there will be more public spaces for expressions of people's arts, entertainment, and equality, and release from rigid social hierarchies. Moreover, they tend to envision a society in which common people will be able to pursue their interests without being hindered by the "moral police" and religious enforcers. Some appear to believe that some form of a "liberal democracy," with protections for human rights, including freedom of expression, would be the best container for such aspirations.[9]

Widespread support for Inul continuing her *goyang*, the refusal of courts to issue any formal ruling against her, and calls from prominent public figures for the country to focus upon more important matters brought the redressive phase into reintegration. In the aftermath of this social drama, we can note that Inul, high-voltage *goyang*, and "people's culture" rose in prominence and normative Muslim authorities have lost, if they ever had, a great deal of respect and legitimacy in the eyes of many common Indonesians. Gradually events began to redirect these contrasting and opposing forms of communitas and the social segments experiencing and espousing them away from the issue of Inul and "body politics" and into other fields. The most significant field for the second half of 2003 and 2004 was the first general election in which Indonesians would directly elect their president and vice-president.

General elections in Indonesia usually entailed acts of violence between opposing parties and their supporters. Civil and religious leaders and authorities, out of fear of a repetition of past violent scenarios, began to call early for a peaceful general election and organized prayer vigils around the country supplicating for one. Political leaders and mass media labeled the election "Pesta Demokrasi Berbudaya" or "A Cultured Celebration of Democracy," and political parties locked themselves into a competition of using cultural arts and performances to attract and get their messages out to the people. Political parades and motorcades circulated through city streets and held rallies usually featuring some forms of popular cultural arts. The buzz of commentators was about whom Inul would come out to support and perform for, swinging the election results on the power of her hips. Although Inul remained neutral in public, just making statements to the effect that she supported the people, most other artists, including *dangdut* stars, began to join forces with particular parties. The incumbent president, Megawati Sukarnoputri and her party, PDIP, led the way organizing prominent film and music stars into a support group. Most presidential tickets paired up a secular nationalist candidate for president with a traditional religious figure, prominent NU personalities, as vice-presidential candidate. These campaigns used *dangdut* widely, as these parties did in the earlier local and regional parliamentary elections, but the modernist and reformist-oriented Islamic parties were at a disadvantage in this regard because their use of the most popular form of "people's culture" would alienate their main base. Although many Islamic parties used popular cultural arts such as *campursari*, *angguk putri*, and even *jathilan*, they did not venture to present *dangdut*, especially in its most popular sensual form. This left them at a distinct disadvantage in appealing to the masses in the aftermath of a social drama in which this form of *dangdut* emerged triumphant.

Dramaturgy and Equalization

In addition to local views discussed above, many of my respondents have also mentioned the economic aspect of this social drama. Some male and female contacts have complained about the use of female bodies for advertising as exploitation of women. A young feminist activist who wears a headscarf (*jilbab*) told me that although she disagrees with the style of dress and dance of many *dangdut* performers, she supports their right as women workers and opposes any attempts to restrict them from earning a living. Some female students have expressed concerns about how the *dangdut* phenomenon is not all about *goyang* but it has to be looked at in relation to the broader Indonesian society in which women are "second-class citizens." Again, we must address and take to heart these lay anthropological perspectives, which place this public cultural form within its macrocontext.

Taken together these local perspectives point out the paradox common to pop cultural phenomena in many countries, in which, on the one hand, there is exploitation of a social strata, while on the other hand, this same social strata is gaining access to economic resources or other benefits via the same cultural form. In this case, *dangdut* supports the continued structural and cultural subordination of women and the perpetuation of patriarchy as television stations, advertisers, and capitalist companies commercialize women's bodies and sexuality to market products (see also Pioquinto 1995:82–83). Women are turned into the objects of the male gaze, *goyang* fetishes, named and unnamed, which capitalist corporations, many of them multinational, scramble to use to fulfill their profit motives. Cafes and hotels also often use female bodies as *atraksi* catering to upper class customers. Women also gain economic benefits as a higher paid entertainment workforce and thereby improve the material conditions of their lives. *Dangdut* also supports the inclusion of some sexual minorities in this entertainment workforce, despite reinforcing constructions of them as mere objects of entertainment and pleasure. In addition, *dangdut* as a form of deviance, breaking the norms of the broader society that tend to emphasize a greater degree of *malu* (restraint and shyness) for women and control over their devalued persons, constitutes a form of resistance.

On a national and global level, the emergence of *dangdut* is a mixed bag. Nationally, it represents the development of a popular cultural form, *budaya rakyat*, to a more universally distributed level reaching all social strata in ways it hadn't before, in its more raw forms, with female sexuality and flirting on display and hot, nasty, sexually suggestive lyrics. The increased exposure of this cultural form opens new opportunities for *wong cilik*, women, and sexual minorities to speak and express their concerns to a broader audience. Their existential communitas has not become highly ideological or organized. Yet, its triumphant emergence on a national stage also creates opportunities for elite *priyayi* to use this cultural form, as they have used others in the past, to deliver their political messages and to further their interests. In addition, it provides another example of the cultural basis for continuing polarization between modernist, reformist-oriented, and secular, "syncretistic"-oriented social segments, with their opposing interpretations and senses of communitas. On a global level, *dangdut* not only represents another vehicle of integration into the global marketplace, but it also entails the flow of many cultural models and values from the West that are being absorbed into this cultural form and local cultures. In contrast to the aristocratic "revival-of-tradition" sort of response to globalization, Inul's *dangdut* "revolution" localizes Western and Asian cultural influences, combining them with local musical and dance styles and producing a new "modern" Indonesian identity. For many local youth who have grown bored with traditional cultural arts, contemporary *dangdut* packages an Indonesian creation incorporating many foreign ingredients into something they can enjoy.

Notes

*Reprinted by permission of the publishers from "Social Drama, Dangdut and Popular Culture," in *Islamic Spectrum in Java by Timothy Daniels* (Farnham: Ashgate, 2009).

1. Ceres Pioquinto (1995) conducted an ethnographic study of female representations in *dangdut* performances during *Sekaten* events in Surakarta (Solo).

2. Pioquinto (1995, 73–74) reports that in 1991 in Surakarta, seating for the audience created a boundary to direct contact between the audience and performers on raised stages in the *Sekaten* night market tents. There were no such boundaries in these *Sekaten*, Gembira Loka, and Purawisata events in Yogyakarta. Men stood around the stages in these venues and occasionally made direct contact with female performers.

3. The Indonesian category for male transgender and transsexual persons, *waria*, is formed through combining parts of the words *wanita* (woman) and *pria* (man).

4. Chamim et al. (2003) discuss some of the performance arts such as *tayub* or *gambyong* in rural East Java involving female dancers doing sexually suggestive moves in social settings associated with alcoholic drinks, gambling, and prostitution. On March 5, 2004, the serial "Peristiwa" aired on TV7 presenting a documentary about *waria* in the traditional melodramatic theatrical form, *ludruk*, most popular in East Java. It stated that *waria* have been a part of these performances for forty-two years and that one *waria* can sexually service around twenty men per night. It showed

waria from the troupe Warna Jaya, one of the roving *ludruk* groups dancing in *ludruk* style, while in the grounds around the performances *waria*
sex workers serviced male customers.

5. *Goyang patah-patah* involves a movement of the hips in a circular motion
   broken (*patah*) with stops at several points, and *goyang ngecor* involves hip
   swinging while standing on one leg.

6. During the last ten years of its rule, the New Order regime turned to give
   a more public, though limited, space for politico-jural expressions of Islam
   (see Hooker 2003:20; Daniels 2007:242; Tanthowi 2008:13–16).

7. In October 2008, Indonesian lawmakers passed a highly controversial anti-
   pornography law supported by several Islamic parties, organizations, and
   the government of President Susilo Bambang Yudhoyono (MSN 2008).

8. Pioquinto (1995:74) states that the "egalitarian nature of dangdut performances" was suggested by the way seating arrangement at the shows were
   "not mapped out to form or endorse prevailing social relations or power
   structures."

9. The small but influential Liberal Islam Network (JIL) espouses ideas
   along the line of Abdurrahman Wahid, Nurcholish Madjid, and other "liberal" Muslim reformers. Ulil Abshar-Abdalla (2003:3), coordinator for
   this group, wrote: "Islam is a personal activity; while organizing public
   life is entirely the product of social agreement reached through proce-
   dures of democracy" (my translation). Hooker (2003) discusses Wahid,
   Madjid, and two other "liberal" Muslim reformers, Hazairin and Harun
   Nasution.

AFTERWORD: COMMENTARY

James Peacock

Timothy Daniels has inspired and organized an excellent volume, neatly pairing two countries, Malaysia and Indonesia, with two kinds of forms from each: electronic media (including cinema, television, and recorded music) and live performance, including ritual theater, dance, and song. Together, these fields span a wide spectrum and they reflect virtuoso fieldwork. First, let us applaud the virtuoso fieldwork. Fieldwork of this depth demands expert performances parallel to the artistic performances; such fieldwork entails language skill, scholarly knowledge, technical recording, physical stamina, and psychic sensibility plus toughness and courage, all of which can be appreciated only by those who have done such work. The fruits of this immense labor are huge and will be appreciated and treasured increasingly as time erases the forms disclosed. The primary value of this volume, then, is in the detailed descriptions of these art forms, captured at a certain juncture in time and place.

Surveying this spectrum of performances, one faces this question: what are the key themes and issues? The volume juxtaposes piety and popular art, the piety of concern being primarily Islam. A guiding question, then, is, what is the influence of Islam on all of these forms? More broadly, of religion on artistic creativity? And how both these forces, religion, and creativity—especially the creativity that is rooted in localized and syncretistic theater and culture—meet global forces?

A blunt answer is that the live performances, including the folk ritual theater forms (e.g., *topeng*, *ludruk*, and *main puteri*), struggle more but perhaps achieve better than the electronic media such as cinema in sustaining the deep genius of culture against restricting ethics such as Islamic piety. However, both live and electronic forms accost not only Islam but also global forces, which can also threaten local culture by dissolving and eradicating it in favor of foreign and global culture, pop or otherwise. Islam, which itself is global in a special way, is arguably a strong defense against global tidal waves. As the chapters in this volume demonstrate, Islamic and local cultures can unite as well as compete, and so can global and local cultures. Even more, some synthesis of all three, syncretic, Islamic, and global may be the most viable survival strategy. However this may be, let us consider each chapter.

Main puteri or *mak yong*, for example, in Malaya and *topeng* and *ludruk* dance in Indonesia, the three ritual theater forms, are described elegantly, by Hardwick and by Ross and Sunardi. All three draw on long localized histories with remarkably rich dimensions. *Main Puteri* heals, seduces, entrances, deploying a pan-Southeast Asian resonance between micro and macro cosmos, treating the body as microcosm of the universal macrocosm. Also, the body is conceived as having a female and a male half; hence women play refined male heroes, expressing the refined masculinity of a divine king fused with the "quotidian femininity of a Kelantanese villager." *Main Puteri*, then, combines a "vertical" hierarchy (micro and macro) with a "horizontal" opposition (male and female) to produce a supercharged bodily symbol of unity of forces and energies. No wonder that dance/drama/ritual can heal and empower!

Topeng, too, mines an incredibly rich spectrum of meanings, symbols, traditions, sexualities, many of which are documented by Laurie Ross's footnotes that point to her dissertation, and lead us through layers of history, culture, and context to the power of the form itself.

Both of these ritual theater forms, *Main Puteri* in Malaya and *Topeng* in Indonesia, are threatened by Islamic orthodoxies and ethics, for example, PAS ISLAM in Malaya. Both survive and even thrive by adapting, perhaps drastically changing, for instance, when *Topeng* players become *ronggeng* dancers thence prostitutes for the Japanese forces who occupied Indonesia during World War II. Today, illustrating a more recent adaptation, *Topeng* has won a battle though perhaps not a war by being adopted by one of the largest Islamic schools (*pesantren*) in Indonesia as a required curriculum within an Islamic framework. *Main Puteri* also assumes an Islamic shape, which makes it possible for a talented *dalang* (the narrating singer of puppet plays, the *wayang*) to continue performing. Adopting a religious guise by *Main Puteri* rather than employing his beautiful voice in *wayang* as *dalang* singing, he forsakes a less acceptable expression to pious Islam, than *Main Puteri* because *wayang* is more a "popular" art than a "pious" religion, while *Main Puteri* apparently has some degree of religious identity. But the gender ambiguity and Hinduistic cosmos of *Main Puteri* also clash with Islamic orthodoxy as does the magical underlay of *Topeng*.

Daniels' study of *dangdut* highlights an intense conflict and mix of piety and popularity, with the latter focused on female sexuality that also conveys an aspect of Islamic culture. The *dangdut* singer/ dancer is usually female, though one star performer is male. While the music and song style reflects near Eastern cultural influence in contrast to Indonesian forms such as *krontjong* or classical court singing such as *majapat*, the singer's display of body, in clothing and dancing, is very sexually provocative, perhaps akin to "belly dancing" in the near Eastern and Mediterranean style. Buttocks and their movements are especially provocative. The performers flirt with Islamic authority, pushing the conflict between popularity and piety skillfully back and forth between attraction and oppression. The trick is to intensify attraction while or by violating piety but not to cross the line into evoking arrest or termination of performance.

The Malay singer analyzed by Thompson (2002) also plays on the counterpoint between piety and popularity but in a different and less physically provocative mode. Romance, both personal and ethnic/ national, is her vector of power. While conveying an Islamic identity she also conveys a Malay identity, capturing the convergence of the two in the Malaya (as well as Malaysian) context: *Masuk Melaju* (becoming Malay) is also to *Masuk* Islam (become Muslim). This connection of Malay identity with Muslim identity is interwoven with the idea of romantic love (*cinta*). Romantic love in this Malay (and Indonesian) context is in turn interwoven with global, especially Western, youth culture, expressed in much popular culture but set against a backdrop of contrasting norms, such as arranged marriage supported by both Islamic and *adat* (localized, regional, ethnic) custom and values. Thus, the songs translated here may seem simple, even naive and stereotyped, but are played against a multilayered societal backdrop.

That backdrop would seem even more multilayered for Indonesia. Such a convergence of ethnicity and religious identity (*masuk Melayu*) would seem less possible in the Indonesian context, where not all Indonesian ethnicities identify with Islam. At the same time, Indonesia separates what Sukarno termed "the romance of revolution" from Islam and renders it an anticolonial nationalism. Here the stronger history and experience of nationalistic revolution for Indonesia separates from Islamic identity; recall Sukarno's NASAKOM (NAS is nationalism, A is *Agama* [religion], and KOM is Communism). Sukarno thus separated these three identities while also integrating them into a single, syncretistic identity. In fact, conflict between the piety of Islam and hopes by some for an Islamic state versus Indonesian (especially Javanese) nationalism and cultural identity has been a dominant theme since Diponegoro through Gestapu; Diponegoro fought the Javanese court under the banner of Islam while Gestapu pitted Muslims against nonpious or non-Muslim ethnic Javanese and others, ostensibly Communist but usually simply not pious Muslims and frequently Sukarnoist nationalists. Such complexities prevent a simple equation of national and Islamic identity in Indonesia and hence complicate readings (or hearings) of the Malay song playing on such identity.

Sunardi's account seems to point to less conflict between Islamic orthodoxy and syncretism and between gender identities. One actor/ dancer (Lestradi) on whom she focuses appears to move comfortably between a male role in life and a female role on stage. Sunardi enriches considerably other excellent work on gender identity (cf. Boellstorff 2005), on the one hand, and on popular theater and dance, on the other. Note, for example, my own work on *Ludruk* that she cites. Her account greatly enriches mine because my contact with female impersonators was limited to conversations and mingling backstage at performances and interviews of several hours each with several impersonators who shared a meal with my wife and me at our residence and narrated their life stories. These actors dressed as men off stage, so far as I saw, but they did not, so far as they recounted, function as husbands to women and as fathers to their own children. One of them, as Sunardi notes, told of origins in a strongly Islamic and perhaps Arab family and recounted that he had to give up his status as the oldest son in order to live as a female impersonator acting in *Ludruk*. Later, I did fieldwork among a pious Muslim group, Muhammadiyans, and I did not see female impersonators among the Muhammadiyan men or women participating in the wide range of activities of Muhammadiyah, whether in Java, Sumatra, Ternate, Sumbawa, or Sulawesi. In this context, then, Sunardi's account is particularly suggestive. It may imply, as does Laurie's, that while Islamic orthodoxy or reformist puritanism (as in Muhammadiyah) and piety may oppose or exclude androgynous gender identity, on the whole, certain Muslim contexts open a space for gender identity flexibility that is either new and evolving or apparent "below the radar" of orthodoxy.

To turn to cinema, both in Indonesia and Malaysia, Islamic values have become salient but differently. In Indonesia the Islamic focus has struggled against secular culture, as in the vivid example of the Islamic film that drew large crowds of the pious to the unfamiliar setting of Menteng, where they were accosted by pictures of bare-breasted women advertising the normally secular and even lurid or pornographic films usually shown in this privileged suburb of Jakarta. One gets an impression from this very thorough survey of Indonesian

Islamic films that the Islamic worldview squelches human experience or directs it into somewhat narrow channels. An example is the film showing the biography of KH A. Dahlan, founder of Muhammadiyah. Dahlan was an extremely admirable leader but one who led through subdued rather than charismatic actions; such an action is the incident noted from the film where Dahlan chalked in the correct directions of a mosque. He then replicated this corrective chalking for a neighborhood chapel by also correcting the Sultan's palace mosque. Such a portrayal is of piety expressed by a technical act; it was not a highly dramatic volcanic eruption as in the case of a Martin Luther who announces "here I stand!"

The Malaysian films are described by Daniels in excellent ethnographic richness by narrating plots that focus on the place of Islamic ethics in controlling romance. While the ethic is controlling, diversity does loom in earlier films, as in the affair between the Malay Muslim woman and the Chinese lover. The death of the earlier female filmmaker Yasmin Ahmad, who was considered "too pluralistic and impious," ended this time of diversity. Yasmin was succeeded by a male director who led a transition to a stricter less pluralistic Islamic ethic and plot in the Nur Kasih series. Daniels shows how PAS Parti Islam SeMalaysia and UMNO-led federal government *dakwah* creates a Muslim cultural sphere that imposes more piety.

These clashes between religious orthodoxy, for example, PAS piety and art, culture, creativity, and tradition is, of course, not restricted to Islam or to Malaysia and Indonesia or to the current time. I recall a clash in 1970 between the great poet and dramatist Rendra and Muhammadiyah who brought him to a trial I witnessed accusing him of misquoting scripture in his play *Barzanji* about the birth and life of Muhammad. He responded: drama is not about scripture but an "oomph, an oomph and an oomph," punctuating each "oomph" by punching his fist into his hand. Here, five years after Gestapu, Islam asserted control. Rendra entered prison and also converted to Islam. Earlier, before Gestapu, in the early 1960s, the *Ludruk* plays that I studied put Islamic piety on the defensive, with clowns scapegoating pious Muslim capitalists. I estimated that in these 1962–1963 plays the most deadly conflicts were not between classes or nations as in colonies but between pious Muslims, *santri*, and impious syncretists *abangan*. At this time, Sukarno's time, communists and nationalists were dominant, and Islam was a minority culture. Piety was swamped by popular culture, one might say, and the popular culture exemplified by *Ludruk* often was allied with a Marxist or Communist perspective but also a richly indigenous syncretic one, *Kejawen*.

Today, these cinemas and plays suggest that Islam gains firmer and more comprehensive control while syncretic culture with its innuendoes of gender, magic, and art loses force or goes underground perhaps sustaining deeper roots, as may be the case with the ritual dramas such as *Topeng* and *Main Puteri*.

Another question, though, is the force that both Islam and syncretic culture faces, globalization. Islam may suppress syncretic culture but by its very puritanical strict and aggressive posture may be better suited to defend localized culture against globalization. Or does a combination of syncretic, doctrinaire Islam, and a global outreach offer best chance to survive and thrive?

These comments accentuate the conflicts between Islam and syncretism while losing richness of the ethnographic portrayals of the plays, rituals, and films themselves, so the reader is advised to turn to these in the individual presentations.

Whether or not these comments are on target, the chapters offer excellent account and analysis of these very lively arts within Islamic SE Asia.

PIETY, POPULAR CULTURE, ARTS: GENERAL CONSIDERATIONS

Expand our lens now beyond Southeast Asia and the particular forms explicated. What general dynamics both illuminate and are illuminated by these Southeast Asian studies?

"Deceptive bedazzlement . . . a realm of irresponsible indulgence and secret lovelessness" is the beguiling comment Max Weber offered to contrast the arts with religion, thereby comparing popular culture and piety (1961:211). Weber saw the arts as offering an ersatz (substitute) salvation from the drudgery of everyday and pragmatic life and work. That is, the arts provide momentary "salvation" through the sensuous forms and performances while requiring no ethically guided creation of community (brotherhood of man) in return. Religion, by contrast, does require such ethically guided "brotherhood" as part of the salvation one gains by religious commitment. Put simply, an audience goes home after a performance without obligation to fulfill ethical community work, while a congregation retains such an obligation even if a religious performance concludes.

Weber's theoretical and "ideal typical" formulation, that is, art is a "deceptive bedazzlement" offering symbolic salvation without ethical obligation, echoes theologies and ethics espoused by major religious traditions, notably the Abrahamic ones, Judeo-Christian, and Islamic. These traditions tend to demean and mistrust the arts because of their deceptive bedazzlement. By comparison, the Hindu Buddhist traditions, which Weber termed "exemplary" rather than "ethical" are perhaps less rigidly judgmental of the arts. (A visual illustration is Borobodur, the great Buddhist monument. It is organized in levels from bottom to top, with bottom depicting sensuality of living humans and top spiritual purity of meditating Buddha figures. The teaching is presumably that the spiritual unity encompasses the fleshly levels instead of repressing them. One must caution against "Orientalist" idealization of mystical or meditative paths such as the ones Borobodur suggest, but the comparison is along the line Weber intimates.)

Loosely following a Weberian (or similar theoretical direction), other comparisons are implied. These include flexible interplay of spiritual and ethical emphases, of gender identities, and a somewhat paradoxical acceptance of hierarchy in some domains (e.g., divine kingship and caste or class hierarchy) with equality in others (e.g., status of women and of the feminine in comparison to men and the masculine attributes). A related flexibility is acceptance of interplay of mind and body. Examples range from meditation to dance. *Kebatinan* (meditation) is claimed to enhance awareness so that a somewhat meditative state while riding a scooter is said to create "eyes in the back of the head" and refined heroes such as Arjuna (sometimes performed by women) defeat crass physically powerful monster opponents by tranquil mental and spiritual states that send the monsters tumbling with a flick of the wrist or finger. Further flexibilities include accepting rituals, shrines, and other material manifestations of faith by contrast to puritanical condemnation of such manifestations as idolatry or "shirk." Still further possibilities include communal union with spiritual energy, as in nationalism and revolution (what Edith and Victor Turner deemed *communitas*), which contrasts with reformist movements that destroy culture and community in order to purify the faith (Turner 2012).

Granted, this is a large menu of tendencies and connections, but they sum up as a kind of holism. We can test or explore their plausibilities through the examples provided in this volume.

Obvious is the tension between piety and the arts, where Islamic piety opposes the artistic performances of dance, *dalang*, and other arts that have grown up nurtured by Hinduistic, Buddhistic, and syncretistic civilization. That this syncretic civilization (*kejawen*) is sustained by the kingdoms and courts, including a syncretic sultanate, may seem paradoxical since the courts and quasi-caste system imposes hierarchy that is restrictive and oppressive in some respects, compared to the ostensibly democratic thrust of Islam that places God above all humans, hence no human is God or god-like. Spirituality, too, is sustained by the court civilization, even though logically the spirit transcends any objective hierarchy. But the courts and their civilization nurture the arts and spirituality while purist Islam often suppresses arts and spirituality.

How do gender identities fit into these patterns? Islam gives and takes away empowerment for women. Court dancers manifest a certain empowerment, that of the arts, of refinement, of sexuality, while pious Islam restricts women in these ways. However, reformist Islam, such as Muhammadiyah, offers a limited degree of empowerment, notably freedom to take initiatives, as in cooperatives and business. The photograph (see cover image) that I took at the opening of Muhammadiyah 2010 congress or Muktamar juxtaposes court dancers and Muhammadiyah women, the former displaying their bodies and the latter covering them, but the latter are energetic in work while the former are displayed in dance.

This brings us to gender identity. The arts appear more open to crossing identities. Hardwick, Sunardi, and others write about dance and drama where men play women, while others forms (e.g., *Wayang Wong*) have women playing men. Still other forms, for example, in India connect such crossovers to theological arguments about rebirth as another gender or to androgyny of gods and spiritual figures in Hinduism. Whatever theological arguments are generated, the phenomenological or psychological aspect is apparent also; Sunardi describes an actor's feeling as a woman when playing onstage and as a man when offstage. "Liminality" is the broad concept or field within which such transformations and crossovers occur. The art forms open a field for shifting and joining identities separated in life. Such shifting and joining can become rigidified, however, as when a sex-change surgery is performed or can be institutionalized, as when the Southeast Asian equivalent of a *berdache* (the native American role, often shamanistic, whereby a man lives as a woman) becomes a social role. In Southeast Asia as in Native American and other cultures, such a role can be part of being a shaman.

Witnessing such juxtapositions of gender identities expressed in performance, one is reminded of the internal juxtapositions that Carl Jung and countless Jungians name anima and animus. While recent dramatizations such as the film *A Dangerous Method* crassly simplify, major point of the Jungians is how such interplay psychologically can be part of "individuation," a "journey into wholeness" that entails mythological, ritual, and dream or other symbolic representations of male and female (animus and anima) forces or identities at work in life and in therapy. The performative expressions both illuminate and are illuminated by such psychological explorations. In turn, the psychologist and psychiatrist need the enrichment of performance studies to get beyond abstracted texts of myth or symbol to the live richness of performance in living complexity.

These patterns, whether general or illustrated in Southeast Asia, connect to the wider world of Islam or of global forces. Questions to ponder: How do these artistic instances connect to tendencies in Islam, for example, evangelism, commercial deployment, or politics and violence? What are implications for peace and conflict, as Islam's evolution joins religious movements and directions in other traditions, for example, Pentecostalism or Hinduism? What comparisons can one make to India, for example, where pious reformist Muslims attack shrines of Sufis, whose artistic manifestations somewhat parallel those described here for Southeast Asia? (Umashankar 2012). Another very pertinent example is the interplay of the Zar spirituality in Cairo in contrast to the Muslim Brotherhood and Islamic piety coming to the fore since the Arab Spring (cf. Umashankar 2012 and Hadidi 2007).

These questions invite an interchange that is regrettably rare—between those who treat the political and global forces of the "real world" and those who explore the internal forces of psychology and culture as expressed in the arts. As charismatic leaders such as Sukarno realized, the former are energized by the latter, hence to understand either one must be nourished by the rich diet of the arts, performance, and the study thereof.

References

Abshar-Abdalla, Ulil. *Islam Liberal & Fundamental: Sebuah Pertarungan Wacana.* Yogyakarta: eLSAQ Press, 2003.

Ahearn, Laura M. *Living Language: An Introduction to Linguistic Anthropology.* West Sussex: Wiley-Blackwell, 2012.

Ahmad Fauzi, A. H. "Islamist Realignments and the Rebranding of the Muslim Youth Movement of Malaysia." *Contemporary Southeast Asia* 30, 2 (2008): 215–240.

Akbarnia, Ladan with Francesca Leoni. *Light of the Sufis: The Mystical Arts of Islam.* Houston: Museum of Fine Arts, 2010.

Al Chaidar. Sepak terjang KW. *IX Abu Toto Syech A.S. Panji Gumilang Menyelewengkan NKA-NII Pasca S.M. Kartooewirjo.* Jakarta: Madani Press, 2000.

Algar, Hamid. "Amāma." In *Encyclopedia Iranica*, 1:9. Ed. Ehsan Yarshater, 919–921. New York: Columbia University Press, 1982.

———. "Silent and Vocal Dhikr in the Naqshbandī Order." In *Akten des VII. Kongresses für Arabistik und Islamwissenschaft. Göttengen, 15. Bis 22. August 1974,* 39–46. Göttingen: Vandenhoeck & Ruprecht, 1976.

———. "Some Notes on the Naqshbandī Tarīqat in Bosnia." *Die Welt des Islams. New Series* 13, 3–4 (1971): 168–203.

———. *Wahhabism: A Critical Essay.* Oneonta, NY: Islamic Publications International, 2002.

Andaya, B. W. and L. Y. Andaya. *A History of Malaysia.* Honolulu: University of Hawai'i Press, 2001.

Anderson, Benedict R. O'G. *Language and Power: Exploring Political Cultures in Indonesia.* Ithaca, NY: Cornell University Press, 1990.

———. *Mythology and the Tolerance of the Javanese.* Ithaca: Cornell Modern Indonesia Project. Cornell University, [1965] 1996.

Anderson, Benedict R. O'G. and Ruth McVey. *A Preliminary Analysis of the October 1, 1965 Coup in Indonesia.* Ithaca, NY: Cornell University Press, 1971.

Ardjo, Irawati Durban. Tari Sunda 1940–1965: Karya Raden Tjetje Somantri dan Kiprah BKI. Bandung: Pusbitari Press, 2008.

Arnold, Sir Thomas. *Painting in Islam.* New York: Dover [1928], 1965.

Attar, Farid ud-Din. *The Conference of the Birds.* London: Penguin, 1984.

Azra, Azyumardi. "Islamic Thought: Theory, Concepts, and Doctrines in the Context of Southeast Asian Islam." In *Islam in Southeast Asia: Political,*

Social and Strategic Challenges for the 21st Century. Ed. K. S. Nathan and M. H. Kamali, 3–21. Singapore:Institute of Southeast Asian Studies, 2005.

———. *The Origins of Islamic Reformism in Southeast Asia. Networks of Malay-Indonesian and Middle-Eastern "Ulamā" in the Seventeeth and Eighteenth Centuries.* Honolulu: University of Hawaii Press, 2004.

Babad Djalasutra: Njarijosaken Lampahanipun Pangeran Panggung Ladjeng Karan Kijai Djalasutra. Yogyakarta: Sumodidjojo, Mahadewa, 1956.

Bacqué-Grammont, Jean-Louis, Semavi Eyice, Nathalie Clayer, and Thierry Zarcone, eds, *Anatolia Moderna II Yeni Anadolu: Derviches et Cimetieres Ottomans.* Paris/Istanbul: Librairie d'Amérique et d'Orient/Institut Français d'Etudes Anatoliennes d'Istanbul, 1991.

Baer, Eva. *The Human Figure in Islamic Art: Inheritances and Islamic Transformations.* Costa Mesa, CA: Mazda, 2004.

Baker, Patricia. *Islam and the Religious Arts.* London and New York: Continuum, 2004.

Banks, David J. *Malay Kinship.* Philadelphia: ISHI, 1983.

———. "Resurgent Islam and Malay Rural Culture: Malay Novelists and the Invention of Culture." *American Ethnologist* 17, 3 (1990): 531–548.

Barendredgt, Bart. "Pop, Politics and Piety: *Nasyid* Boy Band Music in Muslim Southeast Asia." In *Islam and Popular Culture in Indonesia and Malaysia.* Ed. Andrew N. Weintraub, 235–256. New York: Routledge, 2011.

Bateson, Gregory and Margaret Mead. *Balinese Character: A Photographic Analysis.* Special Publication of the New York Academy of Sciences, Vol. 2. New York: New York Academy of Sciences, 1942.

Beatty, Andrew. *Varieties of Javanese Religion: An Anthropological Account.* Cambridge: Cambridge University Press, 1999.

"Belanda: Film Fitna VS Ayat-ayat Cinta" (The Netherlands: Film Fitna Vs. Love Verses). October 5, 2008. *Berita Muslim.* http://beritamuslim.blogspot. com/2008/10/belanda-film-fitna-vs-ayat-ayat cinta.html. Accessed August 27, 2012.

Biran, Misbach Yusa. Personal interview, November 9, 2009.

Blackburn, Susan, Bianca J. Smith, and Siti Syamsiyatun. "Introduction." In *Indonesian Islam in a New Era: How Women Negotiate Their Muslim Identities.* Ed. Susan Blackburn, Bianca J. Smith, and Siti Syamsiyatun, 1–21. Clayton: Monash University Press, 2008.

Blackwood, Evelyn. *Falling Into the Lesbi World: Desire and Difference in Indonesia.* Honolulu: University of Hawaii Press, [2005] 2010.

———. "Gender Transgression in Colonial and Postcolonial Indonesia." *Journal of Asian Studies* 64, 4 (2005): 849–879.

Blackwood, Evelyn and Saskia E. Wieringa. "Globalization, Sexuality, and Silences: Women's Sexualities and Masculinities in an Asian Context." In *Women's Sexualities And Masculinities in a Globalizing Asia.* Ed. Saskia E. Wieringa, Evelyn Blackwood, and Abha Bhaiya, 1–20. New York: Palgrave Macmillan, 2007.

Bloembergen, Marieke. *Colonial Spectacles: The Netherlands and the Dutch East Indies at the World Exhibitions, 1880–1931*. Singapore: Singapore University Press, 2006.

Boden, Ragna. "The 'Gestapu' Events of 1965 in Indonesia: New Evidence from Russian and German Archives." *Bijdragen tot de Taal-, Land- en Volkenkunde* 163 (2007): 507–528.

Boellstorff, Tom. "Between Religion and Desire: Being Muslim and *Gay* in Indonesia." *American Anthropologist* 107, 4 (2005a): 575–585.

———. *The Gay Archipelago: Sexuality and Nation in Indonesia*. Princeton and Oxford: Princeton University Press, 2005b.

———. "Playing Back the Nation: *Waria*, Indonesian Transvestites." *Cultural Anthropology* 19, 2 (2004): 159–195.

Bowen, John R. *Muslims through Discourse: Religion and Ritual in Gayo Society*. Princeton: Princeton University Press, 1993.

Braconier, A. de. "Het Prostitutie-vraagstuk in Nederlandsch-Indië." *Indische Gids* 55 (1933): 906–928.

Brakel, Clara. "Character Types and Movement Styles in Traditional Javanese Theater." In *Performance in Java and Bali: Studies of Narrative, Theatre, Music, and Dance*. Ed. Bernard Arps, 59–71. London: School of Oriental and African Studies, University of London, 1993.

———. "Masked Dances, Spirit Worship and the Introduction of Islam in Java." *Assaph: Studies in the Theatre* 9 (1993): 19–28.

Brakel-Papenhuyzen, Clara. *Classical Javanese Dance: The Surakarta Tradition and Its Terminology*. Leiden: KITLV Press, 1995.

Bramantyo, Hanung. *Jagad Pakeliran*. http://hanungbramantyo.multiply. com. Accessed April 14, 2012.

———. Personal interview, February 10, 2012.

———. Personal interview, September 7, 2012.

Brandes, J. L. A. *Pararaton (Ken Arok) of Het Boek der Koningen Van Tumapel en Van Majapahit*. Batavia: Albrecht 'S Gravenhage/M. Nijhoff, 1920.

Bravmann, René A. "Gyinna-Gyinna: Making the Djinn Manifest." *African Arts* 10, 3 (1977): 46–52.

Brenner, Suzanne. "Reconstructing Self and Society: Javanese Muslim Women and 'The Veil.'" *American Ethnologist* 23, 4 (1996): 673–697.

———. *The Domestication of Desire: Women, Wealth, and Modernity in Java*. Princeton: Princeton University Press, 1998.

Brownrigg, Henry. *Betel Cutters from the Samuel Eilenberg Collection*. New York: Thames and Hudson, 1992.

Bruinessen, Martin van. "Origins and Development of the Sufi Orders (Tarekat) in Southeast Asia." *Studia Islamika* 1, 1 (1994): 1–23.

———. "Shaykh `Abd al-Qadir al-Jilani and the Qadiriyya in Indonesia." *Journal of the History of Sufism* 1–2 (2000): 361–395.

———. "'Traditionalist' and 'Islamist' Pesantren in Contemporary Indonesia." Paper presented at ISIM workshop, "The Madrasa in Asia." Leiden,

May 2004. http://www.hum.uu.nl/medewerkers/m.vanbruinessen /publications/pesantren_2.htm. Accessed April 15, 2012.

———. "Wahhabi Influences in Indonesia, Real and Imagined." Summary of paper presented at the *Journée d'Etudes du CEIFR (EHESS-CNRS) et MSH sur le Wahhabisme*. Ecole des Hautes Etudes en Sciences Sociales /Maison des Sciences de l'Homme. Paris, June 10, 2002. http://www .archivesaudiovisuelles.fr/11/163/martin_van_bruinessen-7.pdf. Accessed January 31, 2007.

Butler, Judith. *Bodies that Matter: On the Discursive Limits of "Sex."* New York and London: Routledge, 1993.

———. *Gender Trouble: Feminism and the Subversion of Identity*. New York and London: Routledge, [1990] 1999.

Carey, Peter and Vincent Houben. "Spirited Srikandhis and Sly Sumbadras: The Social, Political and Economic Role of Women at the Central Javanese Courts in the 18th and Early 19th Centuries." In *Indonesian Women in Focus: Past and Present Notions*. Ed. Elsbeth Locher-Scholten and Anke Niehof, 12–42. Dordrecht and Providence: Foris, 1987.

Carpenter, Bruce W. *Javanese Antique Furniture and Folk Art. The David B. Smith and James Tirtoprodjo Collections*. Singapore: Editions Didier Millet, 2009.

Carsten, Janet. *The Heat of the Hearth*. Oxford: Oxford University Press, 1997.

Chamim, Asykuri Ibn, Syamsul Hidayat, Muhammad Sayuti, and Fajar Riza Ul Haq. *Purifikasi & Reproduksi Budaya di Pantai Utara Jawa*. Ed. Zakiyuddin Baidhaway. Surakarta: Pusat Studi Budaya dan Perubahan Sosial, Universitas Muhammadiyah Surakarta, 2003.

Chinyong Liow, Joseph. *Piety and Politics: Islamism in Contemporary Malaysia*. Oxford: Oxford University Press, 2009.

Chong, T. "The Emergent Politics of *Islam Hadhari*." In *Malaysia: Recent Trends and Challenges*. Ed. S. Sweek-Hock and K. Kesavapany, 26–46. Singapore: Institute of Southeast Asian Studies, 2006.

Cohen, M. I. "*Brai* in Performance: Religious Ecstasy and Art in Java." In *Divine Inspirations Music & Islam in Indonesia*. Ed. David D. Harnish and Anne K. Rasmussen, 132–160. New York: Oxford University Press, 2011.

Creswell, K. A. C. "The Lawfulness of Painting in Early Islam." *Ars Islamica* 11–12 (1946): 159–166.

Crill, Rosemary, ed. *Textiles from India: The Global Trade*. Calcutta: Seagull Books, 2006.

Crouch, Gregory. "Dutch Film against Islam Is Released on Internet." *New York Times*. March 28, 2008. http://www.nytimes.com/2008/03/28/world /europe/28dutch.html. Accessed August 27, 2012.

Daniels, Timothy P. *Building Cultural Nationalism in Malaysia: Identity, Representation, and Citizenship*. New York: Routledge, 2005.

———. *Islamic Spectrum in Java*. Farnham and Burlington: Ashgate, 2009.

———. "Liberals, Moderates, and Jihadists: Protesting Danish Cartoons in Indonesia." *Contemporary Islam* 1 (2007): 231–246.

———. "Urban Space, Belonging, and Inequality in Multi-ethnic Housing Estates of Melaka, Malaysia." *Identities: Global Studies in Culture and Power* 17 (2010): 176–203.

Deeb, Lara. *An Enchanted Modern: Gender and Public Piety in Shi'i Lebanon.* Princeton: Princeton University Press, 2006.

Dhamija, Jasleen. "The Geography of Textiles." In *Textiles from India: The Global Trade.* Ed. Rosemary Crill, 263–267. Calcutta: Seagull Books, 2006.

Diamond, Catherine. "Fire in the Banana's Belly: Bali's Female Performers Essay the Masculine Arts." *Asian Theatre Journal* 25, 2 (2008): 231–271.

Dols, Michael W. *Majnūn: The Madman in Medieval Islamic Society.* Ed. Diana E. Immisch. Oxford, UK: Clarendon Press, 1992.

Downing, Sonja. "Flirting with *Kebyar*: The Intrigue of Dynamic Gender in Balinese Dance." Unpublished paper presented at the Society for Ethnomusicology 54th Annual Meeting. Mexico City, Mexico. November 21, 2009.

Dramatic Durian. "'Nur Kasih' Banking on Its Fans." May 14, 2011. http://dramaticdurian.com/2011/05/nur-kasih-banking-on-its-fans.html. Accessed January 10, 2012.

Duranti, Alessandro. *Linguistic Anthropology.* Cambridge: Cambridge University Press, 1997.

Echols, John M. dan Hassan Shadily (Echols, John M. and Hassan Shadily). *Kamus Indonesia-Inggris: An Indonesian-English Dictionary.* Jakarta: PT Gramedia Pustaka Utama, 1994.

Edwards, Penny. "Half-Cast: Staging Race in British Burma." *Postcolonial Studies* 5, 3 (2002): 279–295.

Ensiklopedi Jakarta, "Ernest Alfred Hardouin." *Dinas Komunikasi, Informatika dan Kehumasan Pemprov DKI Jakarta.* http://www.jakarta.go.id/jakv1/encyclopedia/detail/538. Accessed July 31, 2012.

Faruk and Aprinus Salam. *Hanya Inul.* Yogyakarta: Pustaka Marwa, 2003.

Fealy, Greg and Katharine McGregor. "Nahdlatul Ulama and the Killings of 1965–66: Religion, Politics and Remembrance." *Indonesia* 89 (2010): 37–60.

Fillah, Efa. "Merindukan Islaminya Film Islam" (Missing the Islamic Characteristics of Islamic Films). Suara Hidayatullah. June 30, 2010. http://majalah.hidayatullah.com/?p=1242. Accessed April 14, 2012.

Firth, Raymond. "Ritual and Drama in Malay Spirit Mediumship." *Comparative Studies in Society and History* 19 (1967): 190–207.

Fischer, Johan. *Proper Islamic Consumption: Shopping among the Malays in Modern Malaysia.* Copenhagen: NIAS Press, 2008.

"Fitna versus Ayat-ayat Cinta" (Fitna versus Love Verses). *Sigombak.blogspot.com.* April 6, 2008. http://sigombak.blogspot.com/2008/04/fitna-versus-ayat-ayat-cinta.html. Accessed August 27, 2012.

Foley, Kathy. "My Bodies: The Performer in West Java." *TDR: The Drama Review* T126 (1990): 62–80.

Forbes, B. D. and Mahan, J. *Religion and Popular Culture in America.* Berkeley: University of California Press, 2000.

Forum. "Moral Bangsa di Bokong Inul." May 11, 2003: 27–33.

———. 'Selamat Datang di Negeri Dangdut." March 30, 2003: 47–58.

Frisk, Sylva. *Submitting to God: Women and Islam in Urban Malaysia.* Seattle: University of Washington Press, 2009.

Fuad, Muhammad. "Islam, Modernity and Muhammadiyah Education Program." *Inter-Asia Cultural Studies* 5, 3 (2004): 400–414.

Geertz, Clifford. *The Interpretation of Cultures.* New York: Basic Books, 1973.

———. *Negara: The Theatre State in Nineteenth-Century Bali.* Princeton: Princeton University Press, 1980.

———. *The Religion of Java.* Chicago and London: University of Chicago Press, 1960.

Ghulam-Sarwar Yousof. "The Kelantan 'Mak Yong' Dance Theater: A Study of Performance Structure." PhD Dissertation, Department of Drama and Theatre, University of Hawaii, 1976.

———. "*Mak Yong*: The Ancient Malay Dance-Theatre." *Asian Studies* 20 (April–August–December 1982): 108–122.

———. *Panggung Inu: Essays on Traditional Malay Theatre.* Singapore: Unipress, 2004.

———. *Panggung Semar Aspects of Traditional Malay Theatre.* Petaling Jaya: Tempo Sdn. Bhd., 1992.

Graaf, H. J. de. *Chinese Muslims in Java in the 15th and 16th Centuries: The Malay Annals of Semarang and Cerbon.* Trans. and comments Th. G. Pigeaud. Ed. M. C. Ricklefs. Melbourne, Australia: Monash Papers of Southeast Asia, No. 12, 1984.

Grabar, Oleg. *The Formation of Islamic Art.* New Haven: Yale University Press, 1973.

Gunawan, Rudy FX. *Mengebor Kemunafikan: Inul, Seks dan Kekuasaan.* Yogyakarta: Kawan Pustaka and Galang Press, 2003.

Haan, F. de. *Priangan: De Preanger-Regentschappen onder het Nederlandsch Bestour tot 1811.* 4v. Batavia: G. Kolff / Mart. Nijhoff, 1910–1912.

Hadidi, Hager El. "Survivals and Surviving: Belonging to Zar in Cairo." PhD Dissertation, University of North Carolina, 2007.

Hadisutjipto, Sudibjo Z., trans. *Babad Cerbon.* Jakarta: Department of Education and Culture, 1979.

Halberstam, Judith. *Female Masculinity.* Durham and London: Duke University Press, 1998.

Hardouin, E., W. L. Ritter, and H. M. Lange. *Java Tooneelen uit het Leven Karakterschetsen en Kleederdragten van Java's Bewoners in Afbeeldingen naar de Natuur Geteekend.* Leiden: A. W. Sythof, 1855.

Hardwick, Patricia Ann. "Bridging the Secular and the Sacred: Movement, Metaphor and Meaning in the *Tarian Menghadap Rebab.*" In *Global and Local Dance in Performance.* Ed. Mohd Anis Md Nor and Revathi Murugappan, 431–448. Kuala Lumpur: Cultural Centre University of Malaya and Ministry of Culture, Arts and Heritage, 2005.

———. "Stories of the Wind: The Role of Mak Yong in Shamanistic Healing in Kelantan, Malaysia." PhD Dissertation, Department of Folklore and Ethnomusicology, Department of Anthropology, Indiana University, Bloomington, Indiana. On file at the Indiana University Library and available through ProQuest, University Microfilms International, # 3386680, 2009.

Harnish, David D. and Anne K. Rasmussen. "Introduction: The World of Islam in the Music of Indonesia." In *Divine Inspirations Music & Islam in Indonesia.* Ed. David D. Harnish and Anne K. Rasmussen, 5–41. New York: Oxford University Press, 2011.

Headly, Stephen C. *Durga's Mosque: Cosmology, Conversion and Community in Central Javanese Islam.* Singapore: Institute of Southeast Asian Studies, 2004.

Hefner, Robert W. *Civil Islam: Muslims and Democratization in Indonesia.* Princeton: Princeton University Press, 2000.

———. "Islamic Schools, Social Movements, and Democracy in Indonesia." In *Making Modern Muslims: The Politics of Islamic Education in Southeast Asia.* Ed. Robert W. Hefner, 55–105. Honolulu: University of Hawaii Press, 2009.

———. "Islamizing Java? Religion and Politics in Rural East Java." *Journal of Asian Studies* 46, 3 (1987a): 533–554.

———. "The Politics of Popular Art: *Tayuban* Dance and Culture Change in East Java." *Indonesia* 43 (1987b): 75–94.

Hefner, Robert W. and Patricia Horvatich, eds. *Islam in an Era of Nation-States: Politics and Religious Renewal in Muslim Southeast Asia.* Honolulu: University of Hawaii Press, 1997.

Hellman, Jörgen. *Ritual Fasting on West Java.* Götenberg: ACTA Universitatis Gothoburgensis, 2006.

Hesselink, Liesbeth. "Prostitution: A Necessary Evil, Particularly in the Colonies: Views on Prostitution in the Netherlands East Indies." In *Indonesian Women in Focus: Past and Present Notions.* Ed. E. Locher-Scholten and A. Niehof, 205–224. Leiden: KITLV Press, 1992.

"Hidayat Nurwahid: Wilders Harus Menonton Ayat-ayat Cinta" ([Geert] Wilder Must Watch Love Verses"). http://indonesia.faithfreedom.org/forum/hidayat-nurwahid-wilders-harus-menonton-ayat-ayat-cinta-t23929/. Accessed August 27, 2012.

Hjh. Nik Noriani N. B., ed. *Islamic Family Law and Justice for Muslim Women.* Kuala Lumpur: Sisters in Islam, 2003.

Ho, Engseng. *The Graves of Tarim: Genealogy and Mobility across the Indian Ocean.* Berkeley: University of California Press, 2006.

Hobart, Angela. *Healing Performances of Bali: Between Darkness and Light.* New York: Berghahn Books, 2003.

Holt, Claire. *Art in Indonesia: Continuities and Change.* Ithaca, NY: Cornell University Press, 1967.

Hooker, M. B. *Indonesian Islam: Social Change through Contemporary Fatāwā*. Honolulu: University of Hawaii Press, 2003.

Hughes-Freeland, Felicia. "Cross-Dressing across Cultures: Genre and Gender in the Dances of *Didik Nini Thowok*." Asia Research Institute Working Paper Series No. 108. Singapore: Asia Research Institute, National University of Singapore, 2008a. http://www.ari.nus.edu.sg/publication_details.asp?pubtypeid=WP&pubid=1264

———. "Gender, Representation, Experience: The Case of Village Performers in Java." *Dance Research* 26, 2 (2008b): 140–167.

———. "Performance and Gender in Javanese Palace Tradition." In *"Male" and "Female" in Developing Southeast Asia*. Ed. Wazir Jahan Karim, 181–206. Oxford/Washington, DC: Berg, 1995.

International Crisis Group. "Recycling Militants in Indonesia: Darul Islam and the Australian Embassy Bombing." *Asia Report* 92. February 22, 2005. http://www.crisisgroup.org/~/media/Files/asia/south-east-asia/indonesia/092%20Recycling%20Militants%20in%20Indonesia%20Darul%20Islam%20and%20the%20Australian%20Embassy%20Bombing.pdf. Accessed April 10, 2012.

Ismail, Faisal. "Islam, Politics and Ideology in Indonesia: A Study of A Process of Muslim Acceptance of the Pancasila." PhD Dissertation, McGill University, Canada, 1995.

Ismail, H. Usmar. *Usmar Ismail Mengupas Film* (Usmar Ismail Analyzing Films). Jakarta: Sinar Harapan, 1983.

Jager, Y. M. de. *Excerpta Indonesia* 44 (December 1991).

Johnson, Carolyn Schiller. "Performing Ethnicity: Performance Events in Chicago, 1893–1996." PhD Dissertation, University of Chicago, 1998.

Kartomi, Margaret J. "Music and Trance in Central Java." *Ethnomusicology* 17, 2 (1973): 163–208.

Kellner, Douglas. *Cinema Wars: Hollywood Films and Politics in the Bush-Cheney Era*. Hoboken: Wiley-Blackwell, 2009.

Kessler, Clive S. "Conflict and Sovereignty in Kelantanese Malay Spirit Seances." In *Case Studies in Spirit Possession*. Ed. Vincent Crapanzano and Vivian Garrison, 295–332. New York: John Wiley & Sons, 1977.

"Ketika Cinta Bertasbih Insyaalah Pengawalan Syariatnya Ketat" (When Love Glorifies God, Will Be, by the God's Will, Guarded according to the Shariah), *Era Muslim*. http://www.eramuslim.com/berita/bincang/habib urrahman-el-shirazy-film-kcb-insyaallah-pengawalan-syariahnya-ketat.htm. Accessed April 14, 2012.

Khoo, Eddin, Tikamdas Ramdas, and Elizabeth Wong, eds. *Freedom of Expression in the Arts*. Kuala Lumpur: National Human Rights Society (HAKAM), 2003.

Khoo, Gaik Cheng. "The Politics of Love: Malaysia's Yasmin Ahmad." *Metro* 155 (2007): 52–57.

Knight-Achjadi, Judi and Asmoro Damais. *Butterflies & Phoenixes: Chinese Inspirations in Indonesian Textile Arts*. Jakarta: Mitra Museum Indonesia, 2005.

Koentjaraningrat. *Javanese Culture*. Singapore, Oxford, and New York: Oxford University Press, 1985.

KR (Kedaulatan Rakyat). "Goyang Dangdut di Rawa Jombor." November 24, 2003.

———. "Izin Dangdut di Objek Wisata Ditolak." November 24, 2003.

———. "Pentas Dangdut Lebaran Bakal Semarak." November 24, 2003.

Kristanto, J. B. *Katalog Film Indonesia 1926–2007 (Indonesian Film Catalogue 1926–2007)*. Jakarta: Nalar, 2007.

Kuntowijoyo, Naniek Kasniyah, and Humam Abubakar. *Tema Islam Dalam Pertunjukan Rakyat Jawa: Kajian Aspek Social, Keagamaan Dan Kesenian*. (Departemen Pendidikan Dan Kebudayaan Direktorat Jenderal Kebudayaan Proyek Penelitian Dan Pengkajian Kebudayaan Nusantara [Javanologi], 1987).

Kurniasari, Triwik. "An Enlightening Movie." *Jakarta Post*. September 19, 2010. http://www.thejakartapost.com/news/2010/09/19/an-enlightening-movie.html. Accessed August 27, 2012.

Laderman, Carol. *Taming the Wind of Desire Psychology, Medicine, and Aesthetics in Malay Shamanistic Performance*. Berkeley, Los Angeles, London: University of California Press, 1991.

Latif, Yudi. *Indonesian Muslim Intelligentsia and Power*. Singapore: Institute of Southeast Asian Studies, 2008.

Laqueur, Hans-Peter. "Dervish Gravestones." In *The Dervish Lodge: Architecture, Art, and Sufism in Ottoman Turkey*. Ed. Raymond Lifchez, 284–295. Berkeley: University of California Press, 1992.

Lee, Raymond L. M. "Symbols of Separatism: Ethnicity and Status Politics in Contemporary Malaysia." In *Ethnicity and Ethnic Relations in Malaysia*. Ed. Raymond Lee, 28–46. Dekalb, IL: Center for Southeast Asian Studies, Northern Illinois University, 1986.

Lehman, F. K. "Cognitive Science Research Notes." Unpublished papers, 1997.

———. "Symbols and the Computation of Meaning." In *Anthropology for the Future*. Ed. D. B. Shimkin, S. Tax, and J. W. Morrison, 181–191. Urbana: University of Illinois Press, 1978.

Lifchez, Raymond, ed. *The Dervish Lodge: Architecture, Art, and Sufism in Ottoman Turkey*. Berkeley: University of California Press, 1992.

Lohanda, Mona. "Dangdut: Sebuah Pencarian Identitas." In *Seni Dalam Masyarakat Indonesia*. Ed. Edi Sedyawati and Sapardi Djoko Damono, 137–143. Jakarta: PT Gramedia Pustaka Utama, 1991.

Lukens-Bull, Ronald. *A Peaceful Jihad, Negotiating Identity and Modernity in Muslim Java*. New York: Palgrave MacMillan, 2005.

Lynch, Gordon, and Jolyon Mitchell with Anna Strhan, eds. *Religion, Media and Culture: A Reader*. London: Routledge Press, 2012.

Lyndsay, Jennifer and Maya H. T. Liem, eds. *Heirs to The World Culture, Being Indonesian 1950–1965*. Leiden: KITLV Press, 2012.

Lysloff, René T. A. "Rural Javanese 'Tradition' and Erotic Subversion: Female Dance Performance in Banyumas (Central Java)." *Asian Music* 33, 1 (2001/2002): 1–24.

Ma, Huan. *Ying-yai Sheng-Lan: The Overall Survey of the Ocean's Shores.* Cambridge: Cambridge University Press, 1970.

Mahathir Mohamad. *The Malay Dilemma.* Singapore: Times Books International. *Malaysia.* Copenhagen: NIAS Press, 1970.

Malaysiakini. "Remembering Kampung Medan: One Year After." March 8, 2009. http://www.malaysiakini.com/news/10633.html. Accessed January 23, 2012.

Martinez, Patricia A. "The Islamic State or the State of Islam in Malaysia." *Contemporary Southeast Asia* 23, 3 (2001): 474–503.

Mason, Paul. "The End of Fasting: Evolving Performances at *Hari Raya* Celebrations Are a Window into Deeper Cultural Change." *Inside Indonesia* 93 (2008). http://insideindonesia.org/content/view/1126/47/. Accessed May 22, 2009.

Maxwell, Robyn J. *Textiles of Southeast Asia: Tradition, Trade, and Transformation.* Melbourne and New York: Australian National University and Oxford University Press, 1990.

McIntyre, Ian. "Kelantan Refuses to Lift Mak Yong Ban." *Star.* March 1, 2007, http://thestar.com.my/news/story.asp?file=/2007/3/1/nation/17007800&sec=nation. Accessed April 3, 2012.

McPhee, Colin. *Music in Bali: A Study in Form and Instrumental Organization in Balinese Orchestral Music.* New Haven: Yale University Press, 1966.

"Melawan 'Fitna' dengan Ayat-ayat Cinta" (To Fight "Finta" with "Love Verses"), *@moonblog.* April 11, 2008. http://atmoon.multiply.com/journal/item/199. Accessed August 27, 2012.

"Melongok Shooting 'Sunan Kalijaga' Penyebaran Agama Islam yang Luwes di Pulau Jawa" (A Glance on "Sunan Kalijaga" Shooting: A Flexible Islamic Proselytization in Java). *Pelita.* July 6, 1983.

Merdeka Minggu. "Al Kautsar Nafas Baru." November 27, 1977.

Meutia Hatta Kepincut Karya Hanung" (Meutia Hatta Is Attracted by Hanung's Work). *Kompas.com.* January 27, 2009. http://entertainment.kompas.com/read/2009/01/27/e132341/meutia.hatta.kepincut.karya.hanung. 1Accessed April 14, 2012.

Milner, Anthony. "Ideological Work in Constructing Malay Majority." In *Making Majorities.* Ed. Dru C. Gladney, 151–169. Stanford: Stanford University Press, 1998.

Mohamed Ghouse Nasuruddin. *The Malay Dance.* Kuala Lumpur: Percetakan Dewan Bahasa dan Pustaka, 1995.

Mohd Anis Md Nor. "Reinventing Time and Space in Contemporary *Makyong* Dance Theatre of Malaysia." In *Time and Space in Asian Context: Contemporary Dance in Asia.* Ed. Urmimala Sarkar Munsi, 38–54. West Bengal: World Dance Alliance, 2005.

Mrázek, Jan. "Masks and Selves in Contemporary Java: The Dances of Didik Ninik Thowok." *Journal of Southeast Asian Studies* 36, 2 (2005): 249–279.

MSN News. "Indonesia Passes Far-Reaching Anti-porn Law." *MSN Malaysia News, Regional.* http://news.my.msn.com/regional/article.aspx?cp-documentid=1757250. Accessed October 30, 2008.

"MUI: Ahmadiyah Harus Dikategorikan Non Muslim" (MUI: Ahmadiyah Should Be Considered Infidel). *Tribunnews.com*. February 17, 2011. http://www.tribunnews.com/2011/02/17/mui-ahmadiyah-harus-dikategorikan-non-muslim. Accessed August 27, 2012.

"MUI Urges Government to Ban Ahmadiyah." *Jakarta Post*. March 28, 2011. http://www.thejakartapost.com/news/2011/03/28/mui-urges-government-ban-ahmadiyah.html. Accessed August 27, 2012.

Mutaqin Ahmad. "Spirit Progressive and Moderation of 'Sang Pencerah.'" *Jakarta Post*. October 23, 2010. http://www.thejakartapost.com/news/2010/10/23/spirit-progressive-and-moderation-'sang-pencerah'.html. Accessed August 27, 2012.

Nagarajan, S. "Marginalisation and Ethnic Relations: The Indian Malaysian Experience." In *Multiethnic Malaysia: Past, Present and Future*. Ed. Lim Teck Ghee, Alberto Gomes, and Azly Rahman, 369–390. Petaling Jaya: Strategic Information and Research Development Centre, 2009.

Nagata, Judith. "Religious Ideology and Social Change: The Islamic Revival in Malaysia." *Pacific Affairs* 53 (1980): 405–439.

Napier, A. D. *Masks, Transformation, and Paradox*. Berkeley: University of California Press, 1986.

Nieuwkerk, Karin van. "Artistic Developments in the Muslim Cultural Sphere: Ethics, Aesthetics, and the Performing Arts." In *Muslim Rap, Halal Soaps, and Revolutionary Theater*. Ed. Karin van Nieuwkerk, 1–24. Austin: University of Texas Press, 2011.

Nordholt, Henk Schulte, ed. *Outward Appearances: Dressing State & Society in Indonesia*. Leiden: KITLV Press, 1997.

Oetomo, Dédé. "Gender and Sexual Orientation in Indonesia." In *Fantasizing the Feminine in Indonesia*. Ed. Laurie J. Sears, 259–269. Durham and London: Duke University Press, 1996.

———. "Masculinity in Indonesia: Genders, Sexualities, and Identities in a Changing Society." In *Framing the Sexual Subject: The Politics of Gender, Sexuality, and Power*. Ed. Richard Parker, Regina Maria Barbosa, and Peter Aggleton, 46–59. Berkeley, Los Angeles, and London: University of California Press, 2000.

Onghokham. "The Wayang Topèng World of Malang," *Indonesia* 14 (1972): 111–124.

Othman, Norani. *Muslim Women and the Challenge of Islamic Extremism*. Petaling Jaya: Sisters in Islam, 2005.

Ottenberg, Simon and David A. Binkley, eds. *Playful Performers: African Children's Masquerades*. Edison, NJ: Transaction, 2006.

Pätzold, U. W. "Self-Defense and Music in Muslim Contexts in West Java." In *Divine Inspirations Music & Islam in Indonesia*. Ed. David D. Harnish and Anne K. Rasmussen, 161–193. New York: Oxford University Press, 2011.

Peacock, James L. "The Impact of Islam." *Wilson Quarterly* 5, 2 (1981): 138–144.

———. *Rites of Modernization: Symbolic and Social Aspects of Indonesian Proletarian Drama*. Chicago and London: University of Chicago Press, [1968] 1987.

Peacock, James L. "Symbolic Reversal and Social History: Transvestites and Clowns of Java." In *The Reversible World: Symbolic Inversion in Art and Society.* Ed. Barbara A. Babcock, 209–224. Ithaca and London: Cornell University Press, 1978.

Peletz, Michael G. "Sacred Texts and Dangerous Words: The Politics of Law and Cultural Rationalization in Malaysia." *Comparative Studies in Society and History* 35, 1 (1993): 66–109.

Pires, Tomé. *The Suma Oriental of Tomé Pires.* 2 vols. Trans. A. Cortesão. London: Hakluyt Society, [1515], 1944.

Poerbatjaraka, R. M. Ng. "De Geheime leer van Sunan Bonang (soeloek Woedjil)." *Djawa* 18 (1938): 19–28.

———. *Tjerita Pandji dalam Perbandingan.* Djakarta: Gunung Agung, 1968.

Pioquinto, Ceres. "Dangdut at Sekaten; Female Representations at Live Performance." *Review of Indonesian and Malaysian Affairs* 29 (Winter–Summer, 1995): 59–89.

Pos Kota Minggu. "'Al Kautsar' Dakwah Dibalik Cinta." No. 4 November 1977.

Prapañca, Mpu. *Deśawarnana (Nāgarakṛtāgama).* Trans. Stuart Robson. Leiden: KITLV Press, 1995.

Raffles, Thomas Stamford. *The History of Java.* 1817. 2 vols. Reprint, Kuala Lumpur: Oxford University Press, 1965.

Ramage, Douglas, E. *Politics in Indonesia, Democracy, Islam and the Ideology of Tolerance.* London and New York: Routledge, 1995.

———. "Statement to Committee on International Relations, U.S. House of Representatives." 2004. http://wwwc.house.gov/international_relations.

Rasmussen, Anne K. *Women, the Recited Qur'an, and Islamic Music in Indonesia.* Berkeley: University of California Press, 2010.

Raybeck, Douglas. "Social Stress and Social Structure in Kelantan Village Life." In *Kelantan: Religion, Society and Politics in a Malay State.* Ed. Willam R. Roff, 225–242. Kuala Lumpur: Oxford University Press, 1974.

Reid, Anthony. *Southeast Asia in the Age of Commerce, vol. 1: The Land Below the Winds.* New Haven: Yale University Press, 1988.

———. "Understanding Melayu (Malay) as a Source of Diverse Modern Identities." *Journal of Southeast Asian Studies* 32, 3 (2001): 295–313.

Ricklefs, M. C. *Mystic Synthesis in Java: A History of Islamization from the Fourteenth to the Early Nineteenth Centuries.* Norwalk: East Bridge, 2006.

Rinkes, D. A. *Nine Saints of Java.* Kuala Lumpur: MSRI, 1996.

Roosa, John. *Pretext for Mass Murder: The September 30th Movement and Suharto's Coup d'etat in Indonesia.* Madison, WI: University of Wisconsin Press, 2006.

Ross, Laurie Margot. "The Artist Registry. Tracking Itinerant Artists Before and After Suharto's 1965 Coup d'état in the Cirebon Region, West Java." *Indonesia and the Malay World* 39, 114 (2011): 145–169.

————. "Journeying, Adaptation, and Translation: *Topeng Cirebon* at the Margins." PhD Dissertation, University of California, Berkeley, 2009.

————. "Mask, Gender, and Performance in Indonesia: An Interview with Didik Nini Thowok." *Asian Theatre Journal* 22, 2 (2005): 214–226.

Saefudin, Asep. "Resensi: Sang Pencerah, Mengenal Pendiri Muhammadiyah" (Review: The Enlightener, Knowing the Founder of Muhammadiyah). *Antara*. September 17, 2010. http://www.antaranews.com/berita /1284715324/resensi-sang-pencerah-mengenal-pendiri-muhammadiyah. Accessed August 27, 2012.

Sani, Asrul. *Surat-surat dari Gelanggang* (Letter from the "Gelanggang"). Jakarta: Pustaka Jaya, 1999.

Sasono, Eric. "Islamic Revivalism and Religious Piety in Indonesian Cinema." In *Performance, Popular Culture and Piety in Muslim Southeast Asia*. New York: Palgrave Macmillan, 2013.

————. "Pertemuan Baru Islam dan Cinta" (A New Encounter of Islam and Romance). *Kompas*. June 28, 2008.

Schimmel, Annemarie. *My Soul Is a Woman: The Feminine in Islam*. New York: Continuum, 1997.

————. *Mystical Dimensions of Islam*. Chapel Hill: University of North Carolina, 1975.

Schrieber, Karen Elizabeth. "Power in the East Javanese Jaranan and Wayang Topeng." MA thesis. University of Virginia, 1991.

Scott, James C. *Domination and the Arts of Resistance: Hidden Transcripts*. New Haven: Yale University Press, 1990a.

————. "Everyday Forms of Peasant Resistance." In *Customs in Conflict: The Anthropology of a Changing World*. Ed. Frank Manning and Jean-Marc Philibert, 413–448. Ontario: Broadview Press, 1990b.

Sears, Laurie J. ed. *Fantasizing the Feminine in Indonesia*. Durham and London: Duke University Press, 1996a.

————. Shadows of Empire: Colonial Discourse and Javanese Tales. Durham: Duke University Press, 1996b.

Setiawan, Hersi. *Kamus Gestok*. Yogyakarta: Galang Press, 2003.

Sheppard, Mubin. *Cerita-cerita Makyung*. 2 Vols. Kuala Lumpur: Federal Sdn. Bhd., 1974.

————. *The Magic Kite and Other Ma'Yong Stories*. Kuala Lumpur: Federal, 1960.

Sheppard, Mubin. "A Recording of the *Ma'Yong*: The Dance Drama of Kelantan." *Federation Museums Journal* 12 (1967): 55–103.

————. *Taman Indera: Malay Decorative Arts and Pastimes*. Kuala Lumpur: Oxford University Press, 1972.

————. *Taman Saujana: Dance, Drama, Music and Magic in Malaya Long and Not-so-Long Ago*. Petaling Jaya, Selangor: International Book Service, 1983.

————. "The Text of the Sung Portion of Dewa Muda and a Further note on *Ma'Yong* Stories." *Federation Museums Journal* 14 (1969): 45–74.

Shiraishi, Saya S. *Young Heroes: The Indonesian Family in Politics*. Ithaca: Cornell University Southeast Asia Program, 1997.

Siddique, Sharon. "Relics of the Past? A Sociological Study of the Sultanates of Cirebon, West Java." PhD Dissertation, Universität Bielefeld, Germany, 1977.

Simatupang, G. R. Lono Lastoro. "Dangdut Spectacle." *Gong: Media Seni dan Pendidikan Seni* Special Edition 53 (2003): 12–13.

Sinarharian. "Bantah Hab Hiburan." October 29, 2010.

Sloane-White, Patricia. *Islam, Modernity, and Entrepreneurship among the Malays*. Basingstoke, England: Palgrave Macmillan Press, 1999.

Soedarsono. *Wayang Wong: The State Ritual Dance Drama in the Court of Yogyakarta*. Yogyakarta: Gadja Mada University Press, 1984.

Soeradipoera, R. Ng, R. Poerwasoewignja, and R. Wirawangsa, eds. *Serat Tjentini*. Batavia: Ruygrok, 1912–15.

Soetrisman, Drs., Drs. Yudiono, Drs. H. Djawahir Muhammad, Gunoto Saparie, H. Triyanto Triwikromo, and Neneng Dewi Setyowati. *Direktori Seni Tradisi Jawa Tengah*. Semarang: Dewan Kesenian Jawa Tengah, 2003.

Spiller, Henry J. *Erotic Triangles: Sundanese Dance and Masculinity in West Java*. Chicago: University of Chicago Press, 2010.

———. *Focus: Gamelan Music of Indonesia*. Second Edition. New York and London: Routledge, 2008.

Stout, D. and J. Buddenhagen, eds, *Religion and Popular Culture: Studies on the Interaction of Worldviews*. Ames: Iowa State University Press, 2001.

Strassler, Karen. "Material Witnesses: Photographs and the Making of *Reformasi* Memory." In *Beginning to Remember: The Past in the Indonesian Present*. Ed. Mary S. Zurbuchen, 278–311. Singapore: Singapore University Press in association with Seattle: University of Washington Press, 2005.

Stutterheim, Willem F. "A Thousand Years Old Profession in the Princely Courts on Java." In Studies in Indonesian Archaeology, Ed. W. F. Stutterheim, 91–103. The Hague: Martinus Nijhoff, 1956.

Suanda, Endo. "Dancing in Cirebonese Topeng." *Balungan* 3, 3 (1988): 7–15.

———. "The Social Context of the Cirebonese Performing Artist." *Journal of the Society for Asian Music* 13, 1 (1981): 27–41.

———. "Topeng Cirebon: In Its Social Context." MA thesis, Wesleyan University, 1983.

Sumarsam. *Gamelan: Cultural Interaction and Musical Development in Central Java*. Chicago and London: University of Chicago Press, 1995.

———. "Past and Present Issues of Islam within the Central Javanese Gamelan and *Wayang Kulit*." In *Divine Inspirations Music & Islam in Indonesia*. Ed. David D. Harnish and Anne K. Rasmussen, 45–79. New York: Oxford University Press, 2011.

Sumbogo, Priyono B. "Inul Titisan Ronggeng." *Forum* 47 (March 30, 2003): 59.

"'Sunan Kalijaga' Menelan Biaya Besar" ["Sunan Kalijaga" Swallowed Huge Cost]. *Berita Yudha Minggu.* July 24, 1983.

Sunardi, Christina. "Complicating Senses of Masculinity, Femininity, and Islam through the Performing Arts in Malang, East Java." In *Performance, Popular Culture and Piety in Muslim Southeast Asia.* Ed. Timothy P. Daniels. New York: Palgrave Macmillan, 2013.

———. "Errata, *Asian Music* 41:1." *Asian Music* 41, 2 (2010a): 227–232.

———. "Islam in Java: A Powerful Presence." *Seattle Times* (May 31).The Henry M. Jackson School of International Studies, University of Washington and the *Seattle Times* Newspapers in Education Program, 2012.

———. "Making Sense and Senses of Locale Through Perceptions of Music and Dance in Malang, East Java." *Asian Music* 41, 1 (2010b): 89–126.

———. "Negotiating Authority and Articulating Gender: Performer Interaction in Malang, East Java." *Ethnomusicology* 55, 1 (2011): 31–54.

———. "Pushing at the Boundaries of the Body: Cultural Politics and Cross-Gender Dance in East Java." *Bijdragen tot de Taal-, Land- en Volkenkunde* 165, 4 (2009): 459–492.

———. In review. "Stunning Males and Powerful Females: Negotiating Gender and Tradition through East Javanese Dance."

Sutton, R. Anderson. "*Semang* and *Seblang:* Thoughts on Music, Dance, and the Sacred in Central and East Java." In *Performance in Java and Bali: Studies of Narrative, Theatre, Music, and Dance.* Ed. Bernard Arps, 121–143. London: School of Oriental and African Studies, University of London, 1993.

———. "Who Is the Pesinden? Notes on the Female Singing Tradition in Java." *Indonesia* 37 (1984): 119–133.

Syamsudin, Din. Personal interview, August 30, 2012.

Syed Azhar. "Dress Code Spy Squads Mooted." *Star.* October 20, 2011. http://thestar.com.my/news/story.asp?file=/2011/10/20/parliament/9731542&sec=parliament. Accessed April 12, 2012.

Tanamas, Ronald and Iin Yumitanti. "Perjodohan Ala Islam (1) Sosok Fahri di Dunia Nyata" (Finding Life Partner, Islamic Way (1), Figure of Fakhri in the Real World). *Detiknews.* April 21, 2008. http://news.detik.com/read/2008/04/21/092749/926457/10/sosok-fahri-di-dunia-nyata. Accessed August 24, 2012.

Tanman, M. Baha. "Settings for the Veneration of Saints." In *The Dervish Lodge: Architecture, Art, and Sufism in Ottoman Turkey,* Ed. Raymond Lifchez. Berkeley: University of California Press, 1992.

Tanthowi, Pramono U. *Muslims and Tolerance; Non-Muslim Minorities under Shariah in Indonesia.* Chiang Mai: Silkworm Books, 2008.

Taylor, Jean Gelman. "Costume and Gender in Colonial Java, 1800–1940." In *Outward Appearances: Dressing State and Society in Indonesia.* Ed. Henk Schulte Nordholt. Leiden: KITLV, 1997.

Tempo. "Dangdut Generasi MTV." October 7, 2002: 128–129.

Thiong' o, Ngugi wa. *Penpoints, Gunpoints, and Dreams: Towards a Critical Theory of the Arts and the State in Africa.* Oxford: Clarendon Press, 1998.

Thompson, Eric C. "Rocking East and West: The USA in Malaysian Music." In *Global Goes Local: Popular Culture in Asia*, 58–79. University of British Columbia Press, 2002.

———. *Unsettling Absences: Urbanism in Rural Malaysia*. Singapore: NUS Press, 2007.

Ting, Helen. "Race Paradigm and Nation-Building in Malaysia." Unpublished paper, 2011.

"Topik: Film Ayat-ayat Cinta" (Topics: Love verses the Movie). *Komunitas Dudung.net*. February 25, 2008. http://forum.dudung.net/index.php?topic=2812.285. Accessed April 14, 2012.

Turner, Edith. *Communitas: The Anthropology of Collective Joy*. New York: Palgrave Macmillan, 2012.

Turner, Victor. *The Anthropology of Performance*. New York: PAJ, 1987.

———. *Dramas, Fields, and Metaphors*. Ithaca: Cornell University Press, 1974.

U.S. Committee for Saudi Arabian Cultural Heritage. *Palms and Pomegranates: Traditional Dress of Saudi Arabia*. Washington, DC, 1989.

Umam, Chaerul. Personal interview, January 15, 2010.

Umashankar, Rachana Rao. "Defending Sufism, Defining Islam: Asserting Islamic Identity in India." PhD Dissertation, University of North Carolina, 2012.

Utusan Malaysia. "5 juta dijangka tonton episode akhir Nur Kasih." (5 Million Estimated to Have Viewed the Final Episode of Nur Kasih) November 27, 2009. http://www.utusan.com/my. Accessed January 10, 2012.

Van Groenendael, Victoria M. Clara. *Jaranan: The Horse Dance and Trance in East Java*. Trans. Maria J. L. van Yperen. Leiden: KITLV Press, 2008.

Veldhuisen, Harmen C. Batik Belanda, 1840–1940. Dutch Influence in Batik from Java: History and Stories. Jakarta: Gaya Favorit, 1993.

Veldhuisen-Djajasoebrata, Alit. *Weavings of Power and Might: The Glory of Java*. Rotterdam: Museum voor Volkenkunde, 1988.

Vernoit, Stephen. *Occidentalism: Islamic Art in the 19th Century*. London and New York: Nour Foundation and Oxford University Press, 1997.

Wahyudi, Setiyono and G. R. Lono Lastoro Simatupang, eds. *Cross Gender. Idea of Didik Nini Thowok and Yohanes Sigit Supradah*. Malang: Sava Media and Yogyakarta: LPK Natya Lakshita, 2005.

Walton, Susan Pratt. "Heavenly Nymphs and Earthly Delights: Javanese Female Singers, Their Music and Their Lives." PhD Dissertation. University of Michigan, 1996.

Weber, Max. "On Religious Rejections of the World." In *Theories of Society: Foundations of Modern Sociological Theory*, 2 vols., ed. Talcott Parsons, Edward Shils, Kaspar D. Naegele, and Jesse R. Pitts. New York: Free Press of Glencoe, 1961.

Weintraub, Andrew N. *Dangdut Stories: A Social and Musical History of Indonesia's Most Popular Music*. Oxford and New York: Oxford University Press, 2010.

————. "Morality and Its (Dis)contents: *Dangdut* and Islam in Indonesia." In *Divine Inspirations: Music and Islam in Indonesia*. Ed. David D. Harnish and Anne K. Rasmussen, 318–336. Oxford and New York: Oxford University Press, 2011.

————. *Power Plays: Wayang Golek Puppet Theater of West Java*. Athens: Ohio University Press, 2004.

Weiss, Sarah. *Listening to an Earlier Java: Aesthetics, Gender, and the Music of Wayang in Central Java*. Leiden: KITLV Press, 2006.

Wertheim, W. F. "Moslems in Indonesia: Majority with Minority Mentality." *Occasional Paper No. 3*, James Cook University of North Queensland, Queensland, 1980.

Wieringa, Saskia. *Sexual Politics in Indonesia*. Houndmills, Basingstoke, Hampshire; New York: Palgrave Macmillan; The Hague: Institute of Social Studies, 2002.

Wolbers, Paul. "The *Seblang* and Its Music: Aspects of an East Javanese Fertility Rite." In *Performance in Java and Bali: Studies of Narrative, Theatre, Music, and Dance*. Ed. Bernard Arps, 34–46. London: School of Oriental and African Studies, University of London, 1993.

————. "Transvestism, Eroticism, and Religion: In Search of a Contextual Background for the Gandrung and Seblang Traditions of Banyuwangi, East Java." *Progress Reports in Ethnomusicology* 2, 5 (1989): 1–21.

Woodward, Mark R. *Islam in Java: Normative Piety and Mysticism in the Sultanate of Yogyakarta*. Tucson: University of Arizona Press, 1989.

Yunita, Niken Widya. "Perempuan Berkalung Sorban: Musdah Mulia: Tak Perlu Ditarik, Jangan Gampang Marah Kalau Dikritik" (Woman with Veil Does Not Need to Be Retracted, Don't Be Easily Angered Whenever Criticized). *Detik.com*. February 6, 2009. http://news.detik.com/read/2009/02/06 /174610/1080758/10/musdah-mulia-tak-perlu-ditarik-jangan-gampang -marah-kalau-dikritik. Accessed April 14, 2012.

Zoetmulder, P. J. *Pantheism and Monism in Javanese Suluk Literature: Islamic and Indian Mysticism in an Indonesian Setting*. Trans. M. C. Ricklefs. Leiden: KITLV Press, 1995.

CONTRIBUTORS

Timothy P. Daniels is an Associate Professor in the Department of Anthropology at Hofstra University. He earned an MA and PhD from the University of Illinois at Urbana-Champaign. He has conducted research as a Fulbright scholar and Wenner-Gren Fellow in Malaysia and Indonesia. His research interests include Islam, public cultural forms, and discourse, and urban space and social difference, and *sharia*, economics and politics in Southeast Asia. He is the author of several journal articles and *Building Cultural Nationalism in Malaysia: Identity, Representation, and Citizenship* (Routledge, 2005), and *Islamic Spectrum in Java* (Ashgate, 2009), which won the Lawrence A. Stessin Prize for Outstanding Scholarly Publications at Hofstra University.

Patricia A. Hardwick completed her PhD in the fields of Folklore and Anthropology from Indiana University in 2009. Her dissertation, titled "Stories of the Wind: The Role of *Mak Yong* in Shamanistic Healing in Kelantan, Malaysia," explores why rural *Mak Yong* practitioners continue to perform the traditional dance drama during healing ceremonies despite a ban on *Mak Yong* performance instated by the ruling Islamic party of Kelantan in 1991. Patricia was a Jacob K. Javits Fellow from 2000 to 2005. She conducted her fieldwork in Malaysia funded by a Fulbright Fellowship. She contributed an article on *Mak Yong* dance to the book *Global and Local Dance in Performance* (Cultural Centre, University of Malaya, 2005). Patricia has also done extensive fieldwork on the use of dance and costume by performers in California, Singapore, and Malaysia in the negotiation of complex ethnic, religious, and historical identities. Her research has been published in the *Midwestern Folklore Journal of the Hoosier Folklore Society, Folklore Forum,* and *Humanities Diliman.* She has also written book reviews for the *Journal of Folklore Research.*

James Peacock is Kenan Professor of Anthropology and Professor of Comparative Literature at the University of North Carolina at

Chapel Hill. He received a BA from Duke and PhD from Harvard. He is a Fellow of the American Academy of Arts and Sciences and has received various grants and awards including Guggenheim, Rockefeller, the Thomas Jefferson award at UNC, the Franz Boas award of the American Anthropological Association, Citizen of the World by the International Affairs Council, NC, Johnson Award for Teaching, and Massey Award for public service. He has served as Chair of the UNC faculty senate, chair of the Anthropology Department, and Director of the University Center for International Studies. He was President of the American Anthropological Association. His field research is primarily in Indonesia and Appalachia. His publications include *The Anthropological Lens* (Cambridge University Press, revised edition 2001, Chinese edition 2009) and two books published in 2007: *Grounded Globalism: How the U.S. South Embraces the World* and *Identity Matters: Ethnic and Sectarian Conflict*. Current positions include director, Carolina Seminars; codirector, Duke-UNC Rotary Center on Peace and Conflict; chair of board, Worldview.

Laurie Margot Ross is currently a Social Science Research Council (SSRC) Transregional Research Postdoctoral Fellow and Visiting Fellow at the Southeast Asia Program at Cornell University. Her interests focus on cultural and religious exchange in the Indian Ocean region, emphasizing Indonesia. She is attentive to the localization of mystical Islam (Sufism) there through the study of its visual culture and performance. She earned her doctorate in South and Southeast Asian Studies from the University of California, Berkeley, and her MA in Performance Studies from New York University. Her current project is a book manuscript that situates masks and their use in Cirebon as an important contribution to Islamic art, where they function as conduits for working through local concerns not addressed in the *Quran* and *hadith*. This project has received additional support from the Netherlands Organization for Scientific Research (NWO) and the Royal Netherlands Institute of Southeast Asian and Caribbean Studies (KITLV). Her recent publications include articles in *Indonesia and the Malay World* and *Asian Theatre Journal*.

Eric Sasono works as a public communication consultant for some government agencies in his country, Indonesia. Besides that, he is also a well-known film critic who won multiple awards. He is one of the cofounders and editors of www.rumahfilm.org, an online media dedicated to writings on film and other cultural issues. He is also a board member of the Indonesian Independent Cinema Society Foundation who organized the annual Jakarta International Film

Festival (JIFFEST), the first and the largest international film festival in Indonesia. He is also board member and international honorary advisor for Hong Kong–based Asia Film Awards. His writings, especially film reviews and criticism, have been published in prominent media in Indonesia. Eric has been active in conducting independent research on film and media in Indonesia. His research covers many aspects of film, including both content and the industry context. Eric has a special interest in studying the Islamic content in films. Recently Eric cowrote and published a book on the political economy of the Indonesian film industry.

Christina Sunardi is an ethnomusicologist in the School of Music at the University of Washington, where she has been teaching since 2008. Her interests include performance, identity, spirituality, and ethnography in Indonesia. Her work focuses in particular on the articulation of gender through music, dance, and theater in the cultural region of east Java. Her publications include articles in *Bijdragen Tot de Taal-, Land en Volkenkunde, Asian Music,* and *Ethnomusicology,* as well as reviews in the *Journal of Folklore Research Reviews, American Journal of Islamic Social Sciences,* and *Indonesia.* Dr. Sunardi has been studying and performing Javanese arts since 1997 in Indonesia and the United States, earning her PhD in music from the University of California, Berkeley, in 2007. She is currently working on a book about the negotiation of gender and tradition through dance and music in east Java. In addition to her academic work, she enjoys playing gamelan music with the Seattle-based ensemble *Gamelan Pacifica* and performing as an independent dancer.

INDEX

CPSIA information can be obtained at www.ICGtesting.com
Printed in the USA
LVOW10*1651040314

376006LV00012B/497/P

9 781137 320025